Children and Sexual-Based Online Harms

This sensitive guide for carers and professionals working with children and young people explains the serious issues of sexual content and harm that children face online. Covering technologies used by children aged two through to adulthood, it offers clear, evidence-based information about sexual-based online harm, its effects and what adults can do to support children should they see, hear or bear witness to these events online.

Catherine Knibbs, specialist advisor in the field, explains the issues involved when using online platforms and devices in family, social and educational settings. This guide offers an accessible explanation of how online harm impacts developmental, neurological and social development, as well as young people's mental health and well-being. Examined in as non-traumatising a way as possible, the book covers key topics, including consent, pornography, online grooming, sexting, live streaming, revenge porn, ASD sexuality and gender, and vigilantism. Offering guidance, and proactive and reactive strategies based on neuroscience and child development, it shows how e-safety is not one-size-fits-all and must consider the vulnerabilities of individual children and families.

Children and Sexual-Based Online Harms will equip professionals and carers with the knowledge to support their work and to direct conversations about the online harms that children and young people face. It is essential reading for those training and working with children in psychological, educational and social work contexts, as well as parents, policy makers and those involved in the development of online technologies.

Catherine Knibbs is a clinical and academic researcher, consultant in the fields of cybertrauma and online harms, director of privacy4 Ltd, and a UKCP-accredited child and adult trauma psychotherapist.

Understanding Children's Life Online

Books by Catherine Knibbs

Children, Technology and Healthy Development: How to Help Kids be Safe and Thrive Online

ISBN 9780367770150

Online Harms and Cybertrauma: Legal and Harmful Issues with Children and Young People

ISBN 9780367770112

Children and Sexual-Based Online Harms: A guide for professionals

ISBN 9781032427584

Children and Sexual-Based Online Harms

A Guide for Professionals

Catherine Knibbs

R Routledge
Taylor & Francis Group

LONDON AND NEW YORK

Cover image: GettyImages/Vinh Nguyen Phuoc/EyeEm

First published 2024
by Routledge
4 Park Square, Milton Park, Abingdon, Oxon OX14 4RN

and by Routledge
605 Third Avenue, New York, NY 10158

Routledge is an imprint of the Taylor & Francis Group, an informa business

British Library Cataloguing-in-Publication Data
A catalogue record for this book is available from the British Library

Library of Congress Cataloging-in-Publication Data
Names: Knibbs, Catherine, author.
Title: Children and sexual-based online harms : a guide for
professionals / Catherine Knibbs.
Description: Abingdon, Oxon ; New York, NY : Routledge, 2023. |
Series: Understanding children's life online | Includes bibliographical
references and index.
Identifiers: LCCN 2022059848 (print) | LCCN 2022059849 (ebook) |
ISBN 9781032426808 (hardback) | ISBN 9781032427584 (paperback) |
ISBN 9781003364177 (ebook)
Subjects: LCSH: Online sexual predators—Great Britain. | Internet
and children—Great Britain. | Computer sex—Great Britain. |
Child sexual abuse—Great Britain—Prevention. | Child welfare—
Great Britain.
Classification: LCC HV6773.15.O58 K65 2023 (print) |
LCC HV6773.15.O58 (ebook) | DDC 362.760941—dc23/
eng/20230524
LC record available at https://lccn.loc.gov/2022059848
LC ebook record available at https://lccn.loc.gov/2022059849

ISBN: 978-1-032-42680-8 (hbk)
ISBN: 978-1-032-42758-4 (pbk)
ISBN: 978-1-003-36417-7 (ebk)

DOI: 10.4324/9781003364177

Typeset in Bembo
by codeMantra

This book is dedicated to my 4-legged furry baby who stayed with me through almost 18 years of friendship, and company and was the best co-regulator through thick and thin. I miss you every day.

I want to thank my children for those lifelong moments of sanity, groundedness and humour, I love you both, I am so proud of you, you are amazing.

To my Flow For Writer Buddies: Heidi & Kathleen – I love you, ladies!

My writing mentor Maurice Irfan Coles whom I miss so very much.

Gary and Sue, Adam, Helen and Sarah who as my real-world friends allowed me to grow and spend time in the corporeal world taking time with them and celebrating everything fun!

Thanks also go to the reviewers: Caroline Humer and Jean-Christophe le Toquin, Elizabeth Milovidov, Darryl Edwards, Chloe Combi and Andy Briercliffe.

To my Army buddies Bob, Dave and Robbo and their partners Carol, Sarah and Dawn. Thanks for every silly moment and here's to the life of Bob sadly taken from us. Let's keep the party going.

And a large thank you to the Flow for Writers at FRC: Steven Kotler, Michael Mannino, Brent Hogarth, Karen Darke, Ryan Wickes and Chris Bertram for all the coaching. Every session made a difference.

To each and every one of you that makes a difference for children as practitioners, staff, moderators, managers and more, YOU ROCK and the children need you.

THANK YOU

Contents

Introduction

Now this book is about online harm(s) and so the caveat here is: I'm only going to write and talk about the negative and '*bad*' things. The book is going to sound scary because of this and so it is important that we consider the *balance* of positives that exist in the space of the Internet and digital technology, and boy, are there plenty!

I love technology, I have so much of it in my life and I depend on it to carry out my professional life, using biofeedback and gaming with my clients; personally, it enables me to watch TV (streaming or films, or casting to it whilst I potter with housework or whatever), to listen to podcasts on the go and the other technologies I need such as my car, fridge, alarm clock and more gadgets than I can count. Where would I be without tech? I'd be a nomad living in the woods and probably less of a pain in the posterior to those whom I challenge here in this book or in the spaces of online harm and child protection.

This whole book is about the harms and their trauma impact, spanning each chapter and idea and of course, here in this book, I can only address some and not all of the ills and issues. Please do not misunderstand this book as Misery literature, click-bait or negativity sell as it will be heavy going at times for you and in line with my training caveats *you may put the book down at any time you wish and return to it when you are ready*. The book is not the easiest of reads and because of this I even took breaks writing it. I needed to for my health, well-being and ability to keep coming back to write more. I do not apologise for the depth of the conversations here and continuous page after page of 'stuff'.

This is to provide information and the necessary skills for practitioners to be able to work with this in clinical and outreach practice, youth work, policing, social work, adoption and fostering, residential settings and home settings – after all, many practitioners are parents too. If you are finding this stuff difficult to read and absorb, please consider how this feels for the children going through it. To walk in the waters of trauma, you will inevitably find yourself getting wet and perhaps needing to tread water at times. Please do this rather than drowning in the pain and suffering. Compassion and empathy can be from the side-lines *with* the lifeline rather than *in* the depths

DOI: 10.4324/9781003364177-1

of the rising tides and waves. Compassion does not mean feeling everything the person does, and knowing which type of compassion will be helpful can also prevent this fatigue. These are learnable skills: Goleman (1995), Goleman and Davidson (2017), Gilbert (2011) and Kirby (2022) offer perhaps the best insight into reducing vicarious trauma that I can recommend, and these are just a few of them.

References versus the bibliography

A quick note here at this stage: I am going to use references where needed, these are likely to be books with a large volume of information pertaining to the subject being mentioned. I do not apologise for the lack of specific paragraphs or sentences from the book cited, as the whole of a book provides a better understanding of the point I am making. Also, as you progress through the volumes you will see the ethics, dilemmas and lack of robust research into many of the topic areas that involve young children and so an overall understanding of a topic seems to be a good starting point for these books.

There will also be a bibliography and further reading section at the end of the volumes as there is a broader spectrum of knowledge that informs the contents of the book herein. These book recommendations are given as further reading and some of the books I recommend I do not agree with entirely, and others, not at all; however, they are books I have read to broaden my own knowledge and read another person's perspective in order to gain the approach of the middle lane driver mentioned below. No endorsements for these books are made unless otherwise stated at the time.

Middle lane driver: not left, nor right but balanced as much as can be

When I write on the subject matters around development in the child or adolescent years and the influence of technology on this stage of a growing child, I am writing from neither a far-right nor far-left perspective, with all of the anger that often accompanies such views. Neither am I writing to say that the space we are in as a society for these young people is particularly great, or is this woke position too often cited? I will not be claiming that it is all about acceptance and that no one should be judged, as this liberal freedom narrative is creating its own set of harms, which will be discussed later in the book. We need balance and integral thinking, beyond what Ken Wilber calls the mythical and rational levels. We need to go higher in terms of our critical, inclusive and broad thinking and aim for integral thinking and life (Wilber, 2000), given that we now have more technology and landscapes to integrate.

And so, one of the most important things I will write in this book is: the beliefs about the isms and ists we face today are rooted in a lack of knowledge and understanding *throughout history*, in *all* aspects, by *many* people who may not have completely comprehended; for example, it was not okay to burn someone at the stake, drown them, throw crow feathers at them, or sacrifice them to the gods to remove the evil spirits once thought to inhabit the corporeal body. (We only know newer types of knowledge as we progress and learn; what seemed a good idea at the time, with reflection and the space of hindsight, may be a bad idea.)

Even so, some cultures around the world still have these kinds of beliefs and when we can all get together in a virtual space our ideologies, deeply held in generations of unquestioning loyalty, are 'bound to surface', and with them the venom, toxicity and abundance of the mythological monsters we all fear.

We may be intelligent human beings, but we are also slow to learn, respond and change over time. This is abundantly clear when considering the time it has taken us to reach the space we have today, where old ideologies and thoughts are now changing, being challenged by people, and calling to witness the issues we face as evolving human beings. This is happening in the spaces where children are growing and developing, often doing so without the reins of their parents holding them tight and without a generation of wise people to balance the scales of knowledge, because many of them are not in these spaces, frightened or delayed by the ubiquitous nature of integrated living *in*, *with* or *through* technology.

And, moreover, … we ain't there yet in terms of balance. We still stereotype, blame, judge, criticise and more, and whilst this is part of being human, we cannot always recognise this is us and so project outwards the 'them' and 'us' groups. The groups, however, exist in multiple planes of time and space and occupy so many arenas that the children and young people who go there are subjected to aeons of history of 'them versus us', and you can be sure that divisions, polarisation and separation are rife today, and will continue to be so for some time as we jostle and settle into the digital space. Trauma-informed practice, living with and in, and communication in this space is far off in the distance, but I hold out hope for the light to shine through, one day. And if you read Stephen Pinker's work you will see we are heading into a less violent world when it comes to weapons and war (Pinker, 2012); however, the digital space is only in the infancy stage of human development so I don't know how that fairs, or will fair in the history books.

The new learning, thinking and knowledge that changes our thoughts, beliefs and practice only occurs once we have spent time, and quite a bit of it, learning and listening wholeheartedly. Terrible acts have been carried out in the past and people have been castigated, tortured, punished and killed in the process of progress. For example, we now no longer use Phrenology (the study of bumps on the head) to assess and diagnose psychological or criminal issues, nor do we (I hope) still carry out operations on infants without anaesthesia because we believe them to be incapable of feeling pain (this practice was still carried out in the 1980s so we really are still rather slow in learning (Boffey, 1987).

This means, in this book, that I am attempting to write from a balanced place, not blaming but explaining. I will not be arguing for issues per se.

However, political, religious and cultural aspects will be discussed. Neither will I side with sociological-based arguments about patriarchy or radical feminism, nor the conversations about sex and gender (though these are indeed discussed in this book), nor diagnosis and pathology. But this is taken from the perspective of all I have learned from my clients over a decade, and how this marries up with theories about human behaviour because you as the reader have a history, filled to the brim with generations of religion, culture, race, sex and gender, and an approach to life that I could not possibly know unless I spend time with you and listen.

The information throughout the book is provided here for the practitioners and professionals to assess and make their own minds up on the matters. I do not claim to not have unconscious biases and blind spots and of course, this is my caveat that, if these exist, they do not remain unchallenged, but in the process, being attacked is unlikely to produce the change we wish to see in the world. Challenge me, yes, strawman or attack me, and it could produce a talionic response, so I'm told.

Some references may not appear on some of the subject matters as they are speculative, lacking research, or perhaps only small numbers exist, or even just one article, new, undetermined and so on. Robust research takes time and as you'll see in some of the chapters some of the citations are even challenged. Cognitive and attributional biases are sometimes in play in the early exploratory processes of research and some of these biases have made their way to the Internet and some books, which tend to side with a hard left or right leaning, and hence these are often citations left out for this reason. I also use anecdotal evidence from my practice, for which no research-backed citations exist. The cases are anonymised in line with my ethical profession and all cases have been discussed with the client, parents, or carers as to the amount of information I am sharing. This means some of the things I wanted to share have not been added to this book. My training events have more exploratory cases and challenges in them to highlight the issues raised in this volume as I can guarantee in these cases something I cannot with a written book, which is that I would be speaking to adult practitioners, and where this is under therapeutic training I am working with a code of ethics not present in the written format it is herein.

The sword of Damocles in writing this book

Dare I write and speak out? Cancel culture is a real phenomenon and one I have watched spill over into the real world with consequences that I personally have had to make choices about, even to the point of considering attending events (or not) and asking people not to photograph me or the people I am with, because I do not want confrontation if this appeared on social media. When did this become such a peer-pressured space that I cannot choose whom I can spend time with, even if they have extreme views about me? What a societal mess!

After all, as a therapist, I listen to people who do not share my views about the world and it is my professional ethic to listen, lean in and learn. And so the first question for the practitioners reading this book is: where will your work take you into the pressures faced by young people and children, what are you aware of regarding what it is like to live in twenty-twenty something and how does that feel? Where does the virtual influence the corporeal and how do you understand a young person and the harms they face if you cannot see the influence and overlap of the Venn diagram for their experience?

What they see, interact with and encounter is out of your awareness, and often even if you know the peripheral you are not in the centre of the knowledge. What must it be like to work with a fraction of the issue and why is it perhaps not a great idea to say we understand, when in reality we probably don't? Does this remind you of being young and hearing this line from the adults around you?

The deficiency of body knowledge, trauma applied and embodied practice and the chasm of technological knowledge is present in so many adults today. What has been called the knowledge gap by the Center for Humane Technology has been increasing over the last 27 years or so and we think we know what's at the bottom of the mountain these children are being asked to climb, when we might just be on a different mountain to the young people and their issue. So I'm going to throw you a rope with which to abseil down and meet the young people where they are. However, this is only one mountain and I cannot possibly know them all – accepting this is part of our journey toward understanding the harms children and young people face in a world of technology. Get your climbing gear on, so to speak, we have lots of work to do.

Polarisation

In the space of social media, there are far too many extreme, polarised spaces being built with which to demonise and slaughter those who disagree or oppose and create an in-group out-group society that results in opinionated information based on human flaws and biases rather than balanced conversation, and it is this separation, interpersonal discord, intolerance, misguided loyalty to causes, people and things that is leading down the rabbit hole of mis-attunement and disconnections. This does not mean that technology is creating disconnections but, rather, the intense desire to feel wanted and needed by your group and the unwillingness to listen and engage with those who do not share your views (Knibbs, 2019).

If *The Social Dilemma* documentary produced by The Center for Humane Technology (2020), see www.humanetech.com) taught us anything, it is that even creating a documentary about the social dilemma was fraught with the competition of making their documentary visible to many, and indeed could this have been driven by a desire for *ours as: the one to watch because ours is the truest form of truth* in comparison to the other films and documentaries that were being produced at the time? Ironically, at the time this appeared, the

media seem to have been using the same marketing tactics and online discussions that the documentary addresses in order to promote the film. When
a company or people pour their heart into creating something they feel is
important to share, this results in the desire to knock down the competitors
because that feeling of creating something that goes unnoticed is a terrible
feeling. Some documentaries aired less, were talked about less and this must
have felt terrible in comparison to the popular one (whether this knocking
down of others is not actioned, it still exists). It can re-create the feelings tied
into attachment styles that I have so frequently mentioned in my writings
because we are hard-wired to be seen (and noticed and revered etc.).

The polarisation of professionals online and the 'truth'

Is there really such a thing? And given the current landscape of large organisations and governments arguing for the version of the truth that exists in their
approach you can see that social media and online spaces are filled with human
behaviours. I see many online posts targeting the virtue signalling of some
people, where the people that post them signal utter contempt for the radical
views of others, while holding potentially radical views themselves; a post
appearing from professionals laced with their own histories and narratives,
which may be a trauma response, attachment-based reaction and response or
virtue signalling of their own. Conflict and discord; it's what we '*do*'.

We don't come to the social media space (or indeed authoring books as I
am here) without our own demons, desires and need to be seen in some way.

I, like many others who write or post online, am not here free of prejudice,
judgement, biases and flaws. And, of course, the passions I have are often
driven by a frustration with the system that isn't in favour of trauma-applied
knowledge, compassion and empathy towards our fellow humans; and we are
not there as a society yet, and so my frustrations air at times, just like yours.

This book is primarily another push of my own to educate the next round of
new practitioners, to inform those already in practice and hopefully to make a
change to a percentage of children who are facing harm online from the space
that will never be free of these harms. This is an attempt to reduce, mitigate
and offset the harms, a book to provide new interventions and help direct
children out of the depths of human depravity, abuse and ills that have always
existed in the corporeal world, and to bring a light to those dark spaces and
times. You are the hope of becoming informed enough to do that for them.

Better than life: meta-sphere, meta-verse and meta space ... Red Dwarf already did it through a novel

Many moons ago, Rob Grant and Doug Naylor wrote some books discussing
'The Game of Life' that the four members of *Red Dwarf* fame played (Grant &
Naylor, 1990). It was an immersive game that became the backdrop for a bril-
liant comedy series on TV ... making the parallel of where we are heading

almost funny. Dwayne Dibley just got his second life. Second pun intended because that was another early version of a metaverse. We just got better at designing and integrating the new 'Game of Life'.

Just what is this universe that people and organisations keep telling us about, considering that some organisations are claiming it is theirs, or they own one, or 'it'.

So lets consider how this space is often described as being:

> Web 3.0 ... But that's not 'it'.
> Virtual reality then? This, it is not.
> So augmented reality? Neither that, nope.

And so the seed of confusion is nothing new here because in tech we often give names that sound like they are nebulous, only to be understood by nerds, geeks or Silicon Valley entrepreneurs. So I will give the best explanation that I can:

'Life' is the moment we are born into a world outside of the womb, this space many of us refer to as IRL or *in real life*. However, so is the womb to the developing baby. We have a mind that begins to develop alongside thoughts, beliefs and attitudes and this space we tend to call consciousness. Even though consciousness is a term we cannot accurately measure or define, we accept it as a thing. When we use the Internet on a device we call this 'online' or what is referred to as Web 2.0 and we understand that this 'online' space is made of many facets, arenas, pages of information and of course shopping and social media channels.

But when we talk to the metaverse, the many marketing videos and experts that have appeared on the Internet (for a space that hasn't been fully developed yet, I'm not entirely sure how they can be an expert on it, whatever it is) claim the metaverse to be in 'there'. As in: virtual reality. And this conjures up an image and sense with which we can pull children 'out of it' or 'off it' and even 'ban them from it' and so on.

However, here is a thought experiment that can explain this metaverse: I want you to imagine looking into a fluffy cloud in the sky. At first, it seems to resemble cotton wool balls and looks light and fluffy. And as this descends you notice that it is made up of water droplets, and as it becomes level with the ground it looks more like fog than the white fluffy item up in the sky. It is a thing of beauty in the air against a backdrop of blue hues, and can bring rain, which when it descends is nothing more than droplets of water, mist and fog that float about blurring our vision.

And so the metaverse is the cloud that we are all walking into, changing our vision and our sense of navigation, how we experience life, how we see the world, and what may be the blurred boundaries of deep connection to the person next to us. And I've seen the film *The Fog*.

Ambient, it ain't.

Life is becoming the cloud that surrounds us and is no longer the space we send our photos and files to – it is becoming the space that we inhabit. We are enveloped in digital technology and life is now '*digital-us normal*'.

How our cyber synapses are adding to the complexities of harm, online spaces and the metaverse: how being human is changing tech and how tech is changing being a human

What was once a space in our heads for thoughts about ourselves and others is now a glass-head-style vortex of spaces in the cyber universe to see through and into those spaces that humans *really* go to in their heads.

To continuously outpour our stream of consciousness, say what we think and in doing so where we would, once upon a time, be able to walk down the street and wonder what people thought, we can now '*read their bubbles of thought*', whether we want to or not. It's almost like being in a cartoon and being able to see neon signs above people's heads where they are thinking, processing and emoting.

We can now find spaces online where, akin to being a toddler, we are surrounded by the narration of what everyone is doing. For example, if you watch an attuned mother with her small child, she will be telling her child what she is doing as she goes task to task, educating the child in language, behaviour and contact. In parallel, as many of us are doing this online at every moment, the Artificial Intelligence and Machine Learning bots are also watching us, learning and developing a copycat knowledge of what it is to be human. The online space is littered with all the kinds of emotions we feel, activities we engage in and of course ways we treat each other in order to relate and connect deeply, and where we disagree – psychologically, physically and as a species.

We are moving too fast for our own 'good' and in doing this we are not thinking ahead, because our own motivations for profit and progress overlook the principles of that golden thread. That thread suggests we treat others as we would like and expect to be treated ourselves, and if we can, *shifting from individualism and consumerism to service and collaboration* (Coles, 2015; Coles & Gent, 2022).

And so this book is about collaboration, service and change. This book is my step forward in doing this.

To my dearly missed friend Maurice Irfan Coles, thank you for your unwavering support and friendship, I miss you dearly and I take to heart the message you gave me.

'Be good in the world and create the change you want to see missy'

This book is that step.

References

Boffey, P. (1987). Infants' sense of pain is recognized, finally. www.nytimes.com/1987/11/24/science/infants-sense-of-pain-is-recognized-finally.html.

Centre for Humane Technology (2020). *The Social Dilemma* (documentary film). www.humanetech.com/. Aired on Netflix 2021.

Coles, M. I. (2015). *Towards the compassionate school: From golden rule to golden thread.* UCL.

Coles, M. I., & Gent, B., Eds. (2022). *Education for survival: The pedagogy of compassion.* UCL.

Gilbert, P. (2010). *The compassionate mind. A new approach to life's challenges* (revised edition). Constable.

Goleman, D. (1995). *Emotional intelligence.* Bloomsbury.

Goleman, D., & Davidson, R. (2017). *Altered traits: Science reveals how meditation changes your mind, brain and body.* Avery.

Grant, R., & Naylor, D. (1990). *Better than life.* Viking.

Kirby, J., (2022). *Choose Compassion. Why it matters and how it works.* University of Queensland Press: Queensland

Knibbs, C. (2019). *Fit, fat or frumpy? The effects of social media (writ large).* BACP Private Practitioners Conference, London, 28 September. BACP.

Pinker, S. (2012). *Better angels of our nature: The history of violence and humanity.* Penguin: London.

Wilber, K. (2000). *Integral psychology: Consciousness, spirit, psychology, therapy.* Shambala.

1 Communication

From wise apes in clothes to glass heads?

Communication processes have changed somewhat in the last 27 years or so. This chapter looks to introduce you to the subtle changes, and the not so subtle.

Wise apes?

We are often called 'wise apes', along with 'naked apes', who incidentally need to wear clothes most of the time because it's by and large too cold in many countries to be naked most of the time, so – wise; I think not?

Evolution removed hair over time because we wore clothes or was it the other way round? And why am I talking about clothes at the very beginning of a book about online harms? Well, the proof is in the pudding, they say, and the concept of the requirement of clothing seems to be that our species moved into areas that were too cold, so we required the furs of animals; or could it be the loss of hair was due to being in hotter temperatures through time – but it is debatable as to which way round it occurred and so to the first metaphor of the book. Hair, fur or skin matters not; we need clothing to protect us from elements in the environment such as cold, heat and chemicals. Moreover, some of the clothing itself can be the cause of harm, such as chemicals used in or on them, or deliberate restriction of blood flow via accessories such as belts, that have resulted in death by asphyxiation (either through the act of one human using the clothing to harm and kill another person or use on one's self). Clothing is not the demon, nor is it the panacea of protection. Think about shorts in the Sahara versus the Arctic. They are use-dependent and applicable to the environment!

Next time you get dressed you may think about this, or perhaps you will automatically pull on your underwear, tops or bottoms and before you know it, voilà – fully clothed! This is the metaphor for *the use of technology that we engage with daily so much so that's as automatic as getting dressed.*

Technology is not evil, great or neutral (Hare, 2022; Consilience Project, 2022). It is what it is, and the use, application, or lack of is inherently an issue when harm occurs along the way of the progress, adoption and adaptations

DOI: 10.4324/9781003364177-2

we make with it, through it and for it. Technology can have side effects that were not intended, such as the diminishing skill of remembering people's phone numbers which was a triumphant marker of my youth. Yet now I am not entirely sure I know anyone's number off by heart because I outsourced my device to do that and neither do I have a completed 'phone book' sat in the hallway should I have a 'brain fart' (loss of memory for a moment) and need to dial, not type the numbers into a telephone.

Speaking: but not on the telephone per se

Communication is a skillset that allows us to live and work together and progress as a species. To denote our ability to employ our thinking into language and actions that mean others can understand us and our intentions, and understand what we are interpersonally relating 'about', is the function of language both verbal and non-verbal; however, those wordy-based 'things' that are uttered in sound waves from our mouths or written down are made up of phonemes, morphemes, graphemes, syntax and grammar and make the job a whole lot easier when we consider the following:

Lions do not sit on the plains of Africa holding meetings about the other prides local to them, upon whom they are going to take action. They do not have rallies by holding a loud and noisy demonstration with signs, protesting the perceived state of cub-raising practices by those other lion prides. I am not sure, but I also think they abstain from deciding as a group which new variant of 'lunch' should be on the menu for these meetings, given Kevin's new approach to plant-based dietary information, which Norman recently spoke to him about after watching a Netflix documentary.

Lions work together using sounds, body movements and intuitive prey instinct in order to work as the pride: eat, sleep, poop, procreate, hunt, repeat.

Without language we are less than able to have complex skills in the hunting arena; for example, *Homo sapiens* in the past did not have the language to convey, in one grunt alone, what the grunt meant:

> 'you go that way, and when you see the animal at a distance of fewer than 10 feet, you distract it by running to the left, and I will move around to the right and capture it with this contraption tool thing, for which I have no name yet but I'm thinking "sharp pokey stick with a pointy end". I think that sounds good, although I may have to reconsider my marketing strategy in order to outdo the local competition, I'm just not sure yet. Anyway … Okay, on my mark: 3,2,1 … go!'

We needed language above and beyond the eye glances and bodily movements to convey the past, present and future (and still do to operate as a community). We need concepts, categories and hierarchies to formulate a way of communicating that we can all understand so we all know we speak to the same 'thing'. We are not lions.

And so language became our primary way to convey the intricacies of what we wanted to let others know about our state of mind, intended actions and processes of cognition (especially as this improved with our understanding of the world and technological advances). However, our deep relational capacities of noticing micro-movements in the eyes and face, and the Wi-Fi feelings discussed in my original book (Knibbs, 2022), were referred to as neuroception. These communication patterns run much deeper than many subjective words can ever convey. It is the lack of this skillset that is creating some of the problems we face today surrounded by technology and perhaps, even more, going forwards too. Emoticons may not cut the mustard as far as micro expressions are concerned; though they do reveal much about us – perhaps just not the most important aspects (Wall et al, 2016; Kaye, 2017).

The eyes have it: once we can see the eyes of the other this will resolve the issues of communication online.

Well, that is until we have our 'eye contact' in the virtual space known as the metaverse. However, the paradigm around eye contact is not enough to articulate all of the nuances of human connection and, as in my first book, we *need* our vagal neuroception to be an exact 'carbon copy' human in the digital space. We cannot emulate human relatedness in a digital environment … yet. Even with the proposed measures taking place as this book is being written, who knows if we will have achieved that by the publication date?

Why is this changed communication a problem, issue or harm?

What is it about the communication patterns of humans, communication online and what this is potentially doing to us (bearing in mind this is not a thing we can isolate to study robustly) What is it that needs addressing for this book and the next? Well, the patterns of communication as they relate to sexual harm are the major reflection throughout this volume.

As humans that live in close proximity to one another we are a smörgåsbord of thousands of tiny and large complex processes, all running in parallel helping us to make sense of and understand the world around us. We can in a fraction of a second know whether someone is heading towards us to attack us, or not, and when we get the 'error' processing this it's because the other person is a 'great actor' and has confused our biology through the trick of pretending. We can, in a fraction of a second update our error and go from fear reactions to humorous responses (sometimes). Or perhaps, in the case of some people, move to an outburst of calling someone a '****' for giving us the 'jump-scare fright'.

I am suggesting that our biology forms our communication patterns, and it is this that has been violated in many surreptitious ways through technology that has resulted in micro, slow forming and superhighway neuroplastic changes to these communication processes and the ability to understand the world. This has affected our relational capacities. Therefore, polarisation online is more than the 'limbic' hijack quotes so often discussed in the *Social*

Dilemma documentary (and others). As my previous book discussed, we are bodies *and* brains and our biology right now is to quote young people: '*wrekd*' (Knibbs, 2022), which is hardly a surprise given our history of evolution. So, no, I am not really making a large hypothesis here, or claiming hyperbole or making 'mad' claims, but rather suggesting we need an inkling of acknowledgement and not the scaremongering approach of the doom and gloom brigade telling us technology has hijacked us as a species. *It is changing us, rapidly* and we don't know exactly where we are heading until those changes begin to surface. We are only just beginning to find out.

What I am saying, though, is our ability to critically appraise information and utilise non-verbal cues and other extraneous variables that help us create meaning *and* make sense are changing. How? Well, that is something to pay attention to over the next decade as we move into spaces that our minds and bodies were certainly not designed for, given the biology we were handed at the design phase in the factory of 'teh species'.

Meaning making is a crucial part of our species and this crisis of knowledge, sense making and attributing meaning has been discussed in courses, blogs and videos from The Centre for Humane Technology, The Consilience Project and Rebel Wisdom, with names such as John Vervaeke, Jonathan Pageau, Daniel Schmachtenberger and more taking part. Additionally the academics, highly educated and influential thinkers, once called the Intellectual Dark Web, now seemingly disbanded of sorts, have also added to this conversation and there is much you can research here, but word constraints limit my discussion of this.

What I can say here, particularly for this chapter, is our thinking and feeling patterns about others, based in our biology, are changing too. Our thinking is almost 24/7/365 in an environment where others can now see 'into our heads' and as such this has *never* happened in our evolution, even with language, because private thoughts were just that – private. This meant that our internal dialogue of 'what it is to be human' was reflected upon alone and in our own minds unless we discussed our thoughts with another person. Whether we spoke about these thoughts with others was determined by our thoughts and feelings about that person, and this meant elements of these thoughts and the carrying out of that communication were curated, changed, omitted or provided in a way that pleased others or to defend us from rejection by the crowd, based on our own feelings about sharing our thoughts (and what others think).

These feelings might be shame, or guilt, considering that we may be laughed at, or considered weird for thinking x, y or z etc. And so others only heard the thoughts we decided to share. Private thoughts remained just so. If we got angry, for example, and had 'an outburst', then only those who could hear us at this time were privy to the reactive 'audio' shared at that time.

Though now there is always a curated version of our 'selves', often being aware that, as soon as 'you leave your house', all manner of your behaviour, responses and utterances can be captured by others, leaving you open to attack. And so my questions here are: are we 'acting' more than being and are we authentic to ourselves outside of our homes? Has human behaviour changed because of the ever-present devices 'at the ready'? (our homes can be inside our minds, or physical house so to speak.)

Echo chambers, influencers and your knowledge of knowledge

And so, we can find our 'in group' in spaces online that we will discuss throughout this volume and the next. However, it is noteworthy to keep in mind that as practitioners reading this book you are also influenced by the thinking, teaching and exposure to the knowledge you have encountered over your life. And, of course, now we can find someone somewhere who thinks like us, or not like us, too much like us, way off from us, has abhorrent views, is in our echo chamber, surprises us, educates us, terrifies us and of course makes us feel 'normal' for thinking in this way.

The histories and thinkers of the world make up our brains of today, e.g. Confucius, Lao Tzu, Plato, Descartes, Beethoven and the Egyptians putting images, words, music and rhythm in front of us, and now we are interacting with 4 to 4.5 billion others who can influence us at any time. Cyber connections are exactly this with the potential for each of our cyber synapses, cyber-neurons to connect to any other, almost infinite number by use of the computer highway or what Lexlighter called *the intergalactic highway*, as cited in *The Master Switch* (Wu, 2010).

Practitioner's pause for thought

What weight would you give to the influence of online spaces that have altered the course of your own knowledge and thinking? What skewed, alternative or hard views do you hold and where did these come from? How will this influence the work you do with children and young people? How will this influence your practice and what will you provide for the children you work with based on the factors of how life has changed in the past few decades? Where do you 'sit' with certain topics and how is your own internal thinking, feeling and being open to the conversations the children bring? How much do you know about the spaces online that change the way children are developing and of course the harms they encounter and what this may be doing to their neuroplastic brain architectures and newly forming communication processes?

Memetic traditions outdo historical forms of information

Critical thinking in the online space is the most needed form of inquiry and belief system, and of course it only takes one meme to change the path of least resistance!

As we have just established, communication has changed, in a myriad of ways. What was once a waited thought, reply or question is now actionable immediately and may be coming from a reactive place, not a considered and reflected one. To give the reader some context behind this (and bear with me as I geek out to explain this; there is a slightly more simple version below so you can skip to that section if you wish): what was once a process that took time, could lead you down many paths of the default mode network where you replayed the conversation in your head in many ways, using your reticular activation system linking ideas, novel information and assimilating what you had just engaged in, well, that is now seemingly obsolete and re-placed with instantaneous and reactive rather than responsive actions online (on many occasions). Adding to the noise that you encounter online, your busy mind may not have a chance to absorb and question the knowledge you have just encountered, nor does it seemingly give you a 'moment to think'. Children are struggling with this – what is called information overload or detecting signals from the noise, to use an engineering term.

When short message services began, what we now refer to commonly as texting or messaging, young people found the tech laborious, due to the phones at the time needing multiple key presses just to get to a letter on the number, e.g. spelling squirrel (7x4, 7x3, 8x2, 4x3, 7x3, 7x3, 3x2, 5x3). Short-term memory has limitations on the numbers of 'items' it can hold at any one time (Miller, 1956), a skillset that is possibly now further reduced in terms of what we outsource to our devices as extensions of our own memory. And so, text language evolved to become short with 'mate' becoming 'M8' and so on. This also means that reading complexity was possibly changing, and shorter duration pieces like blogs and memes were sought, rather than tomb-based books. This may in actuality only be a standard 70,000 word piece like a dissertation thesis (unless you are Iain Mcgilchrist (2019, 2021) writing his latest book(s), and this is an in-joke here as I think his recent work has to be the biggest book I ever purchased!).

These short burst, rapid informational pieces are likely to be creating neu-roplastic changes in the land of infinitesimal space. It seems as though all thoughts that escape the cortex and cranial prison are coagulating, touching and seeking over space, time and binary dimensions, synthesising, binding and forming as the synapses do in a human brain (and 99% of it will poten-tially be traceable in the future). This image is how I feel the space of the digital landscape would look if it were a piece of art.

This is also the emerging, maturing voice of AI created by human thinking and expression in real-time in the digital realm. This is the supercomputer of cyber synapses. In opposition to the residents of Alderaan, this is the sound of billions of voices crying out all at once, unsilenced, multiplied by all people who can communicate now, from the peak before the millennium past, to the future, wherever that may be. We are one, now and forever. Meta, chapter and verse.

And the memes, oh the memes that paint a picture of a million or more pixels in one fell swoop. How do young people see the Instagram gurus, life coaches and more via the rapid, densely edited informatic video, post or indeed photo that can, at the drop of a hat, change the thinking pattern of a young person exposed to this new, without context, headline and clickbait. No questions asked, nor should they be if it's shared by someone they admire or who 'influences them'. Don't forget, children, tomatoes give you cancer today and are healthy tomorrow!

John Piaget would be turning in his grave if that were possible. (And the odd things we say?) Critical thinking requires context, processing and 'sorting' so to speak, short- and long-term memory consolidation, assimilation, and an updated schema where necessary (implicit rules of the world) based on the new additional piece of information that you encountered (Piaget, 1926, cited in 2002). We don't have time for this anymore and because X or Y person(s) said or did 'this' online, and we are fascinated, enthralled, or bewitched by them, we don't go through that process with the same grace, effort and required complexities that previously seemed to make up the slower pace of 'real life'. If indeed critical thinking was employed by the general public as a rule; and yet here we are.

You may even find yourself doing this with the content of this book and updating your existing knowledge or arguing with the fact and assumptions herein. Don't believe all I write because *until I am faced with a black swan, all swans are white*, so the logic goes.

Easy speak content follows here: why communication changes are so important for the issues in this book.

Our communication patterns have changed because of the digital realm. Where we could once hold in our thinking, pausing and reflecting, writing and deleting those MSN messages to find the 'right words' (or leaving a trail of ellipses for what seemed an eternity to the recipient), now it's 'Instant' messenger systems requiring replies at the speed of light. Where we once could spend time in the creation of professional emails we are now creating a voice of 'neutral' tonality and PC correctness for fear of offending someone, before sending our thoughts through cyberspace akin to Mike Teavee in *Charlie and the Chocolate Factory*. Now we must reply within the time frame that is often unknown to us, but is certainly less than three days before we profusely apologise and fib to the sender, saying it was in the spam or the outbox (just me?).

Being online consists of having immediacy devices, and those 'relationship provocateurs' are close to one or within arms reach (well, mine often are anyway). And so blue tick distress, delayed gratification and impulse control are perhaps external to our executive functioning? Does the way we now 'speak' in cyberspace mean that we are at the beck and call of everyone all at once and divided by politeness and utter contempt for each other and all through these Internet-ready devices?

A reflection

Where has patience, compassion, acceptance, tolerance and empathy gone in our daily conversations? Why are we so driven to take to the keyboards like Bach, Mozart or Tchaikovsky playing 'chopsticks after consuming amphetamine' to make our point?

Where has our ability to pause, or consider the digital communication that falls from our speedy fingertips gone when sending the recipient to their (psychological) death based on our need to be triumphant with our side of the debate and argument? When did our egos get in the way and where has humanity 'gone'?

And when did the idea of potentially making a mistake around introductions and sign-offs in these communications become so heightened; should it cause distress to someone for the improper pronoun, title or 'ism' surreptitiously contained within the text?

Yours sincerely, … of course.

A socialising dilemma

As regards the scaremongering that has appeared on television, in documentaries and of course on social media, I think that this framing above is not entirely true, or helpful, though as I wrote these lines sat at my computer, I considered that someone may take these questions and reflections of doom and gloom, quote them and perhaps even stick them out into the digiworld citing my level of cynicism. These are headline clickbait questions if ever I saw them. Though, if this was a real conversation with a person face to face this would be contextual, temporal and with many to and fro variations of the meaning behind my thinking and the rhetorical questions I raise. There would be space and time to explore, navigate and work through them as a reflection of 'times a' changing?' There would be a co-created narrative of the mind as per the definition provided by Dan Siegel and colleagues in his book *Mind*, where he explains the mind is created and unbound by skin and bone (Siegel, 2016), elaborated upon by Louis Cozolino (2006) as the *social synapse*. The major difference in this example is the relational aspect of being with someone, face to face and the many cues we receive about reciprocal turn-taking in conversation, sometimes called serve and return, that isn't always afforded in the online world.

What I do know is that our introduction to the space of the 'teh interwebz' was like sending the first human mission to Mars; it needed (and still needs), in the process of colonizing, new norms developing and a level of shared togetherness. I am not entirely sure we have hit this landmark in the online spaces just yet, as the qualitative responses from companies developing and designing these spaces are high in egocentricity, individualism and consumerist greed but not a shared 'me' (what Dan Siegel calls Mwe) or compassion, tolerance or empathy. Like space, the dark needs illuminating. What is needed is light and I fear we only have a small candle at this point. When we learn to manage and regulate our emotions and our own internal narrative about the world and how tech has changed us, our reactive and often righteous 'low road' behaviours, we might stand a chance of changing what The Centre for Humane Technologies calls the wisdom or knowledge gap. Add to this our own body knowledge gap and we stand a good chance of thwarting our Palaeolithic evolution for a more sophisticated version (if I did a good enough job there should be a copy online of my TEDx talk: 'Bodies, brains and technology: The real social dilemma', Doncaster, October 2022 regarding this).

Online learning, communication and real-time reflections.

Take, for example, the blue tick distress that I discussed in my last book, or the zoom phenomenon of being able to direct questions, comments and reflections to the presenter in real-time, no holds barred. When did we move into this new form of 'always on, available and lacking 'wait times'?

Have you ever been sat in a class, lecture or presentation, in the real world, where thoughts can be directed out loud at the speaker as they move from sentence to sentence, construction to idea and thought to words? I don't know about you, but my school learning experience was sitting quietly, internally reflecting, dissecting, assimilating and considering the words that moved through the air like smoke, into my own landscape of understanding, creating a feeling of wanting to ask questions for further knowledge or clarification and being unable to. Learning was a sit-and-listen experience! This was frustrating, but also, 'the way of learning' since maybe the 1900s or before. Children should be seen, sat quietly listening attentively and not speaking. By the time the teacher had finished speaking I either had 40+ questions or had forgotten my salient point when the chance to ask questions was presented. It was considered rude to shout out, and ended in a punishment of sorts such as staying behind for 'a word', lines or some other form of punitive measure deemed suitable for a child who could not hold their tongue. I wrote many lines and became quite proficient at it. If only there was a degree in this, I'd be a PhD already. I am still the same today with a thirst for wanting to know more, more and more!

As I matured, and by this, I mean chronologically only, I have sat in conference halls and events where the speaker finishes their lecture, only to revisit my childhood in a snap, by holding my hand aloft and hoping the person (usually with the microphone) would choose *my* question to be asked so that my thinking could be further expanded and I could go home satisfied with my 'aha' moments being answered (of course, this is my own version of emotional dysregulation around wanting to know the answer to my internal question, my own lack of being able to contain my excitement, curiosity or, for those wise enough to recognise this, my own need to be seen). This indeed is my own personal agenda to become like Jonny5 (the sentient robot in the film *Short Circuit*) and get more knowledge; as Jonny5 requests 'input'. However, I only lift my hand far enough to warrant it being seen by the astute and don't seem to have the prowess of the person who is behaving like Donkey in the film *Shrek* and bouncing up and down almost screaming, 'pick me, pick me!' And my raising of the hand is *only* if I think the question won't be laughed at …

The new paradigm of 'in-real-time' online teaching, learning and education is no longer about self-regulation, norms and what used to be called 'manners'. The individualistic sense of self, perhaps even a level of narcissism or egocentric thinking can be seen on a live zoom call, for example. As such, I was fascinated by this as an evolving new 'norm' when both teaching or speaking on live events as I watched this behaviour unfolding over the last few years (before the lockdowns), and I a willing participator in this process too. In my engagement in this behaviour on several occasions I noticed that the chat function allows for people to send messages 'in front' of attendees as the speaker is speaking.

Now, this messaging function serves two different behaviours in our accepted communication norm changes: firstly, these messages can be to the speaker as in questions about what they just said and reflects the 'shouting out' typical of young children in the class. Or, secondly, the messaging function can be a number of people conversing with each other about the topic, or something else entirely, in front of the other attendees, and this for me is reminiscent of the chatty folk in class disrupting it for everyone else. Furthermore, the speaker can receive direct 'secret' messages from audience members and so the idea of 'teacher's pet' (I went for the polite version here), shy and reserved attendees or otherwise can have a direct line with the speaker without the knowledge of anyone else. So, as you see this behaviour unfolding in text format whilst the 'speaker speaks', I wonder if you noticed that this was a new learning environment/classroom-type experience for you, and if so how did you find it?

Added to this is the fact that some platforms allow you to be seen on camera and so, given that all eyes 'could' be on you, the behaviour of those on camera, on-screen can be intriguing to watch. With 30+ people on a screen nodding and seeming interested, who do you watch? Chances are, it's yourself.

Whereas in your physical classroom scenario these 'audiences' would be to your side, behind you and, likely, you looking a the back of some heads (unless you sat in a circular type format in class), people now find themselves 'performing to the camera' (nodding as a good student/member of the team/employee does) and of course checking themselves out as though in front of a mirror, which can lead to negative body image and thinking patterns about this (Kuhn, 2022).

Those who don't want to be seen turn off their camera. Those with busy backgrounds who have dogs, wives, husbands and children roaming about often do this, or if not cause the viewer to be half and half paying attention to the speaker and to what's happening on 'that screen over there'; and of course the insight gained into people's houses – clutter, pictures, decor, use of blurring or virtual backgrounds – now means many of us are making assumptions about people based on their use of the video-camera.

So, given there is now this freedom to interact in this way, are you a real-time chatter, questioner, reflector, wanting to be seen-er, present and listening with the speaker, distracted, or a sponge for a myriad of inputs all at once? Are you a camera on or off person, chaos in the background, nodder, smiler and clapper, or frozen still? And have you ever reflected on your own behaviour in these circumstances? Did you notice your communication patterns had changed as a human being in these spaces? Did you recognise, somewhat knowingly, that you were 'on show', or speaking out and chatting in order to feel felt by the rest of the 'class' when you could be listening with your whole self, and or are you exhausted by what is now framed as zoom fatigue (Bailenson, 2021)?

Or, since the invention of the hand-raising function, smiley emotes and more, are you now someone who feels that this is a way to let your fellow learners and attendees know that you care, approve or are pushing to be seen? Are you fully present or para-present? And how much time to you devote to watching your reactions, hairstyle, facial features instead of watching others? And did you know that when you can see yourself on camera this is a normal behaviour of the human being to look at oneself much more than the other? I mean, given that you have no head of course, you want to look at 'me' (you the reader, not 'me'); and by this, I mean the concept of being able to see all of your body apart from your face (Harding, 2006).

The days before video chat and 'selfies' meant that we only ever saw our reflection in ponds (Narcissus), glass and mirrors. Now we are reflecting on our reflection moment by moment, in 'self-view' and we are fascinated by it. We see our 'selves' more than we have ever done in our lives and I for one wonder, if we studied this in depth, whether we might just find the emergence of ego-centric, narcissistic and voyeuristic self-perception as a changing phenomenon. '*Self*' perception is changing too as well as communication perhaps?

Video annoyances and multi-task learning?

I have been in a few meetings where a person has reacted and stated that they want to turn the chat function off as it's distracting, and in some cases 'annoying the heckin' flip' out of them. This is both a feature bug of the platforms and of course a feature bug in itself of the human brain paying attention to moving objects for survival purposes (Le Doux, 2015); however, some people are unable to divert their attention away from these flashing little icons, for many reasons, one of which could be that fear of missing something important. Being able to manage this constant stream of information and multiple 'input' sources, i.e. 'multi-tasking', requires a skill of attentional focus to be able to listen, read and even reply all at the same time, which research and literature has shown us is actually impossible, and our self-perception of our ability to do this is way off (Gazzely & Rosen, 2016). This means that cognition may be parsing in far too many directions all at once and slowing us down, ineffective at paying attention to what is being taught, so retaining information becomes that much more difficult and thus we are unable to be present in the same way as in face-to-face learning. Hooray for the corporeal classroom! Or is that hooray? The silence in the classroom was actually a beneficial symptom of learning and we are now in a hybrid model of watching, listening, reading and replying alongside our own thinking processes, and contemplating what the speaker is saying because now we have to contend with the 'input-ters' and other chat functions and faces letting us know that they are engaged, understanding the content or otherwise. Indeed, you can see people who are not engaging as they look down to their device in their hand, out of the window and toward people in their corporeal environment. You can see those who are reading on their screen (for example open tabs on the browser) or editing documents. We just have so much to do that we are now, as Gazzaley puts it in the book title, *A Distracted Mind*. I would say this is changing us and how we converge on our communication patterns and what is acceptable when we are in a group together online (Gazzaley & Rosen, 2016).

And so a small reflection on 'multi-tasking'. You might have noticed that organisations, the media and scientists tell you this is not a healthy way to learn, process information or task orientate with attention, and they would be right and correct (neuro-scientifically). However, I would like to see some research in this area and see how it matches the real-world experience of learning in a classroom, online and through events like this. Is it really possible to take in the information and learn according to the theories we currently have or are we moving to a place where people are developing skills to be able to do this multi-tasking learning, but differently? It is ponderable to consider that we might be able to juggle some of those skills and effectively learn enough to get by, and of course, take in multiple viewpoints all at the same time. Being able to listen to the speaker and read comments (others' thinking) in real time as it happens has never been present in a classroom environment before due to the silence afforded in education settings. Other than working in small groups and speaking one at a time, we rarely get to hear others thinking about a topic, in real-time as it happens. This might just be a way to expand our thinking in a more divergent manner. I wonder what you think? Of course, I cannot hear you as the reader, so would have to wait for a reply in another format; if we were on a zoom call together, who knows!

Paused for reflection

Given that the book is about harm, consider the intrusive nature of session hacking (called 'zoom bombing' during lockdown) and what this would be like for all of the attendees to be suddenly presented with material that was shocking, illegal, or otherwise? Or for people to comment with racist, homophobic isms and ists. Given people in the meetings are usually there for work or educative reasons, then suddenly being in an environment whereby your eyes focus on a terrible image or text and stress response systems engage rapidly, then you can see how this can be a form of Cybertrauma, which is much more pernicious than anything encountered in the real world, where the cues available to you exist of the likelihood of something terrible 'about to happen' being omitted. (Much more on this later; for now, though, imagine the instant shock with no prior warning and what this is like to experience.) There is also another trend that can occur in these spaces, which is the selling of services, items and scams – often called sofa selling, as this was a prank trend created to annoy the attendees. Do you want to buy a sofa? (imagine this a hundred times or more in a chat function!)

Attachment, video events and learning: performing or speaking out and why

When we are small we find ourselves seeking to be seen by the other; in the case of many of the examples given in the literature, this is our caregiver, most often our parents. We may shout out in glee when we are in a reciprocal relationship, or shout out to be seen, e.g. 'look at me mummy!' (perhaps to be noticed in the presence of siblings, relatives or other people). We may indeed not shout out or communicate at all, in the case of the insecure types of attachment and so the digital platform becomes another tool for relationships, the need to be seen, the need to be acknowledged, the need to be in a co-created conversation, the need to be invisible, the need to be secretive for fear of ridicule or the need to ask questions. This is the 'pick me pick me' versus the 'don't ask me, don't ask me' feelings many children encounter in families, education and social settings. Classroom sizes also just increased to the maximal participant volume per platform (e.g. zoom can host 100 people in a meeting and thousands on a webinar).

Imagine what *being seen* means to children; seen by their parents and people they trust, idolise and are connected with (Knibbs, 2022). It's a humongous innate drive to be noticed, revered, celebrated and for survival (remember the bit about bio-survival circuitry (Wilson, 1990)). And so we are drawn to looking at the person on video and looking for those signs that we are 'seen'. And of course, in a classroom, a great teacher, highly versed in social and emotional intelligence (Goleman, 1995) can talk to the whole class, making eye contact with those that can tolerate it, moving their eyes away from those who find it threatening, speaking to the ceiling, door or window when necessary to make a point and containing the whole class at once. They can know and convey that they see you, listening attentively to your non-verbal communication. They see that you are interested and know how to bring the topic to life to create those sparks of excitement and curiosity. And so the transition to the online spaces of video work has left many people feeling like they are watching TV and have what is called a para-social relationship (Horton & Wohl, 1956; Kowert, 2021). This is akin to those pop stars, movies, and TV characters that we can so readily identify with.

And then in a sudden change to our daily norms and life: lockdown! The move into the world of online learning suddenly became the norm for us all – well, for those who indeed had access to the Internet and could access the world of Microsoft Office, Teams and Zoom.

So with the presence of 'immediacy', the open space to be dysregulated and impatient, the visual cues as to whether I am seen or unseen, the capacity and space to hide, and the hidden back door conversations (direct messages), we are moving into a landscape of changing attachment and communication facilitated by *synchronous* technology. What is the best, most helpful, supportive way to do this?

Practitioners pause for reflection

Blank screens and safeguarding

This has commonly been a discussion point with my clients during the lockdown period whereby people can hide behind cameras, forums, chat rooms and online spaces. However, for some children that have been educated online, the need for safeguarding, whilst not necessarily understanding how to do this safely and ethically, has resulted in many institutions asking for cameras to be switched off. This has meant that in the process of taking the stance, 'we don't want to see into the houses where other children may be present', issues have been missed entirely. This camera-off approach, in itself, has potentially been merciless in cementing insecure attachment styles in some children. Being unseen either by camera or in the chat areas has felt beyond cruel and children may not have asked for help, because they couldn't. Not only this but teachers and trainers of online sessions have missed safeguarding issues because they can't see anything, and some opt for screens off so they don't have to.

As a practitioner, if we were in a child's house physically, we 'expect', in fact we are taught, to pay attention to the surroundings, people, visitors and child in that environment to ensure that we 'Work together to safeguard children' do we not? (Department for Education, 2018). So why the sudden change of heart for digital education? Why are people asking children to turn off their cameras? Perhaps this is because parents request it, there may be other children in the house, there may be other parents, visitors and of course their personal items, furnishings and such. And what about if that computer is in the child's bedroom? If the sessions are not being recorded, why do we do this? What did we miss during lockdown education and what can we learn from this?

Screens off or on? Taking responsibility or not and the underpinning reasons of why? What bigger questions need to be asked here and where are the policies for this, developed during or after the Covid-19 pandemic? And where are the standard and ethical operating procedures for this? (I have some available on request as this has been a misunderstood, missed and misshaped situation that we can certainly learn from, going forward.)

References

Bailenson, J. (2021). *Nonverbal overload: A theoretical argument for the causes of Zoom fatigue. Technology, Mind and Behaviour, 2*(1). www.scirp.org/(S(351jmbntvnsjt1aad-kozje))/reference/referencespapers.aspx?referenceid=3174512.

Consilience project. (2022). *Technology is not values neutral.* https://consilienceproject.org/technology-is-not-values-neutral/.

Cozolino, L. (2006). *The neuroscience of human relationships: Attachment and the developing social brain* (2nd ed.). W.W. Norton.

Department for Education. (2018). *Working together to safeguard children: A guide to inter-agency working to safeguard and promote the welfare of children.* https://assets.publishing.service.gov.uk/government/uploads/system/uploads/attachment_data/file/942454/Working_together_to_safeguard_children_inter_agency_guidance.pdf.

Gazzelay, A., & Rosen, L. (2016). *A distracted mind: Ancient brains in a technological world.* MIT Press.

Goleman, D. (1995). *Emotional intelligence.* Bloomsbury.

Harding, D. (2006). *On having no head: Zen and the rediscovery of the obvious.* Inner Directions Publishing.

Hare, S. (2022). *Technology is not neutral: A short guide to technology ethics.* London Publishing Partnership.

Horton, D., & Wohl, R. R. (1956). *Mass communication and para-social interaction. Psychiatry: Journal for the Study of Interpersonal Processes, 19,* 215–229.

Kaye, L. (2017). *What your emoji says about you.* TEDx Vienna. www.ted.com/talks/linda_kaye_what_your_emoji_says_about_you.

Knibbs, C. (2022). *Children, technology, and healthy development.* Routledge.

Kowert, R. (2021). *Jargon schmargon: Parasocial relationships.* Psychgeist channel on YouTube. www.youtube.com/watch?v=Zjl2BFv0Z74.

Kuhn, K. (2022). *The constant mirror: Self-view and attitudes to virtual meetings. Computers in Human Behavior, 128.* www.sciencedirect.com/science/article/abs/pii/S0747563221004337.

Le Doux, J. (2015). *Anxious: The modern mind in the age of anxiety.* Oneworld.

McGilchrist, I. (2019). *The master and his emissary: The divided brain and the making of the western world.* Yale University Press.

McGilchrist, I. (2021). *The Matter With Things. Our brains, our delusions and the unmaking of the world.* Perspectiva Press.

Miller, G. (1956). *The magical number seven, plus or minus two: Some limits on our capacity for processing information. Psychological Review, 63,* 81–89.

Piaget, J. (1926, cited in Piaget, J. (2002)). *The language and thought of the child.* Routledge.

Wall, H., Kaye, L., & Malone, S. (2016). *An exploration of psychological factors on emoticon usage and implications for judgement accuracy. Computers in Human Behavior, 62,* 70–78.

Siegel, D. (2016). *Mind.* W.W. Norton.

Wilson, R. A. (1990). *Quantum psychology: How brain software programs you and your world.* Hilarity's Press.

Wu, T. (2010). *The master switch: The rise and fall of information empires.* Alfred A Knopf.

Resource

Knibbs, C. (2020). *Safeguarding children online: A guide for practitioners.* https://children-andtech.co.uk/product/practitioners-guide-to-safeguarding-when-working-online-remotely/.

Names of people or organisations and websites

Jonathan Pageu. https://thesymbolicworld.com/.
John Vervaeke. http://johnvervaeke.com/.
DanielSchmachtenbergerhttps://civilizationemerging.com/articles/personal-blog-posts/.
Rebel Wisdom. https://rebelwisdom.co.uk/.
Centre for Humane Technology. www.humanetech.com/.
The Intellectual Darkweb. www.nytimes.com/2018/05/08/opinion/intellectual-dark-web.html; www.vox.com/the-big-idea/2018/5/10/17338290/intellectual-dark-web-rogan-peterson-harris-times-weiss.

2 Online harms

Online harms: setting the scene

Henry Ford and the car. It's not the technology, it's the people. Mostly.

I begin this chapter using a metaphor that you may find useful.

Think about Henry Ford and the production of vehicles that could be used by anyone who could afford one, beginning with the few cars that were developed before mass production. Few had them to start with, followed by the many. This early adoption process is not limited to cars or computers per se, but we are looking at technology in this book, so let's think about the new technologies and spaces heading our way as you read. And so, owning a car would be limited at the outset of production to the ones with funds to pay: the rich and affluent. Often what is assumed here is, by default, affluent people would not be the type of people to engage in behaviours such as driving under the influence, speeding, driving with bald tyres, having no lights and the equivalent of no MOT. Would they?

Of course, being rich does not preclude you from these behaviours; perhaps they just weren't observed or penalised as much, especially when there were only three cars in a village, and the laws about these issues were not in place, yet.

However, it was the sudden, sheer number of cars produced and available to the 'common folk' that created the environment of lots of cars on the road, and so we saw 'lots of accidents' and traffic jams occurring. I remember hearing once that three cars too many on a motorway (freeway) is enough to cause a standstill for at least 30 minutes. I have no idea how this would be measured accurately, but myths stick and this thought often pops into my head in a traffic jam (you're welcome).

This metaphor of lots of cars, or too many cars, represents the number of devices and connections that children can own and use to make connections, and this means the likelihood of them encountering a 'bad, distracted or incapacitated driver' and not a bad automobile. This likelihood of encountering

DOI: 10.4324/9781003364177-3

bad drivers is going to be down to the prevalence of 'cars on the road', so to speak, and this number means ... highly likely as there are so many road users today.

A point to note here is that bad drivers existed when there were only three per village and, of course, whilst the regulations, sensibility and knowledge about seat belts, brakes, tread depth and suitability and roadworthiness did exist, it just took a large number of road traffic collisions, deaths and injuries for those rules to come into being. This is almost parallel to the approach taken in terms of regulations around the Internet and harms encountered so far. Many people may die before the changes are applied. This should not be the case, though sadly is a truth.

And yet, the same principles could be applied to the newly emerging space of 'metaverses' and laws of safety-first, profit second are hopefully what the regulatory services are aiming to achieve. Sadly, another truth is that it may also be a retrospective law-making process after the fact. Remember *tech is not neutral* (Hare, 2022).

Jargon and your need to know

You may be hearing these newer words on TV, in the media and of course on social media, and they may be flummoxing and may sound like another form of confusing 'lexicon', words such as metaverse, immersive spaces, NFT (non-fungible tokens), blockchain and Web 3.0. All these are based on the development of another layer to our progress and how such technologies will upscale and work with each other.

These words may well be more popular in the language of children and young people and so we need to learn them too to be able to meet them where they are. For word count reasons, I will not go into explaining all of these, but you can find out more on my blogs via my website and Medium page (see https://medium.com/@nibzy).This technology is ever evolving with great speeds; and with great power and tech come great responsibilities, if of course you are Spiderman, or an adult looking after, working with or know children, or are developing the technology they will be using.

Your responsibility throughout this book is to read, and re-read, digest, understand and implement processes that create safeguarding policies and procedures for your practice and place of work. Those processes should go beyond generic advice, symptom management or signposting to services with words such as online, technology, digital, safeguarding or internet in their titles, confusing the landscape of the ever-present search for the right service, which is an issue for many practitioners who are looking for help in this area. (Note: many services do not have the depth of knowledge or training to work with these issues as many of them are preventative or pathologising services looking at just one behavioural aspect, e.g. 'addiction'.) I'm often met with the following phrases (and faces of utter despair) from practitioners I teach and work with:

'Isn't this just a social care or police issue?'
'But where do I go for advice?'
'What tech can I use to do the job for me?'
'Can I just block, ban or remove it?'
'Is there a website where I can learn more about that?'
'Is there a website that tells me what to do'
'Is there a place I can report this?'
'Who, how, where, when, and most importantly what do I report?'

And …

'Who deals with this?'

The answer to many of these questions is: lots of websites tell you what you should do, along with all of the social media posts about these issues from experts, parents, non-experts and other professionals, non-governmental organisations, governing bodies, membership organisations and other groups online, companies and third sector organisations and sites aimed at a national level in the UK. I have counted over 250 different e-safety type sites all with their own perspectives, recommendations and research.

This is overwhelming for many practitioners, as there are few spaces to have a national, single, coordinated approach to these issues as they are currently so ubiquitous, large and overwhelming that we have not managed to do this – *yet* (I am hopeful!). Some organisations need both policies *and* procedures within them, for example: Social Care Direct. We do not *yet* have a good enough law or legislation, with which we can follow a specific direction, unless it is an illegal issue already deemed in law, for example, child sexual abuse material, or terrorist content.

Unlike the Working Together to Safeguard Children legislation already in place (DfE, 2018), we really have nothing for the online space that has the *same level of guidance*, noteworthy advice and of course level of understanding about harms, issues, processes and how to work with these issues, *yet*.

This is one of the main reasons why I set out to write this book: to provide and educate the professions of adults working with children. It is great when we have lots of knowledge about an issue, but not when we have nothing to lean on other than phrases in legislation about your level of knowledge such as '*understand the online space*'. Why children are falling through the net of being appropriately safeguarded in the space of the internet is the issue. The phrase regarding this that I hear the most is: 'I have been unable to find the procedures that tell me (the practitioner) *what to do*, other than report, signpost and refer on. I don't know how to help, Cath'.

This leaves a practitioner with a deficit in how to help the family or services around the child with guidance or reassurance about what happened (online), is happening now and is still likely to happen once the report or referral is made. Knowing the process requires a process toward knowing what happens once reported.

Notwithstanding this, when someone like myself tries to make a safeguarding concern and report, I am often (and have been for almost a decade), met with a lack of knowledge about the issue, non-existent threshold criteria (for services), and practitioners who are often wary, terrified or reluctant to deal with the issue or even know what services to bring in for the families, or carers (who actually do understand the issue). Unless this is 'sexting', there are currently no suitable forms, guidance and procedures in place. I am often told it's not a safeguarding concern unless I explain *why it really is*. This leaves me worried about those who don't know what they don't know, and so here is a book to change that not knowing. I hope!

As an example of this, I worked for a long time with a case where a child was groomed (not for sexual images or money) and all the forms available to fill out for referring to the services in existence at the time (under the social care banner), were unfit for purpose, lacked the direction needed for this young person and did not meet any of the guidance under Social Care Direct policies for a safeguarding concern outside of the 'real world'. Herein lies one of the biggest issues, which will become crystal clear throughout this book and the next (Knibbs, forthcoming).

As the therapist with the know-how of the issue, even when it was explained to the services why we needed to take action, I was met with blank faces and blank procedures. *This has got to change* and this book is an attempt to begin the processes and understanding, and start to have those documents in place for the safeguarding of all children. Both worlds are one. There is no 'real-life' world anymore.

Too many children have already, over 27 years, fallen through the (inter) net because of this lack of systemic practice and legislation. Let us make the change we wish to see in the world.

Setting the scene:

Online … harms … what are they?

Let me begin by covering old ground on this topic by going back to the 1990s, the birth of the Internet and the laws in place at that time (some still in use today for issues that have occurred using a 'computer'). We need to look at the words we currently have to describe online harms, what the issues might be and how we can classify them, and of course the plethora of typologies that have existed and will continue to emerge with the new technologies. Grab a notebook, there's lots of information to come and you may want to make notes.

In 2011 I began to use the phrase 'Cybertrauma' when I was working in practice with issues that were related to the internet, online spaces and technology. I am not the first person to use this term and so cannot say I coined it (I once naively did say I had coined the term and perhaps I did, but not on paper and an academic search showed me otherwise. So I no longer say I did).

The clients who presented with these types of issues were as young as four, with one lady in her seventies and all ages in between. Each of the issues related to a form of technology that had an internet connection, and so 'online' may have been a good way to describe the issues. However, I hail from the era of language denoting this space as 'cyber', as in cybersecurity, and so I considered that trauma related to this space could be identified in this way.

As we go through this book, it will become clear 'it's not all social media' or the most popular one of these big tech giants at the time of reading who so often feature in the news. Since 2011 I have added to, refined, redefined and adapted my definition of what Cybertrauma is to match the corporeal traumas I work with in psychotherapy. In 2016 I produced a handy guide for professionals and parents describing some of the issues that could be encountered by anyone of any age and, as I look back now, this seems out of date! Yet, it is still imperative to the conversations to be had in this book, there now being many more than I could fit into that guide (Knibbs, 2016).

I intend to go beyond the summaries of that guide in this book and focus on the traumas, abuses and harms that can be experienced. I do not have the word count to cover all of them and, as much as the publishers are able to give me a lot, these issues would take me two days to describe and explain fully in training. The space of the virtual, digital and cyber is so large and increasing it would be impossible for me to think I could do this justice in one writing (I will try though).

However, I will get as much into this volume as I can with a view to creating and writing more along the way, likely over many years. I also have a research study ongoing at the time of handing in the manuscript and so I expect to share these findings once completed too. And of course, the metaverse is likely to bring further writings, so I hope to be your friend and guide in these going forward, a little like a technological Gandalf.

The focus in this book will be mostly on children; however, I may use examples from the adults I work with too, as the children will eventually become adults and some of the traumas will follow these children for the entirety of their corporeal lives and may also live on digitally after their material and cellular body has left the planet. That is scary thought number one. Fasten your seatbelt – from here on in, safety first.

The conversations in this book are primarily aimed at professionals and will include quotes and examples from practice to discuss the issue and highlight how this might be observed, recognised and actioned in practice. For those who have never heard this technology-related language, this can enable them to ask questions about this subject with the children they work with or the adults they are speaking to about it. In 2022 I am still learning new technology-related language as the world speeds into the Metaverse and Web 3.0. infinity and beyond! (Thanks, Buzz Lightyear.)

This book is designed to help you understand the process of technology and arm you, the practitioner (and parent where necessary). The book is also for those readers who are neither parents nor professionals working with children but are curious and here to learn how to protect children, maybe at the level of local authority or government. Often, I find, *if you understand the why* you can begin to create, design and place the policies and provide guidance, law and procedures based on the *what, when* and *how* with tools, thinking and shared intentions.

The topics may not be comfortable to read at times, so self-care, self-pacing of the material and having a person in your life to discuss these issues with is almost a *must have and must do*. I ask that you do this because I do not wish to traumatise or scare you, but I must tell the facts, and this can be a difficult topic for some.

It is imperative that you take personal responsibility for your mental and emotional well-being as you read this book, and of course, know you are not alone in the impact of reading about these issues. I am much further on than many in my understanding of this space and I recognise that this may be the first time you read about and consider the harm occurring to children from this online space; I can sometimes forget that I know this map and landscape well and forget you are first time navigators of it.

You may feel angry, overwhelmed, powerless, traumatised, think I'm a sensationalist, not believe some of the things here, and even take your own child's devices away to stop any of this from happening – and you are not alone. This book is going to be difficult for some; however, the time has come to become accountable for our adultness, and talk the taboo, uncomfortable and scary in order to support and protect children.

It is time to get comfortable with your own discomfort about conversing with children and other adults about these topics.

Many of you will be working in a space where you, the professional may be causing some of the harm, but imagine the harm over time by *not* taking on this topic, due to your own fears and discomfort.

We can and must do better for the children and we must not direct, assume, blame and leave it up to them to learn how to protect themselves. We must work with each other and have these and other uncomfortable conversations. The net has many holes, and we must learn how to seal them up and prevent even one child from falling though them. My wise supervisor used to say to me that I would often get on my trusty steed over matters of child protection and ethics and that I couldn't save the world on my own. So, the only way I feel I can do this is to ask for your help. Are you with me?

References

Department for Education (2018). *Working together to safeguard children: a guide to inter-agency working to safeguard and promote the welfare of children.* https://assets.publishing. service.gov.uk/government/uploads/system/uploads/attachment_data/file/942454/ Working_together_to_safeguard_children_inter_agency_guidance.pdf.

Hare, S. (2022). *Technology is not neutral: A short guide to technology ethics.* London Publishing Partnership.

Knibbs, C. (2016). *Cybertrauma: The darker side of the internet.* Self-published and available on Amazon kindle and blurb books.

Knibbs, C. (forthcoming). *Online harms and cybertrauma: Legal and harmful issues with children and young people.* Routledge.

3 Setting the scene

Online, offline: what's the difference? Surely, it's not that bad?

Let me make an analogy this early in the writing so that we can be clear about online harm and the difficulty with which it can be explained accurately in less than 70,000 words and how it can happen, in this case to a child.

Imagine sending a child you work with into the local city or town park, and not explaining about the path that leads from the main entrance to the safest exit point. You tell them to meet you in a few hours on the other side of the park as you have an errand to run.

Imagine that child wanders into the park and is met with the following harms (these are only some that we will cover in this volume): being followed by or spoken to by strangers and maybe even perpetrators of crimes against children walking with that child (maybe even holding their hand), 18+ sexual content occurring on the park bench, violence, con artists, polarised marches and gangs urging them to pick a side or die, substance or drug use behind the bushes but in full view, animal cruelty and abuse, rapes, murders and muggings – and all you gave the child was a time and place to be out of the park and a warning about stranger danger because that's all you covered in your recent safeguarding course.

It just wouldn't happen. Would it?

You may want to complete the breath cycle you are in. Take your time.

In this scenario, you more than likely would accompany the child to keep them safe. Or establish, create or follow a rule that they couldn't go there alone until they were old enough, which would likely be advised as being into their middle teenage years or even legally an adult. Because that's what we do right to protect our children or each other? I certainly know if I was going to walk through a park during the day, I would likely be given some advice about the 'spots' to avoid. Can you imagine the advice I would receive at night-time? And not because I am female, but because we have an innate responsibility to warn each other of the dangers of spaces to our species. This began way back on the plains when we could communicate the places the lions may be waiting to pounce!

DOI: 10.4324/9781003364177-4

And so the metaphor I use is the ever-expanding local park with infinite entrances, exits and people who visit there. This image may work for you to consider that this online, digital cyberspace is the local park with *no real rules* about what can take place there because there aren't enough do-gooders, police and park 'rangers' to uphold the law, because there aren't enough adequate ones and there are not really enough laws to fall back on, *just yet*. (Note: anyone who has had this thought will have been able to google or find someone else online who shares that thought, ideal, fetish, kink or imagination and meet them 'in the park' with an added potential of recruiting others to their space.)

If you consider the issue here of *'offline'* harm in this context, then I am sure that, as a skilled reader, you can fantasise and imagine how broad *'online'* harm can be. Think more along the lines of how many harms in the real world a child can face on average, and then perhaps double or triple this thinking for the online spaces. Yes, really.

It's not all stranger danger education, nor the ideology of getting them 'bully proof' and capable of defending themselves (as I often see on martial arts posters, group events at school, youth services, local authorities and more); it's about creating a top-down *and* bottom-up approach to child protection and this is *our* role and responsibility as the adults.

The online harms in the online city park ...

'Online harms' is an area of what will soon (quickly I hope) become a bill of law and legislation in the United Kingdom, and hopefully globalised alongside other regulatory actions and laws, so we can begin to address *some of the issues*. The world is moving to this approach, albeit after the horses have exited the barn and ridden off into the distance. And it is only the start of how we manage online harm – it is *not* the panacea. Real-world conversations *must* sit alongside these laws and legislations and they need to be trauma applied. For that, we may be waiting some time. However, we are moving to a space of *the beginning of hope* and child protection writ large.

To appropriately respond to harms and perhaps even regulate the space, to prevent these from occurring at the rate at which they currently do, this bill is intended to focus on the harms that all people, including children, face online. It is still in developmental infancy at the time of this writing and may not be fully read and amended through the legal process by the time this book is published. However, the remit of this bill does not (at the time of writing) cover all the topics you will read about in this book. And my, and others' ongoing research in this area uncovers new issues almost monthly, based on the new and emerging technology, platforms, apps and areas. The bill is expected to be 'future proof', but I am not entirely sure that is possible and so we may need to amend 'as we go' because we know not what is around the corner.

We still have much to do to protect all people. However, as stated previously, this book is primarily to create a learning platform for practitioners to protect where possible and mitigate further harm to children and young people. I suspect we will spend more time on the latter – mitigating further harm – as the gate was opened many years ago and, in my clinical experience, over the last decade; we are playing catch up to a photon of light and we have not been great at proactive protection so far.

The reason the definitions in the bill and the bill itself are so complicated to create, establish and act on is a complicated and nuanced issue. Many of the harms 'defined by people' are based on issues that come to light after the fact, and have often not been previously thought of, because how can we know all the harms yet to be?

Furthermore, in creating this bill, legislation, policies and law, many of the harms are following real-world laws already established and moving them across into the digital space, where borders (geographical, technical and physical) do not exist.

However, if you look at the harms suffered by individuals, they can also be subjective, biased, have attribution errors, and of course then take place in settings not necessarily easy to find, trace or take action in.

The space of 'cyber' and 'online' is fairly difficult to define, and now we have more 'spaces' and places in development that may increase this bill's complexities immeasurably. In spaces where stories of online harm are told, such as to parents, teachers or other adults they can be missed, never actioned, discussed, dismissed or even not understood as such. This is one of the aspects of the knowledge gap cited by The Centre for Humane Technology (CHT, 2020).

Many a time in therapy a client has explained something that happened to them over a platform, something their partner did, or indeed they did with or through technology, that leads to a discussion about responsibility, accountability and of course harm in the context of law and ethics, and I cannot say with robust accuracy that a client has or had broken 'a cyber-based law'. What I can say is that the harm they say they felt is real and tangible, and needs a broader conversation with others outside of my therapy office. And here we are.

This has also complicated the issue itself when I am aware of the harm the individual has suffered and yet there is no place to 'take it' in terms of safeguarding, the law or even actionable behaviour for them, post our discussion and session. My work is to be a psychotherapist, confidante, e-safety 'officer', cybersecurity and data protection guru and online harms 'expert'. This has evolved for more than a decade into who I am today, and I know the parts of my professional make-up make me unique as a practitioner, but it shouldn't be this way. All practitioners need this knowledge to effectively safeguard, protect and care for those who use or are surrounded by technology.

Definitions a many, language and semantics?

Which is what, how, when and for whom?

Some issues to consider to date are how do we define any (or more), behaviours that have an overlap with technology, for example stalking and cyberstalking?

This semantic, pragmatic and legal aspect has been the bugbear of policing, law, content moderation, conversation and of course the language we assign to these issues. Where do these issues sit if we call them online and yet they impact a person in their real world, and additionally something in their 'real' world occurs such as fraud, whereby their bank account is now zero after being conned by a criminal? Is the harm the fraud or the impact, resulting in depression and anxiety? Of course, in this example, the law and banks might be able to pursue a 'traceable address' (even if it does not name a person), and the victim may receive a refund of some sort. The anxiety and depression that results from this are in the real world, in the person's mind and body – so does this count as online harm? How do we describe the apples and pears when there may well be oranges too?

As a further delineation away from this, how do we assess accurately what has caused harm? For example, I often say when teaching, what is harmful and distressing to me, may not be the same for you. What is considered harmful to the body in medical settings may be considered art elsewhere, such as tattoos or body modifications (including self-sought surgery) and so on, and you only need to look to the Internet to see how these issues are poles apart in how they are perceived (this issue is also discussed in Knibbs, forthcoming). So how do we create a consensus of shared understanding where we can all agree? Subjectivity is difficult to express as an objective measured truth and this is plainly clear in the research domains.

This point on its own is a major part of this book and hence this sentence can be carried with you throughout the book and beyond. Much of the focus on online harm at this stage in 2022 is impossible for us all to agree on. Lawyers, regulators, parents, professionals and others will have their own perspectives. And that's because we are human and have our own way of seeing the world.

We are in a space of trying to define and regulate human behaviour and this book brings you the harms my clients have encountered over the years through a concept called phenomenology.

To give those of you who are not psychologists a simple definition of phenomenology, it is the perspective a person takes on their own lives and experiences, and how they make sense of their world using the knowledge they have. For example, school is a concept understood by many of us, but we all have our feelings, interpretations and meaning-making about what school is, what it is for, how it felt to be there, how we would explain it to someone and what words we would use to describe it. Phenomenology is a metaphysical, philosophical position posited by Husserl (Merleau-Ponty, 2002; Cited in Pernecky, 2016).

Real life to cyberspace

Much like real life, the Internet is its own space of human interaction alongside machine learning bots, AI, and plenty of anonymous and faceless accounts. Those humans are also known as visitors, users and inhabitants of cyberspace and are not always best intended in their behaviours. They live online in spaces we would really rather not know about or visit, or they are in or create spaces that cannot be tamed or regulated, much like the experience of walking down the street where, in effect, 'anything can happen'. Spaces online are frequented by humans and, as such, anything can, and often does happen and this is where my focus of this book will be.

So let's begin by looking at what harm is and why the phrase online harm is more about a phenomenon that will be contextual, cultural, time and space dependent. Harm, much like the word trauma can be assessed as being about the recipient, victim or person of happenstance. Whilst I repeat myself a little here, I am going to give some examples so we can be on the same page. To give you an extreme example: circumcision is considered barbaric in some Western cultures, yet there are cultures in which this is not looked upon this way. You see harm becomes a moral issue as well as an ethical consideration, as well as the construct of offence and actual harm as defined in safeguarding (in the UK), and is also based on the environment in which it happens. So, let's break this down a little.

A less extreme example?

Swearing is something I do and have done for many years, based on my contextual upbringing of both being in the military and from a military background where some of these words are adjectives, sentence spacers (such as commas) and enhancers to the communication style of the Forces. You'll find plenty of these words in my vocabulary. I am not really offended or harmed by these 'types' of words being uttered, shouted or typed in my presence as I see them as literal words or letters spilling out from the mouth or mind of a person (or bot). The intent with which they are sent in my direction often has an underlying cause and I'm more interested in that, to be honest.

However, you can see that some, but not all people can be harmed by hearing swear words, which are sometimes called foul or offensive language. Children of course may likely feel harmed if sworn *at*, as this often involves a form and level of aggressive behaviour accompanying their utterance (this is a form of emotional abuse because of this fact). Some children may hear these words daily as part of their family dynamics, or friendships and relationships, and of course, these words are rife online in the gaming and social media spaces.

So my point is to suggest that you may think of swear words as both foul and offensive, or not, or prefer some but not all of them, or you may conjecture that they may be harmful, offensive or foul language to some people, of differing ages for differing reasons, but not all. It's a matter of perspective, upbringing, social norms, societal and cultural aspects and more.

And herein lies the difficulty we will repeatedly visit throughout the book about some of the taxonomy and labelling of some of the issues under discussion. In a world of constructs, ideas and cultures we will see the issue of subjectivity time and time again. We will also see that classifications and definitions also bring many issues of their own when we consider how to measure and pursue these 'issues', especially when we are looking to prosecute or create policies around them.

Our language is not substantial enough really to do justice to the process of creating a well-defined, agreed vision of what global online harms actually are. But *we have to start somewhere*! This leads me to share my long, word salad definition of Cybertrauma which has been increasing in complexity since 2011. I do this to begin to consider the enormity of the issue of the *impact* of harm, what I call the Cybertrauma:

> Any trauma that is a result of self- or, other-directed interaction with, mediated through or from any electronic internet/cyberspace ready device or machine learning or artificial intelligence algorithm, that results in impact now or the future.
>
> This event/interaction can be multi-modal, multi-platform and multi-interval, delayed or immediate, legal or not, singular or plural, and may include images, sound, direct sensation or touch, and/or text and may or may not be vitriolic in nature.
>
> Events may include covert and overt typology and may be virtual and corporeal and or at the same time.
>
> This is my ongoing definition taken from my website www. childrenandtech.co.uk (Knibbs, 2016–Ongoing definition 2021). Or simply: any trauma encountered or facilitated via technology.

My suggestion here is online harm can be considered in the same way, *and* also must include the current definitions used in safeguarding, so that we can focus on the type of harm (e.g. emotional, physical, sexual and neglect); *and*, that which may not include social media companies directly, and may indeed include the legal but harmful mass media, charities and organisations who share material and content in this space (more on this in Chapter 10 about harms caused by professionals).

In the world of safeguarding legislation (Department for Education, 2018) and the UN conventions on the rights of children (UNCROC, 1989a, 1989b) there are legal, technical and academic definitions of what is considered harmful to a child, which include the category of *Abuse*. This category is further broken down into types, which attempt to be objective, yet, as we saw earlier, are open to interpretation, especially when, for example, prosecutors and defence use these terms in their arguments in courts and reports.

These terms can be used as weapons against warring parents, or between them, and often these are the terms that the helping professionals become au fait with and use as a common language between them to understand what we are all talking about. It is important to remember that, as we consider harm and abuse categories, these definitions are on a spectrum (as is trauma).

To understand where I am going with this, allow me to explain these typologies and how they describe the effects of abuse under the definition, as taken from the DfE legislation: *Keeping Children Safe in Education* (Department for Education, 2022, pp. 10–11).

Indicators of abuse and neglect

22. Abuse: a form of maltreatment of a child. Somebody may abuse or neglect a child by inflicting harm or by failing to act to prevent harm. Children may be abused in a family or in an institutional or community setting by those known to them or, more rarely, by others. Abuse can take place wholly online, or technology may be used to facilitate offline abuse. Children may be abused by an adult or adults or by another child or children.

23. Physical abuse: a form of abuse which may involve hitting, shaking, throwing, poisoning, burning or scalding, drowning, suffocating or otherwise causing physical harm to a child. Physical harm may also be caused when a parent or carer fabricates the symptoms of, or deliberately induces, illness in a child.

24. Emotional abuse: the persistent emotional maltreatment of a child such as to cause severe and adverse effects on the child's emotional development. It may involve conveying to a child that they are worthless or unloved, inadequate, or valued only insofar as they meet the needs of another person. It may include not giving the child opportunities to express their views, deliberately silencing them or 'making fun' of what they say or how they communicate. It may feature age or developmentally inappropriate expectations being imposed on children. These may include interactions that are beyond a child's developmental capability as well as overprotection and limitation of exploration and learning, or preventing the child from participating in normal social interaction. It may involve seeing or hearing the ill-treatment of another. It may involve serious bullying (including cyberbullying), causing children frequently to feel frightened or in danger, or the exploitation or corruption of children. Some level of emotional abuse is involved in all types of maltreatment of a child, although it may occur alone.

25. Sexual abuse: involves forcing or enticing a child or young person to take part in sexual activities, not necessarily involving a high level of violence, whether or not the child is aware of what is happening. The activities may involve physical contact, including assault by penetration (for example rape or oral sex) or non-penetrative acts such as masturbation, kissing, rubbing and touching outside of clothing. They may also include non-contact activities, such as involving children in looking at, or in the production of, sexual images, watching sexual activities, encouraging children to behave in sexually

inappropriate ways, or grooming a child in preparation for abuse. Sexual abuse can take place online, and technology can be used to facilitate offline abuse. Sexual abuse is not solely perpetrated by adult males. Women can also commit acts of sexual abuse, as can other children. The sexual abuse of children by other children is a specific safeguarding issue in education (see paragraph 29).

Note: My thinking here is as you look at these definitions some become slightly overlapped with each other and of course technology is mentioned as being a part of the abuse process. Yet these conditions, descriptions, and the very definition of abuse (point 22) are currently omitted from the online harms bill.

26. Neglect: the persistent failure to meet a child's basic physical and/or psychological needs, likely to result in the serious impairment of the child's health or development. Neglect may occur during pregnancy, for example, as a result of maternal substance abuse. Once a child is born, neglect may involve a parent or carer failing to: provide adequate food, clothing and shelter (including exclusion from home or abandonment); protect a child from physical and emotional harm or danger; ensure adequate supervision (including the use of inadequate care-givers); or ensure access to appropriate medical care or treatment. It may also include neglect of, or unresponsiveness to, a child's basic emotional needs.

Supervision of a child going online or lack of supervision, is this neglect or not knowing?

What about the lack of adequate supervision for the online space, whereby a child can visit sites and material that are unsuitable as deemed by media (film) classification ratings? Those spaces that in the real world you need to be 18, 21 or 25 to enter, such as casinos, arcades, nightclubs and adult entertainment venues? Should we prosecute parents for this if they did not know their child was visiting such spaces? Should we include this in our approach to online safety messages? Would we speak with, refer, or prosecute parents who allowed their children into the corporeal spaces suggested here and why are we not looking at the online spaces in the same way? Is this worthy of discussion at high levels as well as in everyday conversations in education and professional settings?

The thinking behind the corporeal age restrictions is something along the lines of *Adult spaces where adults can be themselves as: adults.* Language, sexual activities, legal substance use and of course the right to gamble, spend and consume is a choice given to those we deem mature enough to make these choices. So why do we, currently, not see the virtual world in the same way? And what do we age restrict outside of gambling or sex? And to quote Zuboff (2019), *who decides and who decides who decides?* And how do we enforce, regulate and protect those spaces?

That would mean collecting all sorts of data points about children or adults to enforce this. Age verification is going to sit within or alongside the bill and we know that in years gone by children have been able to circumnavigate getting substances, and alcohol and watching films they were not old enough to watch, so why would the digital space be any more of a challenge for them? And how will we know, for sure?

A point to note is there are already services that offer age verification via facial recognition, credit card details and other techniques. However, I ask at a high-brow level whether this is the way we want to go in light of privacy concerns, or do we feel it's our only option to protect, as there is no guarantee that this data cannot or will not be kept, manipulated, harvested, leaked, robustly secured over time, or used for nefarious reasons? I know this is a controversial point to make here and one that sits on the side of the privacy rights and freedoms movement, but as I said I am not here to say what's correct and true, palatable or even what you want to hear. This is to make you think for yourselves.

But why has it taken so long to get to this point of now putting in protective measures for children, young people and the truly vulnerable?

The house of age-appropriate

In my earlier book (Knibbs, 2022), I talked of the house with residents who take approximately 25 years to fill the house and create a coherent, mature system. I talk of the visual and sensory experiences as the foundation of the developing brain exposed to life events and trauma, even to the degree that their thinking and reasoning skills are not developed to be able to 'handle' these experiences as an adult can.

And here is where the buck really ought to stop and why we need to consider the many forms of abuse, neglect and trauma from the perspective of child development and create a bill that is representative of all the spaces a child can visit online. To create a community-based approach from those who design the technology, to those in power and to those who raise children. *Together.*

It's a human and societal issue, and not only or 'just' technological. Technology cannot solve an issue created by humans, as technology is not, well 'human'. No matter how advanced the AI gets, humans will always be human and we are nuanced, and complex and technology is changing us too.

Yet, we may, and I repeat may, create AI that can think like a human and consider the darker side of human thoughts and behaviour in order to provide a technological solution to the issues. However, we start moving into territory where tech would need to track all human behaviours, no matter how depraved. Of course, that means that we would need a system that could infiltrate all forms of encryption and privacy rights, and that moves us into an ethical and moral dilemma about privacy rights and freedoms of the users of technology, or to begin thinking about the learning that AI would need to do about topics such as child sexual abuse and I don't think anyone would be supportive of that.

My question here and it is a big one that I ask is: do we have the moral and ethical right to 'listen in on all digital communication' to protect children from the most heinous of crimes against them? (And some of them are indeed heinous.) Is this not our duty of care? And yet, do we not have the perceived right to privacy and the right to think what we want, and perhaps converse with others who may think the same without intrusion? For example, What about those who are exploring an aspect of themselves they are too ashamed to speak to another human being about, such as their sexuality? Where does the fortitude lie and for whom?

Complexity in the process or we end up in dystopian times

Are we moving to the Cacotopia world of manipulated humans as suggested by writers such as: George Orwell (1949[2008]), Phillip K. Dick (1962, 1969; think *Bladerunner* or *Minority Report*), Aldous Huxley (1932), Ray Kurzweil (2005), Norbert Weiner (1988) and more? (Usually, these writings are suggesting a dystopian future and I am yet to find a jolly happy future in any books that feature technology.)

Will humans become more secretive and find spaces online where they cannot be 'tracked and hacked' and, if so, what do we do as a society to create a solution to preventing harm from being inflicted, created and continued through the use of technology if we cannot create adequate descriptions and consideration for what they may be? And how to find a solution to this with the rights and freedoms of all people?

As I said in the Introduction, I am not here to create scare stories or choose 'sides', but to consider the issues at hand, and that requires that I discuss them throughout the book. Please remember you are in the driver's seat, so to speak, and you can choose the pace at which you read this book and your opinions on the topics.

You do not have to read chapters that could rubber-band you into parts of yourself that are unhealed. Of course, that may happen anyway as you begin to read the book, and so with all my compassion and emphasis here, please ensure you have time, space and safety in which to read this book (this may include the location you read it also).

Please also have someone you can reach out to should you need to and please find the following helplines and services should you feel you could do with someone to talk to or type at.

Helplines

www.ceop.police.uk
www.childnet.com

www.gloablkidsonline.net
www.internetmatters.co.uk
www.iwf.org.uk
www.lgbthealth.org.uk/
www.mind.org.uk/
www.nspcc.org.uk
www.parentzone.org.uk
www.safeinternet.org.uk
www.samaritans.org/
www.stopitnow.org.uk
www.swgfl.org.uk

References

Centre for Humane Technology. (2020). www.humanetech.com/.

Department for Education. (2018). *Working together to safeguard children: A guide to inter-agency working to safeguard and promote the welfare of children.* https://assets.publishing.service.gov.uk/government/uploads/system/uploads/attachment_data/file/942454/Working_together_to_safeguard_children_inter_agency_guidance.pdf.

Department for Education. (2022). *Keeping children safe in education. Statutory guidance for schools and colleges.* www.gov.uk/government/publications/keeping-children-safe-in-education--2.

Dick, P. (1962). *The man in the high castle.* Putnam.

Dick, P. (1968). *Do androids dream of electric sheep?* Doubleday.

Huxley, A. (1932). *Brave new world.* Chatto & Windus.

Knibbs, C. (2016). *Cybertrauma, the darker side of the internet.* Self-published and Kindle. www.amazon.co.uk/CYBERTRAUMA-DARKER-INTERNET-CHILDREN-PEO-PLE-ebook/dp/B01BREKEQW/ref=sr_1_1?crid=2JAEECCNEIFRM&keywords=cybertrauma&qid=1664621620&sprefix=cybertrauma%2Caps%2C47&sr=8-1.

Knibbs, C. (2022). *Children, technology, and healthy behaviour: How to help children thrive online.* Routledge.

Knibbs, C. (forthcoming). *Online harms and cybertrauma.* Routledge.

Kurzweil, R. (2005). *The singularity is near: When humans transcend biology.* Viking.

Merleau-Ponty, M. (2002). *Husserl at the limits of Phenomenology.* Including texts by Edmund Husserl. North Western University Press.

Orwell, G. (1949, republished 2008). *1984.* Penguin in association with Martin Secker & Warburg.

Pernecky, T. (2016). *Epistemology and metaphysics for qualitative research.* Sage.

United Nations Convention on the Rights of Children. (1989a). www.unicef.org/child-rights-convention.

United Nations Convention on the Rights of Children. (1989b). *Comment 25.* www.unicef.org.au/united-nations-convention-on-the-rights-of-the-child.

Weiner, N. (1988). *The human use of human beings: Cybernetics and society.* De Capo Press.

Zuboff, S. (2019). *The age of surveillance capitalism: The fight for a new human future at the new frontier of power.* Profile Books.

4 Parenting

Parenting: don't tell me how to do it

I am aware that some of you reading this, as well as being a practitioner, may well be parents or grandparents, carers, guardians and adopters too, and so this section is needed. But, also for you as the practitioner, this section can help inform you before, during or after working with the parents and carers, as this will also form part of your work.

Who is responsible?

Can we do much about the issues in this book if we only look to others such as the government, social media companies and regulators to be accountable and take responsibility for harms that happen online?

I suspect that perhaps only some of the problems will be fixed if we follow this route. Going back to the car analogy, bad drivers are sometimes parents and parents are sometimes bad drivers. But, as with cars, parents take precautions for their little ones such as car seats and seat belt adaptors, and only when the child is old enough can they begin their driving lessons, which of course varies from country to country. One worry that is common among parents is worrying about the child in the car, be they passengers or the driver. And this underpins one of the reasons road rage exists when parents feel their or their child's life could have been changed or extinguished by the actions of another driver (this is important to note for later chapters and chapters in my forthcoming book (Knibbs, forthcoming).

So, how do we make the conversations about online, internet and digital spaces as pertinent as we do those about driving safety? How can we bring the parents into this conversation without terrifying them at the idea of bad drivers or calling them bad drivers?

I am often asked whether I run parenting classes, and the answer is, not really, but sort of. These are often the professionals I am teaching who go into 'parent mode' as I speak. They will often forget that they are here to learn about the children they work with and become the internalised narrating, fearful parent that says, 'Oh, I never knew that could happen, I didn't

DOI: 10.4324/9781003364177-5

know that', and suddenly they are down the vortex of 'what if what if what if' regarding their own children, or can feel shame about something they did or didn't do, and I have borne the anger arising from this from some practitioners.

And if this happens to the professionals when it comes to their own children, how do we make space for all parents? Imagine if a social worker only took care of their own car, but not the safe seating of the child they are working with, who was getting into their car.

Why does this occur? Well that's simple in terms of parents – they take care of their own children first, as it's how nature designed us. And *these* parents are only just learning some of this stuff about the online world, so they must try and battle with their own sins, failings and misgivings, as well as looking after others' children and, if *they don't know*, then what chance or hope do we have for *all* parents getting this information in a way that is comparable to how we understand the road and driving safety?

I ask you to bear with the next few paragraphs as I believe the issues around online harm are societal, not just one specific discipline, paradigm or approach that can be left to parents, professionals or the big tech companies. Parents form a small and equal portion of the problem; however, they are often let down by the process of not being given adequate 'training', so to speak (about being a parent in a world of technology), and that is because the professions, systems and societal issues are worldwide and lack this too. And of course, the support centres such as the Sure Start ones in the UK that used to be around for expectant parents and new parents (and early years) have been slowly eroded over time or don't exist at all. So where do they get their support and guidance?

The driving test of parenting

This book is being written for practitioners, some of whom will also be parents. But I am not writing for parents per se, because there is this small consideration that we have in the UK (and many other countries), which is that parenting is not something that we can 'make people do' in a specific manner. We cannot enforce a prerequisite to becoming a parent, such as taking a driving test, because that is about human rights, society, religion, politics and, of course, generational freedoms fought for those to parent as 'they see fit', following the laws and legislations in place.

For example, parents can choose how to parent within the scope of the United Nations Convention on the rights of the Child and UK laws regarding abuse and neglect and any laws that get introduced (such as the smacking ban that has been introduced in a few countries). Parents can apply punishments, and these can take all sorts of forms, as long as the parent isn't breaking the law.

For the rest of it ... anything goes, as they say.

We do not make those of childbearing ages attend a class, curriculum or exam before creating a life. We do make people attend driving lessons before being able to drive on the roads and this is perhaps the only 'must do' type of 'training' and learning that we expect of any driver in the country. We have all manner of driving abilities and so many people put themselves in the 'better than average' category. Many of the parents I work with also classify their parenting in this way too.

We do not make children, adolescents or adults take an IT test before purchasing a computer. We do not ask them to learn how to fly a plane before purchasing a flight ticket. We do not require adults to memorise a map of the world before they can travel. And we do not ask potential pet owners to take a neuroanatomy in animals class before buying a pet

We educate medical staff to a high degree before they can operate, draw blood or administer medication. Often professionals that work with mental health issues do not need much more beyond a college diploma level 3 or 4 to give advice, coach or counsel those with serious issues and needs.

Yet we don't provide any real education *for* parents and people who wish to be parents. What is in place currently are lessons for children about life, which we call Personal, Social and Health Education (PSHE); but many of these lessons follow a plan decided by the Department for Education and only some of this covers digital citizenship and media literacy, without the backbone of the contents of my first book (Knibbs, 2022), detailing the 'why we do what we do online' and utilising interpersonal skills, attachment, trauma and self-regulation skills as the basis with which to educate.

Asking children, for example, to 'be kind online' only goes so far when they see their parents 'road raging' at someone else in the real world or online. And, of course, if you look at gaming cheats (Knibbs, 2022) you can see why digital citizenship is about being 'with' others online and this is a skill developed in the real world, with valued, regulated and empathic others. This is about life – as a living breathing sentient being. Where we are 'doing' our human behaviour is irrelevant, it's the behaviour itself that matters.

Rules, or law?

The only real 'rules' about online spaces and children (and their well-being) tend to be those that involve or revolve around any images of child sexual abuse, data processing and the purchasing of age-restricted games (in similar ways to alcohol and cigarettes). To date, if a parent allows their child on a platform, app or game that has suggested age ratings older than their child, then so be it. There is no law to date that says a child playing a 15-rated game will result in the parent being prosecuted. This is entirely why children are on these games and platforms. And who is going to tell? If we treated this activity in the same way we treat real-world 'under-age' activities such as gambling, substances and entering into spaces that were regulated for adults, then there would likely be an uproar from the parents and indeed the industry. As it is, the laws around data processing mean that we currently have quite a hard stop at 13 years of age. However, I have been aware of children in those spaces for over two decades – and still, they are frequent visitors there.

So why aren't there laws about this online space yet? Privacy laws would sum this up quite quickly, although I'm not going to discuss these in this book. But safe to say that if parents knew that these platforms were really about 18+ rated activities, would they ensure their children stayed away? In which case do they really know what's 'out there'?

Is it really the case that parents don't know? Is it the case that they believe the platform or game is going to be safe? Are the parents in denial or submitting to what is called 'pester power' and is this why parents often don't spend time learning about what their child sees or does on and in these spaces? Or are they terrified to look closely, as this would mean responsibility and in turn would require a more hands-on approach when the digital pacifier makes their lives that bit easier?

Parents are not lazy; they are busy and if they had to sit with their children day after day to learn about the environment their children are in they likely would not get much done. And to be fair, the industry has sold a smoke and mirrors approach of a 'child-friendly' platform because many of the parents of today (those older than say 27) grew up with child-friendly TV and the 'watershed' and it therefore hasn't entered their mind that the Internet isn't regulated in the same way. They have cognitive dissonance about where their child is, goes and what they see. Technology promises thorough plausible deniability.

Parents have been surreptitiously, mistakenly and implicitly misguided that the tech giants are going to care for their children in the same way parents do when dropping them into education settings or leaving them in front of the TV. The tech giants never said this, but there has been an error of judgement along the way, exacerbated by the silence of the tech giants that has become a ubiquitous false belief. *Until there is a terrible situation – and only then do we find out what isn't being done.*

So how do we get parents to monitor 'where their child goes'

In short, this is an impossible task – even with the advent of age assurance, age verification and even laws that will require a credit card to enter, because this would require *all* site owners, developers and platforms now and in the future to create systems to verify their users 'properly and accurately'. Of course, this would also mean that parents would need to monitor, or pay for a service that monitored their children's 'whereabouts' (and then check those systems), and to quote a parent from my clinic: 'I don't have time for that. I would only want to know if they did something illegal'.

'Latch-key kids'

Let's face it. Some parents don't have the skills, some don't want to learn and some don't care. This has always been the way, and likely always will (this is about attachment, trauma and educational levels of those parents that is too big to cover here). There are so many latch-key kids online today because parents are busy, need to work, and don't know about these spaces and this will be the framing of this digital world for some time. These parents are absent for many reasons – we cannot blame or shame them – and this deficit will always exist as it does for children who are alone in the real world whilst their parents work, abscond or go awol with substances or people, and so we need to think about this and the digital space where these children are ever present.

So who are we going to get to watch over this space, watch for the little ones and take care of them to prevent the harms they could encounter? Who are the parents gonna call? … The regulators, social media or gaming companies. And so, the buck is passed and we begin to point fingers toward a tech solution, removing the responsibility from us. What we need is a whole-istic approach to this issue. That's why I asked for your help in this matter.

We need to teach parents compassionately and with care; we need to assist and help, nurture and guide, not berate and punish them for choosing to parent in the way that they do. And this includes allowing their child to meander into, use, deliberately circumnavigate controls, accidentally happen upon, run round 'to their mates' to view, play and engage with spaces they are not mature enough to be in – just like you found ways around the rules as a child and adolescent. The consequences for this and the next generation(s) may be longer lasting if those mistakes are digitally based, though. That's why we must do more than our parents did. Collectively.

Jargon-free education

We need to provide conversations, documentaries and books that do not terrify or shame them, or are written by the folks who coined terms such as phishing, end-user or NFTs. They need education they can lean on, learn from and employ in the lives of their children and this is a task that to date isn't 'on the market' in a consolidated format that is accessible all over the world and encompasses what it is to be a person online. Many of the resources I see take a minimalist approach and tick boxes and do what's needed when we need to go further than this. I'm not here to make this book an easy read, nor to kowtow to saying all the resources out there are great. Some are, some have elements that are, but as a whole, it's fair to say we can and must do better.

We are very siloed in this respect, and I wondered many years ago why we needed so many companies, especially in the UK, to promote the idea of e-safety and online participation, navigation and where children could go. I realised that many of these companies were driven at the outset by the legal framework (i.e. policing) and it is this approach that the parents are avoiding because it is often delivered with the shock factor, finger-pointing towards them, blame and shame and persecutory language such as 'don't'! It's no wonder parents 'don't want to engage'. Furthermore, the silos that exist tend to be country-, topic- or platform-specific and not child-focused from a developmental lens. And why would they be? That's the domain of people like me and psychologists. We are often not in this space and when we are we write to our model and discipline. Again, we need a wholistic approach.

What seems to be missing is parenting the parents and this is again a subjective process with some companies choosing the 'musts' and others the 'don'ts'. The language in many of these companies is dictatorial and authoritarian and lacks a trauma-informed lens.

And of course, the biggest platforms could be the ones to do this for parents, but in doing so may well lose some of their customers, as it would be inevitable that if they were educating about online harm, they would have to lead by example and remove *harmful*, *illegal* and *inappropriate content* (all subjective terms by the way) and underage users, or indeed change the way they worked to benefit parents and children worldwide.

I feel that this is also an impossibility – as the metaphor goes, the gate has well and truly been left open, and the horses are nowhere to be seen. And so, we are left with the approach that we are facing in today's world (2022), which is: lots of websites with advice for parents, lots of media horror stories and documentaries that are the epitome of horror and overwhelming, meaning they don't result in changed behaviours. Well, maybe the parents share the stories to 'warn' others and then move on to the next day and forget the warnings themselves – *a typical human behaviour*. Think about the last time you practised your nuclear war drills or checked your smoke alarm?

Top-down or bottom-up education?

So perhaps we educate the professionals first, like we would educate driving instructors, pilots and trainee surgeons? Perhaps the professionals are the ones to assist parents, but this means they must understand human nature, online life and what occurs there in terms of harm.

And so I am joining the crowd, and aiming to educate professionals because *you will, without a doubt* be working with children and young people who face a form of Cybertrauma and online harm.

This book is an attempt to do that because it has to be societal, it has to include all of us, so let's work top down *and* bottom up!

References

Knibbs, C. (2022). *Children, technology, and healthy behaviour: How to help children thrive online*. Routledge.

Knibbs, C. (forthcoming). *Online harms and cybertrauma: Legal and harmful issues with children and young people*. Routledge.

5 No sex please, we're British!

I am hopping over the real depth of these issues due to word limitations and a need to communicate the harm in a way that minimises harm to you, the reader. This a difficult line to hold when writing about this topic, and others in the book, as I am aware that people with a history of sexual assault and abuse may find these chapters uncomfortable, as can people without histories of sexual abuse and assault.

No sex please, we're British!

So begins our descent in the book to the subject matters of harm to children, beginning with the illegality of sexual images of children, viewing adult material, other illegal content and many other issues that are being added to, considered for, and even rejected in the upcoming Online Safety Bill in the UK.

At the time of writing this book, the bill had just gone through the second reading and was approaching the third with lots of speculation about what will be added in the forthcoming debates in Parliament.

I considered the next chapters in various locations throughout the book, moving them up and down the contents list and, each and every time I looked at the layout, I kept thinking to myself, which part is the one people will want to read first as a professional, and which will they avoid or even skip?

That obviously depends on which part is likely to be applicable to the reader; for example, those who work with eating disorders could refer to my forthcoming book (Knibbs, forthcoming). It was decided that this book would be focusing on sexual-based issues, with the next being about most of the other Cybertrauma and online harms.

However, there is something quite predictable about human beings. They want to read, watch and listen to topics that are taboo and can give them a way to encounter the material, without it being seen or acknowledged by others that this is the topic they are really interested in.

We know sex sells. And in placing the word sex anywhere in any of the titles or chapter headings it is likely that's the section that gets read first. We are a predictable bunch. So here I begin with it because this is a topic that *is*

DOI: 10.4324/9781003364177-6

going to be in the online harms section of the bill. This follows the due process of illegal harm that can be monitored and prosecuted.

Starting from the numbers and what led me to this decision

Take, for example, the analytics on my podcast (currently on hiatus whilst I write books and carry out some research). When I was running it, the funny thing, which of course isn't funny, is the episodes that mention sex got the highest level of listens. Though the video versions got higher scores compared to some other episodes, there was not the marked difference I saw when checking the audio analytics.

Under my own hypothesis, this was, I posit here, due to the fact that this is less likely to be seen in 'internet' histories, especially if you have a shared computer or YouTube account. Listening to audio lends itself to the secrecy and shame of sex, which is the driving force behind our Western, and certainly, UK approach of 'No thank you, I'm British!', and sex is something that we do not talk about openly, let alone let others see from our YouTube history (well, unless it's jokes and comments that have a 'Fnar fnar', Monty Python style nudge-nudge wink-wink feeling attributed to them).

I run a training session on porn viewing in children and young people as this is about child protection and understanding some of what is in this book, yet the question asked most often before the session is, 'you're not going to show me it, are you, Cath?' The answer by the way is *no*, you can do that in your own time.

Too often we do not talk about these taboo and uncomfortable 'matters', and so they go undetected, unspoken about and hidden in secrecy and shame, which becomes a problem for children who often feel they cannot speak out and get help. If you can't talk about, you know, S. E. X., or that so often silently mouthed 'bedroom stuff', what hope do children have?

However, one of the most concerning issues (and under discussion in Chapter 7 on porn viewing), with very small amounts of actual ethical research to date, is: the proclivity of porn viewing in children and young people as creating or causing subsequent copycat behaviours appearing in what we call child-on-child abuse and early sexual relationships of young people. Moreover, this is largely media-driven speculation from small sample stories and so myth becomes legend very quickly. Given that balanced view I discussed earlier, crime statistics and research (where I haven't seen the questions being asked of victims, or what acts were measured and so cannot accurately say this is good reporting, yet) suggest that we are reporting, actioning and charging more children with these types of behaviours, yet the newspaper that reported this was not given the facts of the research carried out by a large children's charity (Gayle, 2017). I cannot find to date the underlying causes for this escalation of reporting or cases occurring in any of the literature and I am unlikely to find a cause, but I will find a correlation. This is not to say I am against this speculative answer, but can we please have some more robust evidence and research to back up these claims?

Notwithstanding this, we must remember that porn was on the Internet 27 years ago, is and has been accessible via some of the sites for free and has been on many platforms and sites for many years alongside the mass amount you can find on social media channels since their inception. What is responsible for this sudden boom in what is now being called sexually harmful behaviour, or is this a chicken and egg scenario of more awareness by children and young people or more reporting? And what about MTV getting the blame anymore? (More on this later.)

The modern-day Bobo doll of adolescence

This narrative that watching porn will create harmful behaviours in sexual relationships is creating the doomsday bells of social learning theory with adolescents as being comparable to those three-year-olds with the Bobo doll (Bandura, 1973). The framing I am giving here is that technology is adding layers of complexity to all behaviours and in this case sexual behaviours of adolescents. Previously we knew a small to fair amount about adolescent sexual behaviour; however, having only the retrospective reflections of adolescents about their sexual behaviours, usually, in research (aged approximately 14–16), whereby they revealed *some* of their sexual behaviours, we *could* now perhaps engage with them about their behaviours if we have a link to the viewing of pornography they engaged in (notice the ethical issue raised here with this). For example, you may be working with a young person referred to you for sexually harmful behaviour, coercive behaviour or underage sexual behaviour and part of the assessment process may have revealed porn viewing (in the past or present) and this is important to know about as discussed in Chapter 7.

Online harms in development

This is a legislative law that is still being decided, due to the complexities it poses and how this will be actioned once firmly in place. Given that we are in a world of Web 2.0 and soon there will be a Web 3.0, what I am calling the 'Dolby Space' as in Dolby surround sound (it may well be a Wi-Fi connected world too once Elon Musk's Starlinks fire up), we will begin to see the impact and the connectedness of Augmented, Virtual and Surround Sound style connections in everyday lives of children and young people. The image I have of this is like water droplets forming together to create a stream of flowing water that we will be surrounded by bit by bit. I hope we have our armbands! Sex is going to level up and who knows what harm children and young people will face in their entirety (I have some ideas about this but that's for another book I suspect).

Flood defences and lifeguards

How would you regulate a moving body of water? Well, you would ensure the banks are solid, they guide the water through villages rather than letting the water flood the land. You ensure that gates are in place to slow the speed of rushing water, you create spaces of slower and calmer currents, you ensure people can swim, boat, dive and jet ski and you also have lifeguards.

But as with all water, the rains can create floods and, in the parable, when babies are drowning in the stream we need people to go upstream and prevent them from falling in, or being thrown in. Floods are without a doubt going to happen, so let's build good flood defences and let's think about life rafts, swimming lessons and dry lands. The world is already a vast expanse of water, so let's ensure like Noah we don't need an Arc to get off the watery planet in order to survive. (Unless of course you're Elon Musk and fancy colonising Mars.) Nor, like the *Titanic*, do we want to head to the depths of a cold icy body of water because we didn't see the iceberg in time. That kind of 'oops' costs many lives.

Let us not drown or sink to the depths of the ocean.

References

Bandura, A. (1973). *Aggression: A Social Learning Analysis*. Prentice Hall.

Gayle, D. (2017). *Claims of child-on-child sexual offences soar in England and Wales*. www.theguardian.com/uk-news/2017/feb/03/claims-child-sexual-offences-soar-england-and-wales-police-barnardos.

Knibbs, C. (forthcoming). *Online harms and cybertrauma: Legal and harmful issues with children and young people*. Routledge.

6 Consent

Consent

This chapter is necessary for us to move into the next few chapters that detail issues around sexual content online and to understand why consent is the most basic of principles, yet the most complicated to explain, understand and utilise in our daily lives. Most of the adults I work with in therapy do not understand this concept fully, nor apply it to their lives, and I wonder after reading this if you will feel the same about your use of consent. Or lack of it.

Consent is perhaps one of the most misunderstood concepts and issues of our time and this sees me having conversations on a regular basis with children, young people and, as mentioned, adults, on a weekly basis in my therapy office. I also speak about consent when I'm educating about Data Protection, and in my work when I am researching, but these are different forms of consent. I am indeed talking about the same concept, but with different hats on, so to speak, and so this chapter is aiming to help you understand what consent really is and how it applies to your work with children and young people.

Consent forms micro-moments of our lives from acts like opening a door to let someone through before us, to the eye contact of a stranger wondering whether saying hello will be accepted. This process is often conveyed via eye contact and how we look to the other for cues of safety (Porges, 2011).

When consent moves into the space of the act of sexual activity it can become littered with cognitive biases, presumptions, assumptions, misunderstandings and what you may have seen in current teachings as a need to be 'enthusiastic'. We will shortly come onto why this 'enthusiasm' is a cognitive bias and why consent is deeply misunderstood by framing it this way, and why the very teachings about this 'enthusiasm' to date often leave young people even more confused. Anecdotally, this is the most prolific form of the conversation I have on this topic in therapy.

The most popular framing and the idea of consent often surround the topic of sex and relationships, and that is where we will begin; however, consent is, according to the Merriam Webster Dictionary, an intransitive verb and noun. (Does this sound familiar with the definition I gave of 'vulnerable' in

DOI: 10.4324/9781003364177-7

my previous book (Knibbs, 2022)?) Let's stick with the dictionary entry here and a quote directly reads:

Intransitive Verb

1. to give assent or approval
2. archaic: to be in concord in opinion or sentiment

AGREE
Noun

1. compliance in or approval of what is done or proposed by another
2. agreement as to action or opinion specifically

ACQUIESCENCE

Now let's think about those words: compliance, approval, acquiescence, concord and agreement. Each one sounds like it is a different way of consenting and when you place it in the context of sex, some of them begin to sound inappropriate. For example, compliance (with a sexual act) starts to sound like coercive behaviour or legal language. Acquiesce begins to sound like having a lack of autonomy and choice.

Language and of course its etymology and phenomenological meaning for the person must mean that we take an individual's worldview and sense of self and others into account, including our own view of what these words and behaviours really mean. When it comes to consent around sexual activity, the process of 'my body' and what 'I', meaning the person conveying consent, feel okay, happy and on most occasions, mostly enthusiastic to engage in without coercion, manipulation or fear of abandonment, starts to create the idea of a self who can make these choices.

Given the previous writings around self and trauma, we can see how and why this subject matter begins to be more complicated the more we delve into it. This is the biggest grey area and requires us to see the individual, their history and ability to have autonomy, agency, and sense of self in order to be able to consent in the first instance.

This is such an important factor to acknowledge here, and we will discuss this below; however, for a better understanding of this issue, deep understanding of attachment, trauma and child development is a must.

Our first question that arises here would be to consider, as you read this section as a practitioner, whether a young person can truly and fully know, if they have never tried, what act or behaviour in sexual activity they are 'okay' to engage in? And once they have tried it, are they consenting because *it is okay* or because they want to please their partner for many reasons, which means it isn't necessarily a coercive act but an altruistic one; and how would you know the difference when speaking to a young person? Did they try the behaviour and find out they didn't like it, not want to try it but did, didn't like the sound of it but liked the sensations, didn't want to try and did for the sake of their partner and so on and so on.

Comfortable or uncomfortable? Discussing sex with children and adolescents

Let's get uncomfortable! What's your sex life like?

And for this question, I am going to invite you to think about your own sexual experiences with your partner(s) and consider how many times you have engaged in an act that you were not 100% happy with, on that day, at that time, or just didn't feel like it and perhaps did it anyway? What about the new variants, positions, fantasies and 'let's try this' moments there have been in your sex life and how did these really feel to you? Would you like to talk about them with a stranger who says they understand? Have they tried these things? What if they *Ewww* at you? What if they say something like 'did you know that was sexual assault or rape?'

Now, let's just visit the latter part of the sentence about 'my body' and think back to the topic of attachment. We can see that consent is layered when it comes to feelings of rejection, abandonment and our introjects about our self-worth, esteem, value etc. If we take this topic and further merge it with psychological, sexual and philosophical game theories (Berne, 1964, 1970; Carse, 1986), then we can see that consent is a very complex process about 'why I am saying yes *in this moment*' and '*what is the outcome I am hoping or aiming for?*'

Perhaps an unconscious drive in all of us, even in the process of sexual activity is: I don't want to be rejected, ridiculed or humiliated and so I may not be able to convey my discomfort, reticence or disgust at this act or moment and so I won't say anything at all, which is then misconstrued and misunderstood as consent. When I am talking to adults about sexual activities they have engaged in with their spouse I am often discussing this very process and I hear:

> 'I didn't say anything as I thought they liked it',
> 'I just went along with it',
> 'I thought it was pleasing him/her/them',
> 'I just thought it was my duty', or
> 'I didn't want them to get angry with me'.

Do any of these moments feel familiar to you as the reader, and are there moments outside of the bedroom too, which can include eating food you dislike, going places and doing things with your partner that you really would rather not? And do you speak out about this in these scenarios, let alone the ones in the bedroom?

And to coin the phrase from sports, 'post-match analysis' (so here this would be 'post-coital'), this is often a conversation missing in terms of consent about next time. Post-match analysis helps us decide what our gameplay will be next time, how we can improve our play and what works well and what doesn't. So I ask, do you have these post-event conversations with your partner about the sex you have just had and do you think young people do?

Practitioner pause for reflection

How was that to think about? You are an adult, would you be happy discussing this with other professionals?

Before, during and after

Consent is a process encompassing before, during and after an interaction and is limited to a specified time and space. This is a helpful aspect to educate young people around – that it is not something we *are*, but something we *do*. Consent is not ongoing permission granted to the other person to utilise to their advantage or to consider permission for continued 'use' for evermore. It is subjective and in relation to a specific act for a specific moment in time.

Whether you say hello, or not

For example, I might not want to say hello in return to that stranger today because I am lost in thought, feeling grumpy or just don't want to; versus later in the day I may make that eye contact and say hello back – maybe I'll even do it *enthusiastically*. The stranger does not get to decide when I am in a place to exchange pleasantries – that is my decision. And how they think about my response or lack thereof is up to them.

Now … can you feel the societal messages in your head and perhaps even feel them in your body right now that might go something like this:

'That's rude though',
'They may be offended',
'They may not speak to you again',
'They may say hello anyway',
'I'll just say hello, even though I don't want to, because … manners',
'It's only saying hello'.

And this is 'just' about saying hello. Perhaps your cogs are whirring that complexities of human histories and behaviours make this more … well, complex!

Consent, therefore, is a person-specific permission, co-created in space and time and subject to the alteration when or wherever necessary by the creator of that permission (which is now beginning to sound like legal speak!). This might just be the way we need to think about this in terms of the depth to which consent is understood and taught.

Parenting and the almost daily overriding of consent

Let me tell you a story of consent override in its most basic format, and one that may have practitioners umming and ahhing, feeling denial and anger at my pointing this out, and of course those who have engaged in this behaviour may potentially feel guilt, shame and remorse or become defensive as these feelings are evoked in you. Take your time and see below the behaviour stories to the why reflection and explanation.

This topic is complex and to explain this as a core concept of human rights we have to begin at the beginning and really break down the concept and discuss *when* we are able to begin 'giving' and 'doing' consent and how this comes to be in our society a speculative topic of, '*how would I know for sure that I have been given consent by the other person*', and of course when can a person begin to give consent and at what age?

So come with me on the following examples and consider this for your practice, how you work with young people, what their rights really are, whether you consider this 'liberalism' and of course how these fit into your life (as something that you may never have considered at this depth before). Please bear with the stories and read them through before getting to the discourse after them.

The stories are evocative, and they are possibly going to challenge a lot of people because they may jar with the parent in you, the practitioner, the sceptic, the extremist – and the reason I know this is I have been watching the fallout from these questions on social media, and this is a polarising subject for sure!

Story 1

Lucy is two months old and in the arms of her mother. She is being gazed at adoringly by her mother, who is making cooing noises and talking to her daughter in the motherese tongue and Mum feels like her heart could burst. Lucy is gazing back at Mum and reciprocally making noises back. At one point in this 'conversation' Lucy feels overwhelmed by something; a feeling in her body, a sound off to her left, a moment in time where she has had enough of this dialogue (and who knows what it is to be sure as babies cannot speak to us, nor can we read their minds, yet). Lucy turns her head away from Mum to regain some 'downtime' for a moment.

Mum, who feels rejected, or in charge of the conversation, overwrought with joy and love, hurried, or impatient (again, who knows) gets hold of Lucy's face by her chin and turns it back towards her to continue the chatter and smiles. This happens on several occasions and Lucy learns on a bodily level, that she is not able to exercise her rights of being in control of her body and her feelings, and of course regulating her sense of overwhelm. Lucy is 'regulated' by Mum and is unable to make her own choices. *Is this consent or consent override?*

Reflection

Often when you see the laws surrounding consent we tend to favour spoken language to acknowledge or debate and argue against whether consent exists or not. Lucy is not able to give 100% 'enthusiastic' consent because she cannot speak. In this case, would we see that her own bodily feelings are violated? I ask, would a lawyer for example be able to fight for the rights of the child here as not giving consent in its truest form?

Story 2

Thomas is four and does not want to get ready for school. He is feeling tired, grumpy and overwhelmed by the rushing around of the adults and older siblings. He is refusing to eat his breakfast and is attempting to get down from his chair at the table. Dad is late for work and confronts his son: 'Eat it or I will smack your bottom!' he declares. Mum is sitting with him and takes up the spoonful of breakfast cereal and pushes it in Thomas' mouth whilst he is crying. Is this consent being overridden?

Reflection

Thomas has clearly 'spoken out' about not wanting to eat his breakfast. If he does not eat now, he may have to go hours without food and he is diabetic, so Mum knows that he must eat for his own health. Is this good parenting to prevent her son from having diabetic issues or consent override?

Story 3

Marley is six and knows what he wants in life as a forthright child. He is visiting Granny with his sisters and Mum as they get ready for Carnival weekend. He is adamant he wants to wear the Tutu like his sisters and Granny is 'having none of it'. She demands that he puts on the clothes she bought for him so he 'looks smart like the other boys'. If not, 'he will not be getting his favourite treat for supper', she tells him. Marley is adamant he is going to wear the tutu and complains vociferously as Granny is pulling it from him and swearing at him through gritted teeth. In vain he gives up and is sat on the floor wailing. Granny picks up his feet and begins forcing the trousers over them, lifting him up and 'hoiking' (a term to mean lifting with force) them up to his waist. Is this consent being violated?

Reflection

Granny believes that boys should dress like boys and is against the trans ideology. Granny also doesn't believe that children can play at being whomever they want, and thinks Marley should 'do as he is told' because that is how she was brought up. Is this consent override, manipulation and coercion or a strict upbringing with a closed mindset due to her age? Was the process of forcing the trousers onto him abusive as she did this with force?

Story 4

Dora is at her grandparents' home whilst her parents work. They chose to use Dad's mum to do the childminding so that Dora was given a familiar adult to stay with. She is turning four next week and is busy preparing the party bags with Nanny P and is very excited. Dad comes to pick up Dora and as they get her ready to leave, excitedly talking about the party, Dad says 'Go and give Nanny a kiss goodbye'. Dora says, 'I don't want to' and Dad looks embarrassed. 'Why don't you want to give Nanny P a kiss? Go on, she's getting your party stuff ready for you. Go and give her a kiss' and with that pushes Dora towards Nanny P, who at this point leans down and holds Dora's face and plants a big kiss on Dora's cheek, saying 'ah, of course, you wanted to gimme a kiss and say goodbye, you cheeky young lady'.

Is this consent being violated?

Reflection

Dora has spent a few hours with Nanny P and perhaps feels that a simple goodbye would suffice. Dad's behaviour is both hurried by embarrassment and the societal rules of giving goodbye kisses to relatives. Nanny P, however, tells Dora that she did not know what she really wanted when she tells her that she really did want to give her a kiss goodbye. Is this consent override or emotional intelligence override or both?

Are you still with me?

Each one of these examples probably sounds familiar, is often witnessed, or is carried out up and down the country on a daily basis. Those of you reading this who are parents will know all too well the 'battle' of eating, dressing, schooling and the 'goodbye' routines. Some of you may be feeling a slight outrage at me here, citing the 'need to' get children ready for school, bed, outings and more – the feeling of 'customs' of kissing relatives goodbye, saying 'hello' and 'thank you'.

Does your body belong to you?

And so the point of this page is to introduce the concept of body consent and the message children receive from us the adults as infants, as young children and into their adolescent stages. Which stands as *'consent is your right, given by you until I decide otherwise as the adult, older person or one with the power dynamic that says so. You can decide to consent, but this can be violated and changed at my say so if I give reason'.*

So you can have it, until I say you can't

Mixed messages

And we currently wonder why consent in a sexual context is misunderstood, confusing and sometimes given, or perhaps overridden by adolescents in sexual relationships, because we currently place the onus on developing brains that do not fully understand the meaning and application of this concept in their lives; especially if they received mixed messages in the process of growing up, being told what it was, how it 'works' or, in the cases above, does not, when someone else decides so.

Childhood trauma and the concept of consent

Now, given this confusion, as discussed above, the next layer to add to this is the consideration of children who have suffered harm, violence and sexual abuse, and their ability to consent.

We can begin to see that more complexity arises when we consider children who are sexually, physically or emotionally abused. Many of them do not know how to give consent after abuse because this basic concept is violated at such a pernicious level and so they may have an internal belief that they cannot really give consent, because it was taken away from them in such a devious manner. The word, body language and process of saying no can often be useless because a perpetrator used their power to override consent, even if it was explicitly stated as a no! And so consent becomes a feeling associated with powerlessness. Children who present in the therapy room, in courts, or even during questioning after abuse would go along with whatever the practitioner, police officer, teacher or social worker wants, because who are they to even try to exercise their rights to not do so? This may be the underlying reason why these children become reactive and rebellious in situations where they can say no in other ways, such as withholding faecal matter, not sleeping, eating, doing homework, going to school and so on – you get the picture.

Where are the places children look to see others exhibiting and modelling consent? Adult relationships, employment and online in spaces such as pornography.

Consent in porn: is there any?

Now as we move into the chapters on porn viewing you will see that within this area of material the word no can often mean yes, and that visual consent is confusing when the body language of one or more of the active or passive participants often reflects 'non-consent' and yet the vocal expressions say 'I am consenting'. So the concept of how consent looks, sounds and is acted out becomes more confusing, misunderstood, and to some children falls outside of the conversational space because who and how do you speak to about consent in this type of content? It's not like you can show a video and slow it down, frame by frame to discuss the process. *Do not do this*, it is merely a philosophical reflection and way to explain why we are quite stuck in being able to discuss consent with children.

Conversations with young people

How do we explain nuanced sexual 'conversations', when role play is occurring and when it is not, when consenting aggression but not violence or harm is part of the sexual activity, when harm is, and to what degree, when the rules are violated and how this is dealt with, how people talk to each other about their kinks, desires, likes, squinks or dislikes before and during the sexual activity? Can we talk to them about the intelligence needed in this sphere of mating and sexual activity? What do we mean by this and is this different to contextual moments and consent? Is mating intelligence something that needs to be taught in PSHE or Sex-Ed, part of which will require the subject matters in this volume. For more information on kinks, squinks and mating intelligence see Ogas and Gaddam (2012) and Geher and Kaufman (2013).

All of these questions are mainly unanswered in pornography videos because we do not see the lead-up to the activity or how the participant got to that point. I mean who would want to watch and wait before the 'exciting' aspect of the video?

However, the process of consent is not necessarily explicit in these circumstances either. And hence the most important aspect of consent is not present for the viewer to learn and consider, nor is this an educational video as easy as understanding drinking tea. We need to look at the idea of shopping for tea, the many types of tea, making the tea and the offer of tea, rather than jumping to the drinking of said beverage.

In my therapy room I often have long conversations with young people about how to speak to their partner about sex, which includes what words they can use. And, yes, these words include the sweary, colloquial and vulgar versions (often seen as crude by the embarrassed, or taboo), because these words *are* acceptable to *some* people in *some* situations of sexual activity, and of course, you have to know what your partner is happy to hear and speak. This often confused the students in the Sex-Ed classes when I explained that words need to be discussed as a part of your pre-sexual activity conversations so that you know what words to use during the act, so that you both know where you stand, beforehand! Very few people are likely to speak anatomically correctly about genitalia when it comes to sexual activity or they are in the throes of passion and excitement, and this was always quite the conversation in those lessons.

Many of these lessons delivered by other tutors seemed to explain to children and young people *not* to use these words when talking to professionals and so they would try and describe to me the parts of the 'downstairs', creating more embarrassment for them.

Correct language when visiting the GP for example and words people are comfortable with in the bedroom?

And here's the thing, young people get embarrassed with words like knickers or breasts when adults are present, so you can imagine if they want to discuss contraception such as dams, anal sex or fellatio, commonly not referred to by this name but BJ for short with their peers or partners, and the adults are saying not to use these words. It's likely silence will befall them rather than try the anatomical or medical versions. They need to be able to use acceptable words for genitalia and sexual activity with partners of their own ages and this will need tutors who can handle these words, robustly.

We confuse children and young people with anatomically incorrect words, because we are embarrassed to say penis or vulva or we ourselves don't know what a vulva is, and what a clitoris is or is for, which is also a largely unknown fact. For example, the word vulva has often been missed from Sex-Ed because we keep teaching children and young people 'it is called a vagina' when in fact we mean vulva, referring to the skin on the outside of the vagina, and don't explain the internal space is the vagina. It's no wonder these young people are confused and don't know how to 'ask' or discuss bodily parts before engaging in sexual activity. How do they get a concept like consent? This is like teaching the car is the engine or the engine is the car, but not how to inflate the tyres to drive safely.

Body shame, consent and expectations

We have created a world of body shaming, particularly online, and wonder why young people want to do 'it' with the lights off. We don't discuss that bodily noises are part of the process and that these are because the presence of liquid, air and skin-to-skin contact creates vacuums that are sometimes noisy. Many of the young people in my office think they broke something, broke wind or even broke 'it', have something wrong with them or have to break up because they are too embarrassed about what happened.

So how do we expect young people to understand what they see on screen, learn in Sex-Ed and generalise into a real-world setting, what consent is, looks like and feels like when shame and confusion are so often overarching with this topic? When the online world tells them what they should or should not be doing, this is often about the behaviour, *not* the co-created relationship.

Why is my office full of conversations about sexual activity that took place where they felt violated by the fact they didn't know how to express displeasure, fear, pain or dislike and refusal? Why are the populations of children and young people I speak to under the impression you can't say no and if you do then you will be forced, raped or assaulted for saying so? Why is this message so prevalent?

A hypothesis

Perhaps because the adults are too frightened to have the above conversations, don't fully understand how to explain consent, know what consent is at a neuro-biological level, know what it is on a social and interpersonal level, are uncomfortable discussing sexual activity with young people, leave it up to the PSHE or Relationships and Sex Education or Sex Education tutors, who are often skilled at delivering messages about sexually transmitted infections and underage pregnancy but not the nuanced stuff discussed here. I worked in this profession and I talked to the young people about relationships and what they are really like, relationally and developmentally, and what was outside of the scope of the 'do and don't' messages I was being asked to deliver. I met the young people where they were and answered the questions they had the courage (or dared) to ask and did not shy away from them. Because this is what they need.

I was struck by the knowledge gap of many of my colleagues about sexual activity 'other than vanilla and heteronormative'; the lack of depth about sex in all its glorious forms, kinks, same-sex relationships, to the depravities and confusions of rape, sexual abuse and grooming, child development and pregnancies and what this entails and sadly sometimes results in, including abortion and what the females needed to know about this process. The script I was asked to deliver was almost akin to the drug's message of 'just say no' and as long as we reduce the number of issues presenting at sexual health clinics then we have 'educated' people about sex, ... huzzah!

Now we know better, and Sex-Ed is changing. But how much of those extra interpersonal aspects, and permissions from the adults to discuss subject matters they are uncomfortable with will be revoked or granted?

Sex is a part of an interpersonal relationship with many levels of okayness, not okayness and the newer words such as 'kinks' or whatever you want to call them (I use this word rather than the word fetish as that sounds deviant and I am meaning the things that a person likes). It is about touch, non-touch, conversation with verbal and non-verbal gestures and understanding this from the world of emotional intelligence, social intelligence, mating intelligence, empathy, compassion and neurobiology, and not 'practical' based education alone. This is more than the mechanics, and this is the reason why consent is massively misunderstood because it's missing from the early year's education settings *with* parents and carers. We're attempting to educate the top down and we need the bottom up too, no pun intended! Well, okay maybe a cheeky one there (humour is a necessary part of this topic – I hope this doesn't offend too much).

A further issue we have about consent is the ability for this education to take place as a necessary part of our lives now. We currently have and are surrounded by the narrative of, 'it's up to the schools to teach the birds and the bees' (use of this language is an example of the uncomfortableness with sex as a topic!).

Schools feel (to prevent litigation of some sort maybe?) they must educate around basics and 'the mechanics' and I remember it was a Science teacher who delivered my education, rushed in one lesson and – Tah-da, now, go to your next lesson; phew! She was accurate in her delivery of the biological mechanics, the drawings of genitalia were almost correct, as in no women were portrayed to have vulvas and looked like barbie dolls with no pubic mound, and the males were drawn above average size and it was never portrayed they can be flaccid too, but she did her best, given the script of 'reproduction' (where was the knowledge about joy and sex etc.?)

Schools are often expected to deliver this education, sometimes with parents opposing this through letters, protests and religious beliefs or because they have perpetrated sexual abuse and so don't want their child educated about it. Schools may also be faith schools and do not want to deliver this topic and sometimes children are removed from the classrooms at the parents' bequest (this can be embarrassing for these children as they tell me 'everyone knows why I can't be in that class').

What a tricky subject matter to consider. So who consents to this education, what do we do if a parent revokes their consent to this and how do we model listening to that consent or non-consent request or do we plough ahead to teach this?

How do we look at the issue of children seeing porn online and getting their sex education there; do we need to have a national strategy of 'we are going to teach this no matter what or do we leave it up to the parents to decide?' Or do we try to hide pornography and sexual activity scenes from online spaces? And how on earth do we achieve any of this?

What about TV, on-demand services, direct messages, websites, cinema and any other way a child can see sexual activity with or without consenting parties in those scenes and videos? How do we tackle this giant of a 'problem'?

Practitioner pause for reflection

So what can practitioners do about this topic? What is the issue for you to help young people in understanding consent? Is it our duty to educate about consent in and around sexual relationships outside of the family's wishes?

Of course, we must consider those family permissions about this topic; for example, I ask about religion and beliefs about the topic of sex and sex before marriage from the parents or carers. I need to bear in mind that I offer a space to talk about anything and may be working with children who are sexually abused, curious about something they saw online or heard, questioning their sexuality, or engaging in sex underage.

And of course, this is where safeguarding literature needs to include online 'stuff' more so than it currently does. Whilst the viewing of sexual activity, known as pornography, is illegal for those under 18, what if it's a video that 'hints at' or uses other material but is clearly about sex? Would you know what to do, or what the children and young people are even talking about? This stuff is on TikTok, YouTube and Twitch and so we do not even need to broaden our thinking to the porn sites at this point, as they are not viewing illegal activity as per current legislation.

Our children of today are encountering images and messages about sex without it 'being' sexual activity. It is in their social media feeds, their DMs and files shared on apps, it is discussed in gaming, on live streams, by influencers, on TV (satellite and VOD), and of course on everyone else's, so even if we lock down 'our homes' we cannot prevent children seeing this stuff elsewhere. It is inevitable, and I work with children as young as six who can tell me about watching this 'stuff' and wondering what it is.

Again, I say it is time to get comfortable with being uncomfortable and start talking about consent, sex and relationships. We need discussions about pity gifts, persuasion, coercion, aggression, nonverbal cues, checking in, say-ing no, when no actually means no, role play, kinks, fetishes, dressing up, language and how to be assertive and say what we want, mean and need. This could be a most difficult conversation for us as practitioners and adults if we had a childhood of consent override (lots of those 'don't you say no to me' moments).

When parents override this autonomy, they do so unconsciously, out of their awareness, because they are frustrated, want their children to conform to the behaviour of the moment to get things done, stop people looking, or indeed just get out of the house on time. This is not always a malicious act of consent override.

I know as a parent I said to my children many times (and likely still do), eat your greens, put your shoes on, stop jumping on the sofa, go to bed and all of the other parent quotes and, yes, I also said 'don't you say no to me' when I wanted something to be done at a certain time (especially when the behaviour triggered shame in me such as being late for school!)

It happens, and there is a big difference between being far left and liberal with very few if any boundaries, where I was called a soft, liberal, hippy Mum who was 'spoiling my children with love' by giving them autonomy and freedom, and the type of parenting I received, which was authoritarian, institutionalised and strict. I still said those phrases that I am challenging here because some days we (or I in this case) don't want to be late or whatever the thought is and the feeling that goes with it. We do have to remember to get the pacing 'good enough' as Winnicott said (Winnicott, 1971), and we know from models like PACE, which stands for Playful, Accepting, Curious and Empathic, by Dan Hughes that PACE is both a great parenting and therapeu-tic model (Hughes, 2011).

We do have to get the balance right so that children learn about rules and social norms because this is how a healthy society functions. And, that when the occasions appear where those phrases of consent override are ejected from the mouth of the adult, they can be addressed in a way that is not overly intrusive into a child's autonomy, agency and sense of self. We can create sit-uations whereby they have the power to choose with smaller options such as choices for food, dressing and hobbies or games because it is important to be able to make choices consciously and say no, in order to be able to do this later in life with sexual partners. It's often not defiance towards us, but frustration that they cannot articulate.

Where is consent when it comes to online harm?

Is there such a thing as consent online? Do we actively get to make choices about what we see, and are those 'warnings' often disguised as a trigger or content warning enough?

We could discuss consent in this space as the choice about whether we are exposed to text, images or videos as a violation of human rights when that content is played before we make our choice. The autoplay function has been turned off by default on several platforms, not because of this issue, I might add. Some platforms now cover up 'graphic' videos that you need to actively uncover to view, and this is fraught with many issues as the bots and humans currently grading this material are not in line with the world of film and TV classifications of violence and often miss the very ones that are attributed to Cybertrauma.

For a more in-depth discussion on this, I talked to Onlinevents in 2014 about the autoplay feature that Facebook (as it was called then) rolled out and the Cybertrauma I was exposed to … without my consent! You can find this at www.youtube.com/watch?v=fyUyM-eW0L8&t=1907s.

Managing consent to enter an 18+ or the adult world is the one area most focused on to date in the age assurance process because we can, should and will 'do something' about this with a fair amount of ease compared to the issues above, because gambling and pornography are already 18+ rated in the real world and so 'cut and paste' rules can almost shift left into the cyberspace. Age verification will likely be used for this in the first instance for adult sites and gambling etc., and then slowly the other issues will follow suit when we can get objective ways to measure, define and action them. Until then, by 'consenting' to the platform community guidelines (not always easy to understand, actioned or even available with ease), you can be exposed to all sorts of 'stuff' that you don't really get to consent to as you meander through the city park that belongs to [insert platform name].

Consent is not a new topic and when we work with children we need to take into account that trauma is often created by the lack of consent, and so our role as practitioners is to consider how the lack of consent was present in the issue and what the understanding is around this lack of consent for the child, and being able to assist and help the people who care for the child.

So, with your consent, let's move on to the topic of pornography. Now have you really given consent to the chapter's content if you don't know what it will say?

(Don't forget as you read the chapter to take with you what you have learned here about consent.)

References

Berne, E. (1964). *Games people play. The psychology of human relationships.* Penguin.

Berne, E. (1970). *Sex in human loving.* Penguin.

Carse, J. (1986). *Finite and infinite games. A vision of life as play and possibility.* Free Press.

Geher, G., & Kaufman, S. (2013). *Mating intelligence unleashed: The role of the mind in sex, dating and love.* Oxford University Press.

Hughes, D. (2011). *Attachment-focused family therapy workbook.* W.W. Norton.

Knibbs, C. (2022). *Children, technology, and healthy development.* Routledge.

Merriam-Webster Dictionary. www.merriam-webster.com/dictionary/consent.

Ogas, O., & Gaddam, S. (2012). *A billion wicked thoughts: What the internet tells us about sexual relationships*. Plume.

Porges, S. (2011). *The Polyvagal Theory*. W.W. Norton.

Winnicott, D. (1971, republished 2005). *Playing and reality*. Routledge Classics. Routledge.

7 Pornography viewing in children and young people

Pornography

Online supermarket shopping with a very different cost

I am hopping over the real depth of these issues due to word limitations and a need to communicate the harm in a way that minimises harm to you the reader. This a difficult line to hold when writing about this topic, and others in the book as I am aware that people with a history of sexual assault and abuse may find these chapters uncomfortable, as can people without histories of sexual abuse and assault.

As per the last chapter, all about consent, a good idea here is to give you an idea as to what you will read: I am going to describe pornography websites and their content, lacking specific details about the acts on the sites as this book could be picked up by young people and I am aware that in training I can steer and hold conversations differently. This means you will be guided to the elements necessary for your practice and if you wish to understand the subject matter in depth you will have to speak with me in training.

This is a taboo subject; however, this is one of the most important conversations within this book due to the prevalence of and access to a world of sexual activity that we have never encountered, nor had pretty much anyone in history before 1996. It is suggested that an adult (in this case a young person) can now see more sexual images in one hour than could a man in the 1900s see in his entire life (Ogas & Gaddam, 2012).

Does this change child development in any way? Let's find out.

Let's go shopping!

A is for avocado, Z is for zucchini

Online shopping is quick, easy and fairly private. No one can see in your basket or trolley as they would in the real-life version as you muse around the store. There's no pressure to shop to 'eat healthy' in case you bump into that person you admire or want to impress.

DOI: 10.4324/9781003364177-8

And, of course, when you go to your online shopping website you can fill your basket up to the brim with those treats for the weekend with ease, thanks to the dedication of the supermarket website designers making your shopping experience easy to use.

As you browse online, you can see this week's special offers: food is categorised and easy to find, rather like meandering up and down the aisles and popping items into your basket or trolley; you can take your time online without feeling like you look lost, incompetent or have memory issues (this often happens when they change the shelves and you can't find what you're looking for!). You can look at the item, compare it with other brands and, of course, there's always a bargain to be had, when you can have two for the price of one. The offers are strategically placed, mimicking the 'end of the aisle' psychology. The only thing that's missing from the online shopping experience is the bright lights, screaming children and regular announcements about spillages and staff needed at the tills.

Oh, but online it's better, as you can peek at the fruit and veg beforehand by checking the thumbnail, which might just even play a 360-degree tour of the avocado. What a delight! And no one can see which fruits, veg or sweets you're 'eying up'.

You might be on the same page as me at this point as you read the above paragraphs, and if not, allow me to extrapolate and describe the experience of a very well-known online porn website.

Categories: avocado – zucchini

The comparison to supermarket shopping is quite stark and online porn websites are much the same in their layout, and with a tongue-in-cheek framing here I am going to say you can certainly see the fruit and veg and compare their sizes, select their ripeness, view them from a 360-degree angle, compare 'brands' and find exactly what you are looking for through the front page, listed categories or by searching A for avocado through to Z for zucchini.

And of course, the adverts and offers are *very* well placed on the home page. Aiming to lure prospective customers to another supermarket, with what could be a better deal, two-for-one, reduced prices or more exotic fruit and veg! Or, perhaps to the gambling websites because porn and gambling seem to go together like wine and cheese.

However, the difference between an online porn site and a supermarket is that the thumbnails on a porn site contain *the highlights of the video played in short bursts* (maybe 10 seconds or so) when you hover the mouse over the thumbnail. So realistically you never need to click play to see the top five moments of a video, which usually contain the '*money shot*' (discussed later).

And the landing page content here is free, accessible by clicking recommendations, a bit like the YouTube format, which many children are accustomed to using, and so this makes it all that bit easier to navigate and reduces cognitive load, meaning attention can be given to the material to be viewed with 100% concentration. The user experience is 100% set to 'ease of use'.

This, however, is not the most alarming point about these websites, so I urge caution as you read that you have both the time and space (and suitability of space) to read the following paragraphs and the rest of the chapter. You may have several reactions, responses and bodily sensations as I describe the website content.

And on this occasion, I am not referring to avocados.

S.E.X sells!

Sex sells and pretty much always has done, in so far as being described in religious writings, scandalous gossip and the supermassive adult industry that revolves around this. Some of you may find that your curiosity brings you to this chapter and shock and disgust follows, and some of you may feel shame, or that, as you read this chapter, you may find your imagination starts to run quite loud and some of you may notice sexual sensations occurring as you read around the following text. Therefore, stories that contain sexual scenes or hints towards them are best sellers, mainly for females as it turns out, as can be seen with the prevalence of Literotica (PinkNews, 2018) and EroRom (erotic romance) and Fan Fiction (Ogas & Gaddam, 2012).

Please note this: solitary text such as these paragraphs, which contain sexual words and/or suggestions, can create and construct sexual excitement and arousal (thanks to the power of the brain and imagery that appears in your mind as you read). Imagine what the visual space can do. Consider the phrase *a picture can speak a thousand words*. This is the fast-track express shopping lane to sexual excitement, especially for male brains, which we will discuss throughout this chapter, which is not a gender slur but a fact we need to consider. The point for you as the reader is *you* may feel the excitement as you read this, so pay attention to your body responses and imagine a child who is also going through this process and what happens to them.

Sex differences: for example, to return to the concept of female excitement occurring through text. The huge success of *50 Shades of Grey* (James, 2012) highlights that women are drawn to this kind of sexual material, which of course we know logically, and Mills & Boon have been a cornerstone of success in terms of women reading 'raunchy' books, as they have been referred to. The *50 Shades* book sales brought the issue to the awareness of many people that women did 'like sexual content'. Which of course is true, but not necessarily in the same format as men. There are some great books on this topic (Ogas & Gaddam, 2012; Nagasoki, 2015, 2021) and for the sake of word count, it is worth reading outside of this book if you are interested in how we 'get our kicks' as adults. However, I would urge you to remember that the data used in the conversations in my previous book is assumed to be from adults (Knibbs, 2022). As you read this volume, I am sure it will become obvious that we cannot rely on data collected online to be 'only' adults' responses and searches, and more and more importantly, the published dates of those books is over a decade or so ago. Much has changed since then.

So, thanks to the viral emergence of the *'ladies love porn literature dontcha know'* phenomenon, we are now in a space and time where this material is no longer being referred to as being suitable for the *'dirty ol' man'*, as is often muttered in comics like *Viz*, sitcoms and beyond, with the wink-wink nudge-nudge approach of Monty Python.

Pornography is, seemingly *for all people, watched (or read) by all people*. And you can find what you wish to view online as there is always a category labelled as such, so every person can always find what they like! Or press the category, quick link button or website URL to find out. Kink, squink or otherwise; get your curiosity kick here!

This is the allure, excitement and perhaps what can be called wickedness of these adult sites in repeatedly enticing young people to them. The text alone is often enticing and suggests an activity that they are curious about or have heard about; it suggests a new and novel thing, which of course is the way the brain loves to explore, learn and remember, and in this process, akin to what is known about human infants, the viewer may likely exhibit strong preferences for stimuli and situations that they have never seen, viewed or experienced before (Jaegle et al., 2019). Upon landing on one of these pages the initial text can be and often is misogynistic, abusive, straight to the point, contains swearing, colloquially named body parts, new language and is the 'sales' technique to the *'click here to see, view and enjoy!'*

Before the images are seen by the eye of the viewer, it feels exciting, secretive (as it often is), scary, and also illegal (which, of course, it is for children to view this material in the UK under the age of 18). It is forbidden by parents, society and maybe even friends; it is anti-religious, toxic, enlightening, educative (of sorts) and answers a lot of questions for curious young people. *Why wouldn't they click to watch?* Curiosity is a natural part of our evolution as it is part of the survival process (Kidd & Hayden, 2015).

Remember Amy R and her need-to-know things to protect you? What about if this was something that she needed to know? Better to be safe than sorry, right? Yes of course that means you must read and watch the content; this could be a lifesaving moment!

The harms: what we know so far

Here is the more serious section as I move you from humour to curiosity and explanation. Therefore, pornography can be harmful to young people for the following reasons.

Firstly, the videos contain people having sex in some form or another; of course they do, as these are websites hosting exactly that content. However, I am going to explain the text they can read, still images and then video images in terms of the issues, harms and perhaps long-term impact(s). I will use and cite some neuroscience in this chapter; however, I want to emphasise that we are more than 'dopamine hits' and neural pathways. And I include the caveat of: some of the books cited here and subsequent TEDx talks given on these topics are (a) queried by TED the organisation, in so far as they have added text to say they are the presenter's views only, and (b) conducted by people with a seemingly cognitive and even attributional bias in their field of study, as you will see discussed below, perhaps because they want their viewpoint to be true. Going back to the start of the book, I am presenting as many viewpoints as I can find as I think it's necessary for us as practitioners to take a balanced rather than an extreme, political or opinionated view.

What we do know is that we *can not ever* subject children or young people to studies of the nature described in this chapter for ethical reasons and therefore everything we do know is being 'transposed' onto children's development and learning. The neuroscience we currently have on children and young people for other subject matters, such as reading, cognition and behavioural responses, is where we can lean, but we can never directly know for sure about these matters as there will never be an ethical reason justified for showing children pornography with which to study it. Please do remember this when you see articles and reports and experts telling you *they know*.

What is striking here, as we now conduct studies on young people in the fields of neuroscience, is to explore brain architecture changes, such as, how do we differentiate between brain architecture changes that have already taken place due to viewing pornography since the ages of say, 8 years (as some research suggests) and who are now 27 (the age of the Internet), and those who only began viewing at say perhaps 18 or 21? How would we know what the effect of anything is in this space as we do not have retrospective neural data, nor can we isolate pornography from other things a child sees or watches? What about those children or adolescents that are still in the process of maturation and neuroplasticity – a lifelong process? How do we tell the differences and how do we tell the similarities and where, what and when are the causes?

This would be like trying to measure the exposure to weather patterns and using brain imaging techniques such as fMRI data to guess where children are geographically living. Therefore, all we can do, and please bear this in mind when you read articles in the mainstream media and by well-intended organisations wanting to express how *they know for sure* the effects of pornography viewing on young children's development, is make correlation *only*. And even this is a weak link of knowledge on this topic matter.

We can work with children who are telling us their own experiences, which may *not* be the same as other children. We can look for themes, but the likelihood of having causal data for children viewing pornography is nigh on impossible. Furthermore, not all children will see pornography, others will see a lot and all of the quantities in between. Not to mention some will see vanilla porn, and others will see torture, gonzo or hentai for example (these are categories/styles). We will not eradicate this material from the Internet and not all children will speak of the fact they have seen it. Some may not even know it is pornography if it involves animals, children or a whole host of other participants, sentient or not. Furthermore, and a quick reflection here: does this count if it appears in music videos, films or games and what's the difference in the way we adults categorise sexual content in other mediums?

But first, let's look at the research to see what we can claim, evidence, or hyperbolically use for clickbait.

So, let's begin with text on the sites and then 'see' what happens with images (both still and moving) as the children find (accidentally or purposefully) and view this material (for short or longer periods).

Text: sexual words on the screen

In previous book (Knibbs, 2022), I explained that minds are not great at distinguishing (visual) reality from imagination and are said to have mirror neurons that help them notice, mimic and feel what the other person is doing, feeling and showing (Ferrari & Coudé, 2018). Brains or minds are great at constructing emotions from internal and external signals (Feldman Barratt et al., 2016 and reading words has an impact on your visual cortex (Wandell, 2011); often we see the word as an image, for example when you read the following words, notice if you get an image of Big Ben, the Eiffel Tower, a car or your car. You may well glancingly see these images in your mind – what is called the inner eye in psychology. Some people cannot create a mental image in their mind (Nielson Hibbing & Rankin-Erickson, 2003); however, emotive, sexual words may not require these mental images needed for comprehension of this subject matter. And again, this provides us with an ethical dilemma about how we would research or study this. Words, therefore, create and evoke images, and often in turn images evoke feelings, feelings are linked to actions and associations.

The websites, as I have said, are laid out for ease of navigation. Usually with the most recently uploaded, popular, upvoted videos and themes or styles all rallying for your attention on the home page. The categories include easy-to-understand taxonomy such as 'blonde', 'brunette', 'anal', 'gay', 'for females' and 'big dicks'. Some of the categories are not so obvious and are acronyms for the regular visitors to the website and of course if you're not sure what they mean, it only takes a click to find out …

There are usually search facilities where you could and can type out a fantasy (forbidden, fetish or recently introduced to your worldview), and one of the most popular searched terms and 'type' of video is incestual in nature (familial), such as stepmother and son, father and stepdaughter or siblings, for example.

This information is often provided by the websites; for example, Pornhub even has a research section on the website for you to check out the statistics, which can also tell you the average amount of time a person spends on the site (it's not as long as you think but is probably longer than you think). If you want to try this function out, you can find out more about the human psyche and porn site usage than by viewing the material alone. However, most users of the site are not engaging in statistical analysis research, apart from people like me and other sexologists. If they were, I don't know how long the industry would last!

Please also note, you can do this yourself to see what I mean, and I do encourage those who want to understand this subject to courageously visit the *front page only* to see what I mean. You do not have to watch the videos, but that is your choice, and I am not here to judge if you already do this. If you do this, yes, your Internet provider will be able to see that you visited this site, it will be in your search history and as such, you may want to consider whether this is something you want in your Internet browsing history.

Some of you may have already visited these sites, may have deleted the evidence or turned on incognito mode to hide this fact (which is still recorded in history on your computer and with your internet provider, and tech-savvy adults have utilised this knowledge to spy on their children or their partner in the case of a few clients I have seen over the years). *This is only a suggestion*, but the point to take away from this exercise and thought experiment is: most of you reading this will already be adults and old enough to visit the sites legally.

Notice how it feels to think about doing this activity. Notice how it feels as you carry out the activity and what this might be like for a young person doing the same activity and what they might feel. Also, young people are likely to be using other methods for the videos so this is just a thought experiment.

Please remember that if you do visit the sites on a shared or family computer others may be able to also click on the site in the internet history if it is not deleted. This is often how young people find the site in the first place. (Or at least that's what they tell me. Some just google words like sex, boobs, and the ones they hear in the playground, yard or online. More on this in a moment.)

Porn categories: shopping on the front page

These categories, the search facility and the explanatory text of the videos form part of the problem, yet there is a sinister peripheral issue that sits above the actual material contained in the videos themselves, so let's look at this and what is going on here. The text and thumbnail create curiosity about the click-and-view behaviour; however, if the viewer then goes on to read the comments, usually below the video as per the YouTube layout, it can soon turn sour in terms of what is being said about the content and why this sexual, aggressive and misogynist language becomes associated with the content by the viewer.

I am suggesting, through the lens of neuroscience, these two processes overlap and become merged in the way that neuroscience tells us associative memory works (Kandel et al., 2013), so we have to infer and deduce that if memory works on an associative basis then watching videos of people having sex and reading language relating to this event is going to create an association.

I am sceptical when we say we have evidence that watching pornography in a laboratory setting shows us the associations that exist 'in' the brain (mainly because I ask what kind of person volunteers for these experiments … Is a shy, retiring person a participant? I doubt it, but I reckon that an exhibitionist is going to love being on show for this kind of research). Many of the studies look at brief reactions to films, whilst being watched or observed on a reasonably sized screen, sometimes in a machine (fMRI). This is not the average person's day or week as to when they choose to watch pornography or on what device, and of course, the set and setting influence the nervousness, shame, excitement or feelings of egocentricity that a 'participant' will be feeling when they are exposed to such images; consciously knowing their brain activity, pupil dilations, heart rate, skin respirations/sweating or breathing patterns and rate may suggest to the examiners and researchers that they are excited or enjoying the observations perhaps? It's like a version of Crufts but with people watching and or performing for the judges, only in a voyeuristic form of people watching people watching pornography. (Research is strange, huh?)

Narratives and harm

This particular example reflects videos and their comments on heterosexual intercourse between two people. There are many more formats, types, kinks and sexualities present on these websites and videos and these will be briefly mentioned soon; however, the most prolific video content is of heterosexual couples and so this is what I am talking about here initially.

The comments underneath many of these videos would be classified as misogynistic, to say the least, and often have violent, aggressive and sometimes homicidal tones. The women are objectified, and the male actor is cajoled via the comments into harming and hurting the female for the pleasure of the viewer. Where the videos are same-sex or gay men the same can be said; however, the level at which this occurs is nowhere near as prevalent as the heteronormative versions. Of course, the actor cannot and does not see these comments (as they are mostly post recording, not live videos); however, the other readers do see these comments. The language and narrative of the videos can be quite stark, shocking and of course a form of education and exposure to new words and ideas to the newer readers, whilst they can also be confirming, reassuring and familiar to a regular reader. It can also be the assumed normative sexual language to a naive first-time viewer, especially if they are under 18.

Much of the research suggests that the age at which young people access porn is approximately 14, with some seeing it around the age of seven (BBFC, 2020). And with this age is the ability to read fairly robustly and so the comments form part of the process of association to the material, swear words and lexicon between peers. Even where comments are not necessarily read through, titles containing words like 'smashing her back door in' and 'whore gets a pounding' can both titillate, excite and inform new viewers that this is the 'language of sex'. These were often terms shouted out in the Sex-Ed lessons I taught over a decade ago so you can see this is not necessarily a new issue. Where these terms originated from may well have been peers, the playground or grown-up people.

Notwithstanding the learning difficulties or other vulnerabilities a child may have, the title text is quite short and says how the person, often female, is being treated. It uses language that can be misleading or nuanced and for those with learning difficulties this compounds their misunderstanding. And for those younger people who do not understand the nuances of language, sarcasm and social norms, such as those with neurodivergent thinking, it can become something they repeat without understanding the context and appropriateness, and it often occurs in public settings or texted to peers. And the idea of swear words to younger children is often exciting and they practice them with their peers (looking for social cues as to appropriateness). I have often worked with a younger adolescent who was on the autistic spectrum or SEN who made a statement such as 'glory hole' and cannot explain why a vagina may be referred to as such or why their peers find this offensive or confusing. They have then used the language in education or youth settings, only to be further confused as to why they have now been asked to speak with a teacher, adult or even social worker, and as a result, end up in my clinic with a pretext of sexually harmful behaviour and language preceding this.

We must do better when assessing the needs of children and young people who are viewing this type of material and to do so we must understand the language they read and hear and how they understand this. I am circling back to good sex and relationships education which now has to consider the fact that children are going to be exposed to sexual language with a much higher prevalence than before the Internet existed. Children and young people may continue to view this material after the Online Safety Bill comes into effect and the age verification processes are in use.

We cannot eradicate this material, only reduce the exposure to it, but we must have better education in place for the youth of today. The most difficult aspect of this is knowing that material that references or shows sexual activity is available 24/7 on streaming platforms, such as the Big Brother type 'love' or dating programs, in films that have not been restricted with parental controls on streaming apps and TV, let alone via the porn sites that exist. And so the days of the watershed on TV are no longer creating a time barrier, which used to serve as an obstacle to this. In my clinic, I often see and speak with children aged around 7–8 years and upward that have seen pornography, been sent it, and use phrases like 'dirty minded' and can explain what this means.

Would the harm be different if the comments were not there? What about the images? A major piece of information that you require from this point of the discussion in one of the largest regions of the brain is devoted to optical processes of vision at the back of the brain in the occipital lobe. This is extremely important to consider for child development and the issue of viewing material such as this.

(*Note*: To do this chapter's section justice, the work of ophthalmologists and how eyes and brains work together cannot be understated in my approach here. Researchers like Margaret Livingstone and Andrew Huberman have informed much of my work and understanding, particularly in this domain. Given my background in Optronics, eye tracking work in my undergraduate degree, polyvagal theory knowledge about the eye muscles and how this relates to emotions, attachment and socialising, and how this transitions into my work as a therapist with a focus on non-verbal communication (noticing, in particular, the eyes), I feel unique in this space to be able to synthesise this work together to have a credible voice here on this topic. With the many conversations I have had with children and young people on this topic there are still flaws in non-experimental evidence. Data is only ever going to be anecdotal but worthy of further research and conversations.)

Static images

This conversation is way beyond the *Karma Sutra*, which contains static images (pictures and drawings) of sexual positions, or the 'position of the week' as once shared in a magazine in the late 1980s and early 1990s aimed at young females, who were often 12–16 rather than the young adult age of say 18–25. These magazines are now glossy brochure types in print and online. So, I will explain why still images versus moving have a different effect on the viewer.

Static images, i.e. pictures, photos or drawings of a sexual nature, were once forbidden in many spaces and places (as were moving pictures), and yet historical paintings contain images like this, of semi or fully naked bodies and many seemingly in the throes of sexual activity, masturbation or sheer nakedness, and you only have to visit an art gallery to see this.

However, I am discussing here intimate images in magazines known as 'top shelf' material as they were placed out of the reach of children. This out-of-reach idea can be enticing enough for young people (forbidden fruit so to speak) and this is why magazines have been so popular over the years. 'Used' magazines strewn in bushes and under mattresses have likely filled the minds of maturing children of the 20th century as a secret that they could look at only in times when adults were not around, or when other children showed them. They may have been excited or confused by these images and, of course, they lack context about what to do, as often they were images of female genitals or breasts, and sexual penetration was omitted.

These magazines were imagination-based spaces that minds could wander into about sexual activity and what it may look like and feel like, and indeed did not contain many directions for the how-to – these were not Haynes manuals! Moreover, magazines that were designed for women such as *Playgirl* did not show genitalia and history suggests these magazines were taken up by the gay communities and so did not go to waste, so to speak (Rettenmund, 2017). Moreover, any pictures of genitalia did not show erect penises and it is only recently that TV was allowed to even go there, causing uproar regarding this when a program showed an amateur photographer and naked, semi-erect males (Hirrons, 2020). I'm sure many females who have received consensual and non-consensual Dickpics will tell you that they are not the artsiest enjoyable images to the viewer, and I wonder how many of the complaints came from heterosexual men and or women about this program.

For the adults, mainly males, who buy these magazines (*Playgirl* and *Playboy* type), static images allow for the eyes to wander and zoom in on genitalia and naked bodies, taking as long as is wanted, needed or required. Static images allow for imagination, fantasies and desires to take place in the mind of the imagineer. Of course, much of this imagination is based on experience and knowledge; imagination can take a person into what I will call our darker or shadow selves where we can take our mental representations and wishes to a level that no one can see, hear or know about. We can fantasise about events that may be classified as weird, kinky, illegal, immoral or silly. The imagineer can add or take away elements of sexual practices and anything else they can think of and no one outside of that mind's eye view can see it or know it (for now).

What is interesting and worrying here in this chapter is young adults, young people and children will also 'wander' off into their imaginations. Perhaps young people consider what they can, should, ought to have done, have experienced, and want to or not want to do with these bodily parts of theirs or perhaps other people's. For children, this may be an idea presented about what they can now do, and so these images can be the first introductory 'idea' about sexual activity without ethical or moral guidance.

Moreover, children may be seeing images that are represented and associated with sexual abuse if they have been victims of this crime. And notwithstanding that, the static images they are sent via technology are a format of this type of abuse. If we don't let children access the 'top shelf' material in the real world, why are we allowing them to be bombarded with these images via technology through the prevalence of this material online? And it is more than likely they will see videos rather than static images, but to what degree or in what numbers is unknown because children tell me in the clinic that, if they do see 'this stuff', *they don't report it or tell the adults* (for lots of reasons).

Videos: or 'moving' images

Our eyes are innately drawn to movement as our lives depend on it – there could be a predator lurking in the shadows. Life is dangerous as Le Doux (2015) suggests and so the system of sight is tied to our survival as an organism. I deliberately talked about these issues in my previous book on the orienting response, convergent vision and neurobiological underpinnings of technology use, so that when you began to read this part of this book you could start to see the real issues behind these harms and understand them in depth (Knibbs, 2022).

Moving images of sexually related content or nakedness have been around since the invention of technology and I don't mean computers. If you head out to any museum you will likely see how we evolved from photographs to video. Spinning plates, Kinetoscopes and Cinématographe machines were the first kinds of moving image spaces (Science & Media Museum, 2020) before we ended up where we are today with videos, augmented reality and the expansively creative, immersive and mesmerising world of virtual reality. See the work of Lanier (2017), for more on this, and later writings from myself about this space.

These pornography videos tend to follow the same kind of story format and may be in a cartoon-based format or with real people. Many of these videos contain what is referred to as hardcore pornography, which differs from the kind that was previously called softcore (meaning there were no actual scenes of penetrative acts up close and personal, though there were scenes of naked bodies, genitalia and kissing). These were often called 'blue movies' and many of these were recorded on VHS tapes and shared by the physical giving of the tape to a real person recipient. Hardcore videos were likely much more sought after when they were created, as this was the most taboo and was often seen in the same way as contraband alcohol of years gone by. And we know how that worked out.

The idea that you had to know code words to get, borrow or purchase a video, or know someone who had one, could get one, or even made them, makes this more like drug dealing behaviour. And of course, there are many drugs that a street drugs dealer can sell; however, when it comes to the likes, dislikes and more that are associated with sex, then you can begin to see that a metaphor of the drugs deals or underground market street trading becomes fairly redundant when you start to think about how many '*types*' of content can be typed into a search engine, forum and space that exists out of the normal 'Internet' (and what is searched for is often found with a few clicks or details on how to find said search requirements and where these are provided by previous searchers).

This effectively means that any sexual language that appears in films, songs on social media, music videos and computer games, or is shared through chat mechanisms, can be a few seconds away from being entered into searches (though not all of these take place through the search engines), and a few clicks away from being viewed and browsed. No more code words, knowing the person with the dodgy tapes or having to borrow them for a short while. No more asking in shops for material hidden by plastic covers or brown bags. This is now 24/7 and 365 on many platforms, and many search spaces (forums for example) and, what's more, it doesn't have to be 'real' people. And it doesn't have to be searched; it can be sent to you in a direct message.

And so back to the moving images. Our eyes are captivated by moving images in the same way that we notice 'things' in our peripheral vision that could be a threat to us. Our social engagement system is, if you remember from my previous book, controlled by the upper dorsal vagal nerve that controls our facial muscles; particularly those around the throat, mouth and eyes (Knibbs, 2022). When we feel safe our eye muscles are (mostly) relaxed and we focus on the faces of others to understand the social cues they convey. We notice micromovements in other people's faces and react accordingly and, of course, when we are facing someone in the real world we often have other things to look at over their shoulders, next to them, off in the distance and more.

When we face a computer screen our gaze is intensified into the screen through convergent vision which is associated with the fight–flight mechanism and therefore has a high attentional salience at the cost of the peripheral vision around it. (Think small screens on phones and tablets and the zone of false safety I discussed in my previous book and you can see we zoom in like this even more so with smaller screens (Knibbs, 2022)). This tricks our brain into believing that we are looking at a larger space in our environment because in this image the entire 'room' is contained in that screen. We are 'hyper-focused' at this range and size. And our brains are likely to be confused somewhat by this, but can't tell why.

Imagine watching a film at the cinema, where the screen is so large you become immersed in the story and you feel like you are almost 'in' that space with the film characters. The camera direction recreates what we call a first-person view (mostly).

When we focus or zoom into the space in the computer monitor or device screen we make the image in the middle sharp to identify distinguishing features and to pay 'attention' to what it is we are looking at. And perhaps we let the details on the outside of the 'film' fade into a blurry mess as they are not conducive to our intended focus. When we are focusing on the middle of the image and paying attention to certain behaviours, we can miss obvious visual cues or details as has been demonstrated by the 'gorilla in the crowd' video, which also became the name of a book (Wiseman, 2004) after Richard Wiseman carried out this experiment for a tv show (link: www.youtube.com/watch?v=y6qgoM89ekM).

When we look at video images that have within them familiar shapes through our visual perception system, such as faces, edges, cylinders, squares and more (Tovee, 2008), which make up the bulk of everything we ever look at, then our eyes and the occipital lobe of the brain work together in a harmonious dance to produce a reciprocal moving image of the world in front of us so we can understand what is happening.

Our brains don't care 'where' the image is, it just wants to make sense of it, code and decode and re-present it to us as something that we need to pay attention to. And if it's an act that seemingly connects us to an aroused feeling and state then we are going to pay that little bit more attention to it because our brain is likely to be piecing together a story of 'that' behaviour is equal to 'this' feeling and sensation that we 'like' (in most cases it is liked).

And of course, if we are interested in it from a perspective of joy, fear, suspicion, intrigue, curiosity or excitement then our attention will be much more intense as we delight in the cacophony of changing colours and light and sensations that we are perceiving.

In the process of the brain interpreting the movement of the adult being watched (or more than one, as is often the case on pornography videos), in front of us on the screen, our ability to 'feel' some of the things we are see-ing is created by the connection we have with mirror neurons (Staminov & Gallese, 2002). The visual aspect of watching someone else carrying out ac-tions we already know, have carried out ourselves through mimicking and copying, and can do in parallel with the 'actor', creates a feeling of 'sameness' in ourselves. We empathise on a bodily level with the body on the screen and feel similar feelings. If, for example, a child sees an adult masturbating they will likely already know this feeling, but if they are watching behaviours such as penetration they might not have engaged in this behaviour yet and perhaps, due to the connection with an already known, similar feeling, they may now seek out the unknown and, in the behaviour of Jim in the iconic 1999 film *American Pie*, 'an apple pie feels like third base' (video link to iconic film conversation about this: www.youtube.com/watch?v=Ik1NKkN0ysI).

Children or young people may attempt to find something 'in the real world' to emulate what they watched on the screen. If they find something similar this may become an issue; for example, if they find another child with whom to practice, or in the case of a child-on-child sexual abuse, this is where they are re-enacting upon another child. It could even lead to fetish-based ideas copied from the video, comments, or even suggested elsewhere as in the case of the film *American Pie* the film. Moreover, young children are inducted into the behaviours of copying through TV programs, nursery and childcare set-tings, so this will already be a familiar pattern to some children and engaging in these copying behaviours may follow this learned patterning.

In the moving images, the viewer will be paying attention to the micro-movements, and noticing the changes at the level of the skin colour (when it flushes) and the breathing rates of those in the videos, the face at the points of before, during and after orgasm, the words spoken or noises made during this process too and, like the orchestra, will be piecing the symphony together as one experience.

Attempting to recreate this with another person or animal (and yes I did need to say this) might just be the biggest issue we face with children and young people watching and re-enacting these videos. We know to date that we are becoming aware of many cases of child-on-child sexual abuse, and what is now an emerging trend of sexually harmful behaviour with books (Ey & Mcinnes, 2020), training packages and helpline services being needed. And, whilst we cannot point the finger entirely at pornography, we can be-come aware enough to think about this issue when we are facing a case with a child exhibiting sexual behaviours and have this in our minds as a possibility, where previously it was often connected that displays of sexual behaviour could be linked to sexual abuse.

Pornography addiction and reward deficiency syndrome?

Going back to the lab, the performer and the research team, seriously, I mean just imagine the pressure of the researcher and the participant as to what it is they want to measure (and find) and of course what needs to be 'performed'. It's not as clear as is often made out by those authors, researchers and influencers, such as those in the space of the Nofap movement (which is about 'quitting' pornography viewing and masturbation) claiming that pornography creates an addiction, using research from such studies about obesity for example (Benton & Young, 2016), focusing on the marked changes in a pathway called DDR2 (specific to Dopamine in the brain) leading to addiction. DDR2 pathways are cited and compared to pornography 'use and consumption' (words that have a negative and provocative connotation) as this matches the study on obesity, which does not contain any references to pornography use but does look at food and substance consumption. (Note: this is a case for people to read research citations as it can be illuminating what biases they reveal.)

It would be unethical to show someone the amount of pornography that they became addicted to as a method to measure these pathways. We certainly cannot do this with substances like drugs or alcohol for studies and so, of course, we are seeing some research with some helpful findings but, as always, the brain is complicated and so are our sexual preferences and likes/dislikes. We need to ask the person about their activity, behaviour and more, and see things on a case-by-case basis. If a client tells you they feel addicted, then go with their phenomenology and language, whilst leaning on the data. But let's not use the data from *some* studies to pathologise and berate the person we are working with.

For example, Gary Wilson discusses in his book that the protein Delta-FOsB is present in the addicts of pornography consumers (Wilson, 2014), stating high concentration in the nucleus accumbens, and yet this protein is also in people who have other addictive tendencies with substances, but can also be present in people who exercise, eat food that is palatable and delicious and those who suffer with stress. Also, was the protein compared against a baseline? So, I ask that if we started to measure children for this protein could we say it was because they had been viewing porn or could it be from enjoying exercise like football, and playing this four times a week, and snacking on sweets, energy drinks and junk food, or eating out with friends at fast food outlets (Christiansen et al., 2011)? Or what about stress (perceived or real), which also increases this protein (Wang et al., 2016)? We know that stress is certainly something that many of us faced and felt throughout the Covid-19 pandemic – would we say this was porn 'addiction' or lockdown or both? Also, Wilson's book does not state *whether this was true for females who 'consume porn [sic]'*, as this cohort is not discussed in the book.

Pop music or rock?

Think about the type of music you like and the fact that sometimes you have to be in the mood for certain types of music, some days you switch it off quickly, and some days you turn it up loud and dance to it. This basic example here is less complicated than the biologically primed mechanism of pleasure through orgasm, much more complicated than having a boogie.

Now, this is not to say that associations will not be made by watching pornography; of course, they will, and in this case here the sex that children and young people watch may be classified as rough (hurting and harming one or more people) hardcore which includes visible penetration and often includes anal intercourse. Associations are likely to follow the narrative spoken in the films or indeed written about in the comments or by others sharing these videos. Likely, this narrative will also become a norm and associated with this viewing. Ergo: *this becomes the developing internalised framework for a sexual experience for a child and young person watching if they do not have a baseline or education with which to compare it or be able to question and challenge what they see and read.*

If we don't have these conversations with young people about what sex is like, and by this, I don't mean explain in graphic detail what *your* sex life is like to a child (*don't do this!*), but talk to them about relationships, consent and more; then they will have what is laid out by the porn industry or biased teachings from organisations who are completely anti-porn, sex, kink or anything other than heteronormative sexual intercourse (for many reasons, political, ideological, religious or otherwise), and by default that's equivalent I suppose to a form of neglectful abuse? A point for you to muse over.

If we don't explain that these are often films curated to look a particular way by the industry and those who create content for this industry, then they will be left with a narrative that is skewed in the direction of the industry 'standards' as perhaps the standards they are expected to follow. Some young people say they know this is not 'real' sex, yet do they *really* know, if adults don't have these conversations to confirm their knowledge? How many young people have engaged in sexual activity and behaved like they are in one of the films, without challenges, retribution or corrections in that patterning? For example, we need to understand something ourselves to educate around it, and from a balanced perspective. That means that the education we provide is not leaning too far left or right of the politics, religious views and debates about gender, sexuality and identity – a difficult space for many organisations to hold, without personal feelings becoming part of the education itself.

Also, as discussed more in Chapter 12 on autistic spectrum disorder and neurodivergent thinking we need to be truthful with this cohort of children and young people based on where they are on that spectrum, as there are times I have seen educative material, parent and carer responses telling these children 'it's not real', 'it's rude' or 'that's not how sex is'. What I'm about to say may be controversial; it *is* real, people *do* do these things, they *are* real people (especially amateur and home videos), people *do* use *those* words, people do like *some of those* things, no we do not hurt animals or use animals for sex, yes people *do* like to dress up, no you don't have to do anything you do not want to, and more. These children are not stupid and our own embarrassed, taboo discomfort is creating an issue for children who then go on to become adults who are surprised by sexual acts, feelings and desires. I cannot express how so many 18+ autism spectrum disorder (ASD) clients I have seen who have and do enjoy sex but were told lies and untruths about porn and sex by the adults around them and their expressions in therapy are how embarrassing it was 'not to know' things or to be offended by an offer or request for an activity because they didn't know beforehand. To know another human did 'those' things or wanted them to engage in them shocked them and left them feeling betrayed in the same way as '*finding out about Santa*'.

The making of porn: how much do you know?

How many average adults are aware of the processes of making a porn film, what occurs in the creation, how long they take, what is often happening off camera, how much people are paid, or not paid, who is treated well, who is offered substances and promises beyond the movies, what kind of person takes part in these films, what the stars have to endure in order to make a movie that looks good on camera, and why the uptake of this material is now on streaming platforms (see below) and video-on-demand, social media and file sharing apps?

Why porn is not going away any time soon

We may now need to rethink our own taboo processes and learn about this material in order that we can hold the innocence of children for as long as is possible, whilst knowing at any time it can be shattered, changed and taken from them by an accident when seeing something online (or in the metaverse) in the blink of an eye; and of course with the education that informs and empowers rather than disables, punishes or shames others.

Furthermore, knowing how people at home can and do upload material like this to these websites through choice is empowering for some couples (or more), and knowing whether it is legal, or in the fallout stages of a relationship called revenge porn is helpful for answering questions by young people and helps to have those conversations. How we have discussions with children about filming, being filmed and taking part in these kinds of 'agreements' with partners is often about lifelong contracts of mutual respect and trust (can any of us really have that?), and what this may mean for relationship education in a world of technology. Saying 'don't do it' is like saying 'don't do *it*' to children; it isn't going to happen as often as we would like.

Lots for us to consider!

Prevention, prevention and age assurance

Currently (at the time of writing), there are several services, applications, programs, companies and conversations at the level of the Online Safety Bill regarding how we prevent children and young people from accessing this material. In doing so, there have been attempts over the years by internet filtering approaches to reduce exposure to this material. The efficacy of these filters is still perhaps a question of 'how do we know for sure?', with research in 2018 highlighting that internet filters had inconsistent and practically insignificant links with young people reporting their actual encounters of this material (Przybylski & Nash, 2018). In 2022 the children commissioners report (www. childrenscommissioner.gov.uk/report/talking-to-your-child-about-online-sexual-harassment-a-guide-for-parents/) stated that 25% of parents thought their children had seen porn online compared to the figure of 53% of children interviewed who said they had (not forgetting that children may not recognise porn for what it is, not want to say they have viewed it, or that shame may stop them reporting this even on survey type studies, and so accurate figures are always going to be difficult to ascertain here). What is certain is internet filtering stops some content, but not all. Filtering may not eradicate this material as it is shared on many platforms and in many ways, and age assurance apps may only prevent access to the websites themselves advertised as showing pornographic material. Much of the content that is seen by the children I have worked with in therapy is an embedded video in direct messages, apps or websites that have hidden rooms, as well as on social media, TV streaming services with no parental supervision or filters and on shared USB sticks.

Therapy conversations

In the therapy room when questions arise about pornography or sex, young people (and often adults too) are often unaware of the legalities of viewing this material, as previously discussed consent is the most misunderstood aspect of sex. They are often confused or don't know how to talk to a partner about what they may want, like or need sexually, have a prefixed template with which they converse about what sex is, why they *'have to'* (their words) do these things, what's expected of them (both sexes), what happens if they don't conform, perform and copy, what they should say, or not, and how their relationship needs or ought to look based on their knowledge of sexual material that they have watched or read. (I worked with a few young females who read *50 Shades of Grey* and that was a very interesting time for them to learn about kinks as well as the sexual activity I am talking about here).

Both males and females have discussed their fears about the violent nature of some of the acts and this confuses them about 'how' to engage with their partner. I often reflect with them that conversations before sex are needed and if they think chatting about sex is uncomfortable imagine what being in the moment would be like if they had to say they didn't like something. The replies have left me feeling saddened because most of them have said something like, 'I wouldn't' (say something about disliking an act during sex), which leaves me to ask you the question as the reader, 'why are we letting our young people down?' Why are some continuing in a sexual relationship where they can't or don't say no, or they dislike something happening and are wordless, powerless or dismissive, and as a result the abuse continues in this way, by and from each other?

Children who have been sexually abused often tell me they watch pornography or films that include scenes of sex to try to understand it, to see what people look like having sex, to see what faces people pull (orgasm faces), to watch the violent and rape-based versions to empathise and compare, or to permit themselves to be angry about this crime; and much more than I can discuss here.

Where and why has our teaching gone awry or our lack of education arisen and how did we leave them in this space to navigate it alone? Perhaps our discomfort is our justified reason and, if so, what now needs to change?

Add to this, peer pressure, new and emerging sexual normative practices, gender identity and ideology-based practices that suggest to children 'this gender' or 'this sexuality' should be the one to be engaging in, so you can be considered 'this gender or sexuality' according to the rules of the Internet or society writ large? Looking at the expectations from TV, books and videos (which include TikTok and other soc-med platforms) and the lack of balanced and complete education, you can see why so many young people are in a 21st-century state of confusion and why we currently have so many interpersonal relationship issues. I suggest this is why so many therapists are going to need to start asking questions about the taboo subjects of sexual activity when their clients are classified as young people or children because the world has changed over the last 20 or so years and pornography viewing is a thing for many of our children.

Knowing what categories are being viewed can give insight into the what, why and how of sexual and or gender development. I hope that the age verification process can prevent the accidental finding of these sites, especially for young children under 12 (see Knibbs (2022) for an explanation as to why this age is important); however, I suspect that we are late in 'shutting the gate' as the horses aren't even in the field anymore.

However, we are where we are, and this means we now have to match our education to the presenting problem, rather than trying to fix the problem by only going backwards. We as adults need to have those conversations we may feel uncomfortable about, and I can tell you, talking to young people who have been abused or suffered harm through copied pornography content is extremely uncomfortable for both the child and the practitioner. Knowing that actions could have been taken many years ago by the state, government, parents and the educational system to reduce the likelihood of harm occurring in the first place can be so devastating and anger-inducing for the child, parent and practitioner. I have felt this many times and it hasn't become any easier knowing that we don't have the legislation and education in place yet.

Some other areas for you to be aware of follow: an introduction to cartoon and other types of porn.

Comics? From Manga to Anime and Hentai

This category is well worth knowing about as it isn't just on porn sites in terms of its origin. To understand the evolution of these cartoon-based images and videos I need to take you back many years when comics became international and the shops I would go into (in the 1980s) would have an array of superhero-based comics, alongside the comics created for children such as *The Beano* and *Dandy*, *Bunty* and other such titles. There would be the Japanese, Korean and Chinese comics with their amazing artwork and stories that soon came to be the kinds of cartoons that appeared on TV for children.

Remember Pokémon in the 1990s? Well, this is not the first time this kind of artwork has appeared in an animated format. (I remember *Battle of the Planets* but that's showing my age.) However, bringing this up to date with the categories on the pornography sites, you can so often be met with the young-looking (often schoolgirl uniformed) figures with oversized genitalia, breasts and undersized waists overly keen for sex and willing to do anything for it. This is a complete genre of artwork mixed into the world of pornographic scenes and stories and there are lots of children and young people drawn to this because of the artwork and the kinds of films, geek and gaming worlds they inhabit and love to be part of.

It is well worth your time to explore and research this topic area because there is also a major aspect of violence and gore within this category and area; again I am limited here by word count and so I am ensuring that you are alerted to this area for now.

ASMR porn

Autonomous sensory meridian response (ASMR) is a feeling that accompanies auditory or visual stimuli (often tingling akin to goosebumps).

This kind of 'porn' will be found mostly on the streaming platforms like Twitch (or in videos on Snapchat, or YouTube, but may not have the word porn after it and be called 'satisfying videos'). It is unlikely that bare breasts or genitalia will be seen as that is an instant ban for the streamers, but they will, through the '*just chatting*' function, show you their oral and audio skills and use many double entendre hints, likes and mentions, which can direct and guide you to your 'success point' or encourage you to become associated with this person, their skills and the sights or sounds. This is often accompanied by the live chat function of many a 'folk' encouraging (through monetary means of subs and donations) the 'presenter' to become more like a 'cam girl', as the profession is known. Children can access this at any time as there is always someone 'just chatting'. Again, limited by word count this is an introduction here.

Word porn, food porn, robot porn, symmetry porn or car porn. If it's a popular category online for people to share images and videos and discuss their hobbies or day-to-day activity (think Instagram and food porn), then the word is ubiquitous in the lives of us all, including children who are entering this space.

The outcome, side effect or symptom? Sexual issues

Each child will have a different response and sexual behaviour associated with these videos and the viewing. Some may masturbate and some may become more compulsive with the masturbating, some needing to have the pornography on whilst they do this, and some following the pathway of what has been called Fap entropy (more extreme scenes needed to hit climax) by Mary Harrington on a podcast with Chris Williamson (2022). (https://modernwisdom.libsyn.com/episode-444). However, this issue *cannot* be seen in the same way as adults because children under the age of puberty will not be climaxing in the same way as a pubescent child and so we cannot utilise all of the adult literature to say the same for children. We also may need to slow down and consider the differences between children and adults in the cognitive space of 'fap entropy' as sexual experience is going to be different, based on age alone in most cases.

We do know that brains like novelty and become saturated, bored and habituated and so we know that some children may keep exploring more extreme pornography; however, the arc of curiosity could take them there anyway, as they do not necessarily know what the words mean before clicking.

Most of the literature you will read about issues with pornography use language like 'consumption' or 'use' to relate to people who watch and climax with this medium. 'Users' are generally later in the adolescent phase or adults when discussed in the literature. However, sexologists and therapists are beginning to find caseloads increasing with younger clients presenting with issues surrounding premature ejaculation, failure to produce an erection or dysfunction with this process such as satisfaction with sexual activity (personal communication). Some clients attribute this failure to reach climax or erections as being the fault of pornography.

We are currently in a void of research in this area about the damage viewing porn does to a child or young person. I am certain it does cause damage, but cannot say, with clarity and robustness, what and how much. I say *viewing not consuming* because the modus operandi for a child may well be different to an adult looking to 'hit success' whilst watching and they are often watching it, like TV, rather than seeking it out to accompany a need to masturbate with visual stimuli.

Pornography is *not* going away

What is clear at this point in the time and space of the digital age is sex is here in this space because adults frequent this online space. At a 'guestimate', adults outnumber children by 2 to 3 and so the adult's digital playground is going to have child visitors because they can get into these spaces, mostly with ease. These will not always be porn sites themselves and I am sure they will find ways around the age assurance, by navigation, homelife or friends and whatever means they can.

Whether we are in or post the 'sexual revolution', whether people of all genders are now feeling empowered, or disempowered, by being able to create, access and share sexual material with their crowd, we need to ensure that the children we work with are not in these spaces where they can watch, explore and be exposed to the sexual material. Reduction of this is the way to go, as eradication is impossible; so, mitigation of harm after, for those who do end up in the space, seems to be the sensible solution. However, this is so difficult to achieve, given that almost any space a child is in will be frequented by adults too who, looking to recruit and harm children, may show them this material. There are no safe and secure spaces online for children where this material can end up, nor can the adults wishing to share this kind of material in their own spaces be 100% sure that it is only adults who are viewing it.

And this is why we need to talk more openly about it, and not stick our heads in the sand.

Practitioner's pause for reflection

When 'onboarding' your young person into the service, do you ask about accessing such material as presented here and would you know what questions to ask and how? Being trauma-informed, applied and knowing what to ask and how is more complicated than I have time and space to go into here. However, is this something you allow consciously into the space of working with a child or young person?

And, what about the issue of being a therapist, and being asked by parents or carers as you begin your intake, that any conversations about sex or pornography are off the table for religious reasons, for example? How does this influence the therapeutic alliance, and what parts of the healing space are closed off by taking this approach? Do you ask parents if speaking about sex with them and their child is something they had considered in the process of working with their young child?

Would you know what to do about the issues of a child disclosing that they view pornography, whether this is accidentally, intermittently or regularly? What services have a safeguarding process built around porn viewing and how would their services deal with this?

What would your relationship with the child look like if you closed off the sex and porn talk? How can you offer all aspects of yourself as a practitioner if we don't make room for these conversations in practice without being a voyeur?

What about if the child or young person wanted to ask you questions about what they saw, so as to understand it? Are you a sex educator in your role and are you comfortable talking 'rimming, fisting and gang bangs' as denoted by the typology of the videos? Would you know how to discuss about ATM (arse to mouth), BBC (big black cock, not the TV service) and other acronyms without putting your judgements into the conversations about what *you* consider to be acceptable sexual practices?

How comfortable are you really, with this topic?

How was this chapter to read and what did you learn, what offended you, what sparked a curiosity, what children that you worked with did you think about?

How much more do you think there is to know?

And then we have the immersive pornography scene coming soon! The pun intended. (My next book and courses.)

References

American Pie. (1999). *3rd base feels like Apple Pie*. www.youtube.com/watch?v=Ik1NKkN0ysI.

British Board of Film Classification. (2020). *Young people, pornography & age-verification*. Personal Communication.

Benton, D., & Young, H. (2016). *A meta-analysis of the relationship between brain dopamine receptors and obesity: a matter of changes in behaviour rather than food addiction? International Journal of Obesity, 40(1)*, S12–S21.

Christiansen, A., DeKloet, A., Ulrich-Lai, Y., & Herman, J. (2011). *'Snacking'" causes long-term attenuation of HPA axis stress responses and enhancement of brain FosB/delta-FosB expression in rats. Physiology & Behavior, 103*, 111–116.

Ey, L., & McInnes, E. (2020). *Harmful sexual behaviour in young children and pre-teens: An education issue*. Routledge Focus.

Feldman Barratt, L., Lewis, M., & Haviland-Jones, J. (2016). *The handbook of emotions* (4th ed.). Guilford Press.

Ferrari, P. F., & Coudé, G. (2018). *Mirror neurons, embodied emotions, and empathy*. In *Neuronal correlates of empathy* (pp. 67–77). Elsevier.

Hirrons, P. (2020). *Viewers horrified at erect penis onscreen*. www.entertainmentdaily. co.uk/tv/viewers-horrified-at-unacceptable-channel-4-documentary-that-showed-erect-penises-onscreen/.

Jaegle, A., Mehrpour, V., & Rust, N. (2019). *Visual novelty, curiosity, and intrinsic reward in machine learning and the brain. Current Opinion in Neurobiology, 58*, 167–174.

James, E. (2012). *Fifty shades of grey*. Cornerstone Publishing.

Kandel, E., Scwartz, J., Jessel, T., Seigelbaum, S., & Hudspeth, A. (2013). *Principles of neuroscience* (5th ed.). McGraw Hill Medical.

Kidd, C., & Hayden, B. (2015). *The psychology and neuroscience of curiosity. Neuron, 88(3)*, 449–460.

Knibbs, C. (2022). *Children, technology, and healthy behaviour: How to help children thrive online*. Routledge.

Lanier, J. (2017). *Dawn of the new everything: A journey through virtual reality*. Bodley Head.

Le Doux, J. (2015). *Anxious: Using the brain to understand and treat fear and anxiety*. Viking.

Nagasoki, E. (2015, revised 2021). *Come as you are: The surprising new science that will transform your sex life*. Scribe.

Nielsen Hibbing, A., & Rankin-Erickson, J. (2003). *A picture is worth a thousand words: Using visual images to improve comprehension for middle school struggling readers. The Reading Teacher, 56(8)*, 758–770.

Ogas, O., & Gaddam, S. (2012). *A billion wicked thoughts: What the internet tells us about sexual relationships*. Plume.

PinkNews. (2018). *Literotica: 5 websites to quench your online erotica thirst*. www. pinknews.co.uk/2018/09/25/literotica-online-erotica-websites/.

Przybylski, A., & Nash, V. (2018). *Internet filtering and adolescent exposure to online sexual material. Original Articles, 21(7)*. www.liebertpub.com/doi/pdf/10.1089/cyber.2017.0466.

Rettenmund, M. (2017). *Playgirl magazine history*. www.esquire.com/entertainment/a55592/playgirl-magazine-history/.

Science and Media Museum. (2020). *A brief history of cinema*. www.scienceandmediamuseum.org.uk/objects-and-stories/very-short-history-of-cinema.

Staminov, M., Gallese, V. (2002). *Mirror neurons and the evolution of brains and language.* John Benjamins Publishing.

Tovee, M. (2008). *Physiology of vision and the visual system* (2nd ed.). MIT Press.

Wandell, B. (2011). *The neurobiological basis of seeing words. Annals of the New York Academy of Science, 1224(1),* 63–80.

Wang, H., Tao, X., Huang, S., Wu, L., Tang, H., Song, Y., Zhang, G., & Zhang, Y. (2016). *Chronic stress is associated with pain precipitation and elevation in DeltaFosb expression. Frontiers in Pharmocology, 7(138).* www.frontiersin.org/articles/10.3389/fphar.2016.00138/full.

Williamson, C. (2022). *Modern wisdom podcast. #444 – Mary Harrington: Modern society is failing men & women* https://modernwisdom.libsyn.com/episode-444.

Wilson, G. (2014). *Your brain on porn: Internet pornography and the emerging science of addiction.* Commonwealth Publishing.

Wiseman, R. (2004). *Did you spot the gorilla? How to recognise hidden opportunities.* Penguin.

Wiseman, R. Video of gorilla: www.youtube.com/watch?v=y6qgoM89ekM.

8 Online grooming and exploitation

I am hopping over the real depth of these issues due to word limitations and a need to communicate the harm in a way that minimises harm to you the reader. This a difficult line to hold when writing about this topic, and others in the book as I am aware that people with a history of sexual assault and abuse may find these chapters uncomfortable, as can people without histories of sexual abuse and assault.

Online grooming: child sexual exploitation – a model, education and a reflection

Shotgun friending, cocktail glasses and real name tracking

One of the most well-respected and profuse writers around the topic of sexual exploitation is David Finkelhor who, writing about this in 1984, referred to the prevalence of this issue, 'and that stranger danger message ... And if this is the case, surely telling these children will make them cautious about strangers and help prevent this issue'.

He has written many papers on the topic of the perpetrator, and this has been adopted by many services as the theoretical way for us to understand how this terrible crime of exploiting children for sexual activity happens. I'm going to briefly reference him and some of the models. However, for this chapter I thought long and hard about conveying this information to you without scaremongering, filling this chapter full of models, theories and approaches, victim blaming or putting the onus on the children to prevent this from happening.

The stories here are taken from my practice and experience of teaching sex and relationship education. This chapter will include actual comments made by clients and schoolchildren and, of course, to protect them I need to ensure that identifying features are removed and perhaps only the age and sex of the child are mentioned, whilst omitting or emphasising only where necessary.

If relevant, for example when gender, social or learning difficulties were involved in the grooming, these will be mentioned. The stories are about the process of online grooming from the perspective of the young person

DOI: 10.4324/9781003364177-9

and for you, the reader, whether you are a parent or professional; in this case I am going to explain the why and the how and contextually propose why this will continue to happen whilst the current models of 'preventing' online grooming are being taught to young people.

This is not to say that the current models are wrong and should not be used; however, I don't think they fully capture the nuanced issues at hand with the current landscape of (overly) sexualised child development, the body safety I discussed in the first book and the sheer number of people in the spaces online. There are so many ways to groom a child online, or rather so many spaces and types of spaces in which to do this and not everyone is a bad actor in these spaces; so it can be confusing to children when we use the current models, and there is confusion around consent and stranger danger, given the sheer numbers of randomers and gamers online at any one time. To use the phrase separating the wheat from the chaff is something that we need to think about, and add to the existing literature and education.

The children I have worked with have been groomed via gaming, apps, through trends on social media platforms resulting in real-world interactions, spaces such as Comic-Con and events such as this, where gaming and geeky go together and connections are made that then go online, on forums and social media.

This is a fast-moving, at times changing landscape, though a fairly predictable one, once you understand the motivations of a perpetrator in their approach and reasons.

However, in my clinical practice, it has been repeatedly stated to the young people when I reflect and explain this as logical, 'of course this happened like this', as people (i.e. the adults around them) were oblivious to this process in this new digital world and did not consider all the factors involved in technology.

Perpetrators of crimes against children are fast and have such digital literacy that we may not catch up with them, especially when they work together like a coordinated pack of hyenas. Some of them will be caught and removed; however, the majority are, in the words of TV series *The X Files*, 'out there' in a space that is so vast, expanding and exponential that I'm afraid we are looking for aliens using the fermi-paradox.

So we need to know what we as adults can do

I'm hopeful that in conversations with you here in this book, through trauma-informed and applied workshops and education, we can filter out the unhelpful messages and remove the fear-mongering of some current education programmes that approach this topic with a fear-driven message in the hope that it will terrorise children and young people into 'never being a victim' or 'this is the result for you if you make a mistake'. Yet, this is the overarching message given when these programmes and professionals speak in this way and are being run in schools even as you read this.

As a therapist who sees this, I am both mortified and compassionate about the cause, and understand why these programmes are being taught in the way they are. They come from a place of best intent but have the potential to shut down the child to whom this is happening, to traumatise children to whom this *has* happened or *could* happen, and often blame children where they do not mean to. Or perhaps there is also an aspect of this education whereby adults enjoy creating that level of fear in children (see https://childrenand-tech.co.uk/2021/05/21/presenters-media-and-conferences-cybertrauma-by-experts-the-shock-factor/, Knibbs, 2018). Shame-mongering is not the way to educate anybody, let alone children, and so we need a radical change in how we do this.

This is both victim blaming and impossible to achieve and if you read and understood the first book you will know that in circumstances of stress and fear the brain does not learn anyway, and so these messages can traumatise; they create a shutting down and stress response reaction. This is not conducive to learning or helpful in creating change (Knibbs, 2022).

What is 'grooming'?

As a professional, I am always curious as to how we end up using 'palatable' terminology for horrific events, trauma and stressful situations. In the moment, we can 'awfulise' and over-emphasise just how bad something is or was, and with time our minds lessen the lesson and become distanced from the events of the tragedy. When we become politically correct we change the language about these events, which can cause further confusion around the problem.

Over the years we have had phrases such as 'stress head' through to 'drama queen' and 'neurotic mothers', and then some people had a 'nervous breakdown', to denote a person's imploding sense of self and emotional distress (which can include hearing voices, seeing things, thinking one is going mad, and is utterly distressing beyond words – this can be called psychosis, too).

There have been diagnoses such as 'split personality' and the colloquialism to describe something we now call dissociative identity disorder (American Psychiatric Association, 2013) because labelling a person as having a split-ness denotes brokenness (yet does not reveal the depth of the trauma a person suffers with this diagnosis). We have had 'incest' to denote familial child sexual abuse, 'flashing' to denote the exposure of genitalia to others and child sexual exploitation to describe the child sexual abuse of children by (usually) more than one perpetrator.

Car 'crashes' are not road traffic accidents anymore; we now say collision, because accident denotes no responsibility and collision can produce culpability without the accompanying image conveying speed and sounding as destructive as 'a crash' – anything to lessen the horror. Language allows us to do this through a process of separation and disconnect (accompanied by linear time), and allows an apportion of blame where we can. After all, we live in a very litigating-based society now.

So, given that we have the phrase 'grooming', and I started the chapter with this word, we need to unpack what this is. Education for children talks about this process, often as part of PSHE, citizenship or even sexual health lessons and often the educator uses this word in class. I wonder how many parents use this terminology in their house, or in conversations they have with other people and what is understood by this term by those who use or hear it? It is certainly a word that is easy on the ear and does not need 'whispering' around others as do other taboo words, for example 'sex'. And so, it has become a normative and palatable way to describe a process around recruiting children for sexual activity.

This is the paragraph that describes grooming for you; this preparatory sentence is sometimes called a trigger or content warning and in parallel grooms and prepares you for what is to be read by you.

In short, the word grooming denotes the *preparation of a child/young person for sexual conversation(s), images, videos and coercion to engage in sexually related activities with themselves or others*, in this instance and for this chapter, through the medium of technology. It is a crime and can be carried out by other young people and/or adults or groups of perpetrators. These images and videos are often recorded, screen-grabbed and shared with other children, perpetrators and groups/forums (see Chapter 10).

Although this seems a very long-winded phrase, you can see why the word grooming was chosen for this topic as in 'to get ready for show' (horses/dogs, etc.), so think dark and twisted versions of Crufts. It's quite the macabre process, isn't it, when you consider the intent behind the phrasing and what it is the groomer is aiming to achieve. Preparation ... for a show, and who knows who the viewers will be over the years?

I have also been very purposeful in not giving this process a timeline (as to how long the grooming takes) because it is dependent upon several factors that the perpetrator drives, alongside the child's developmental stage, chronological age, beliefs and family scripts and is dependent upon the digital space in which this occurs. It can be as short as a few sentences exchanged or a longer more deliberate process that takes months or years.

What this effectively means is that there is a standard theory of how grooming happens, in stages, denoted by Finkelhor (1984) and approaches of other organisations in this domain such as NCMEC, Marie Collins and NSPCC (see Bibliography). Yet children are often in varying stages of life, geographical locations, social timelines, political landscapes and of course familial patterns, as well as cognitive, moral, emotional and psychological development in these spaces; groomers know this and are looking to exploit all domains and spaces where children are. They are like salesmen and each one has their niche and patter and specialism with which to sell their product, so to speak.

Each child is therefore unique, and the process utilised by a groomer is dependent upon what may be considered the vulnerabilities of that child and family and where they are groomed, e.g. on an app or in real life. For example, one client I worked with was groomed extremely quickly (less than an hour before sharing intimate images) as he was only eight years old and 'did as he was told', coming from a family of strict upbringing (among other factors), and in comparison, a female client aged 14 did not, in her words, 'fall for the tricks' of sending nudes when asked by the perpetrator. However, a child aged 12 sent images to their online boyfriend, to compete with their friend who had also been groomed, as this age is often about peer rivalry, one-upmanship and relationship aggression. The perpetrators may have used these facts knowingly for the process of grooming these children and may well have understood child development too. Who knows, as they were never found or prosecuted, as is often the case.

Grooming as comparative to writing an essay?

Writers will tell you that the process of producing an essay or book requires planning and execution. There is the preparation, action and completion of an essay, thesis or book which has a beginning, middle and ending. As I was writing this, I considered that readers may think I am minimising the grooming process and comparing it to essay writing – which I am, in terms of our knowledge of how this process is carried out. However, there are rarely writers who write a book on happenstance; there is a knowing that this is what you want to do and you toy with many ideas in your head before putting ink on paper or typing out the chapters and verse. You also write the vomit draft which requires that you look at your process and refine it, maybe even rejecting some of the content or sentences as they don't or won't work for the result you are aiming for. Therefore, I consider the parallel here for you to think about between adult groomers and writers as we both know what the end goal is and there is a disciplined process to get there. The research phase is just as important as the execution, as you cannot write without that foundation. You must know the map of the terrain to navigate competently. Or perhaps the vomit draft could or might work. Disciplined or half-hearted writing results in the same outcome, yet I suspect detailed, evidence-based writings do much better in terms of sales over the long run. And I'm not really talking about books here.

Training

I have, and I am sure many of you readers have had the pleasure of being at some excellent training around grooming, and others that talk about the child as a 'commodity' in the process, or as the one who 'ought to have' done x, y, z to prevent it. When we teach the model of grooming in a simple way we say things like: there is a preparatory or getting to know you stage, there is the attachment and friending together stage (e.g. buying gifts, spending time with, saying they love you), there is the rebellious and sometimes exciting stage (e.g. skipping school), there is the pressure to be with the perpetrators (again missing school or not going home), there is the threat and blackmail phase (e.g. 'I'll kill you, your parents and I love you so do it for me or else'), there is the added pressure to do things for the groomer (run drugs or money) and so on and so on.

These signs are also taught to children in lessons such as PSHE and Sex-Ed as warnings to look out for. This is the narrative of the child I encounter in therapy; they tell me that they were looking for the 'signs' that they had been educated about and did not 'see' these other more subtle signs of the process. Or they met an online perpetrator that straight out asked them for nudes, and they complied thinking it was someone they knew, or in some cases someone who had been sent their images and was now engaging in threatening and blackmail behaviour.

What is sometimes missing from these conversations (and it depends on who is facilitating them in education or residential settings) are discussions with the children. It's often a case of tutoring and lecturing models and not co-created spaces where children can tell you what their thinking is or lack of critical thinking, giving the educator a space to educate and inform. It is out of their awareness on many levels due to not understanding human behaviour at these young ages, and why would they? Given that many adults do not spot the signs either, we need to talk to children about feelings and those early warning signals, which of course are different when using technology (discussed in Knibbs, 2022).

Children expect a person who is grooming them to look and sound like the films they were shown, talks they were given and horror stories that appear in the media. Do you know the kind of person? The menacing eyes, the beard, glasses or lots of lavish gifts (which do occur and I am not minimising but being the provocateur of the stereotype). But what if these gifts help on a computer game, to maybe get them past a boss level? What if they cannot see the eyes of the groomer or the facial communication and energy of a person so often needed by our bodies to detect trust and safety, as they are sent an image of someone else? What if they end up in a forum with someone helping them to process their identity, affirming that fursonas are not 'about sex' or fetishes, that dressing up as a film, game or superhero is cool, that being vegan is about a supportive community, that our tribe of hobbyists are the tribe you are looking for, or they are writing fan fiction with and for others (see Chapter 7), and so on (these are all examples of child cases I have worked with regarding what the groomers said to the children and adolescents).

However, when gender, sexuality, early access to pornography, neurodivergent thinking, vulnerabilities like being cared for by family, or looked after in spaces like foster care or residential settings *and* attachment trauma come into this equation, it can become complicated, more so than the standard models currently in use. We must understand the process of attachment as a basic framework for grooming models but we must also update those models to reflect what a child seeks online and what those spaces can offer that is not reflected in the standard grooming models taught to professionals and children alike. And it isn't just children.

Cybersecurity, phishing and grooming, the same scam?

I have worked internationally, educating about cybersecurity or online safety for a long time and can say yes to the preceding question with 100% accuracy: that across the globe live people who are, through technology, conned out of money, phished, scammed, lied to, romanced into giving away inheritance, life savings, house deeds and more. Many people buy expensive metal at a market only to find they bought a brick painted in cheap fool's gold and it is often *the adults* who do not spot the signs of a deal too good to be true. I for one 'fell' for a rug scam in the space of cryptocurrency-based assets (NFT) in 2021 and here I am 'wittering' on about this stuff. The difference: it didn't cost me in the same way that a child being groomed does and it's not left me with scars, trauma and a sense of being watched by those who know or could know about it and I can sleep at night with my mistake (I did blog about it so people do know).

Parents and professionals often reflect this also when they are speaking with me about the classic threats, personality characteristics, and even stereotypical clothing they expected a perpetrator to wear, say or do. It's like Hollywood, soap operas and hard-hitting films are giving you the expectation of being able to recognise these villains. You know, the 'standard robber or burglar' wears black and white stripes and an eye mask? Life is not like that and understanding what these children reveal in therapy settings about the villains, and the impact they feel of not being able to 'spot' it or them drives a victim-blame narrative. One that shoulders the responsibility on the victim and their families to have prevented it in the first place.

Practitioner's pause for reflection

Just think for a moment about the Netflix wave of 'crime' docudramas that are increasingly on the rise. If you watch these, many are about serial killers (e.g. Ted Bundy); do you see the victims as being stupid, 'shudda saw the signs', manipulated, tricked and conned or do you see the villain in the picture as the villain who had the intent to kill people and was good at socially engineering them and luring them to their death? Why would a child or adolescent, far from having mature adult cognitive abilities, life skills and worldwide smartness be able to see through the trickster's smoke, mirrors and magician-like behaviours?

Intent and the nuances of the 'trickster'

And so, looking into the process of intent by the groomer, what children have told me, and countless other therapists I suspect, is the children's lack of understanding about the process and how they were tricked. We must look at how this occurs online and why these children are not understanding what is occurring. Now before there is an uproar against the organisations creating these training packages, or I am seen to be attacking them as being incompetent, they are not, and they are doing their best to prevent children from being groomed and for that I applaud them wholeheartedly. Yet we need to have conversations with children and utilise people who can work with varying levels of critical thinking skills or lack thereof, and find non-judgemental or scary educators to help children learn. We need not shout and scream, so to speak; we need to develop child-focused, trauma and attachment-aware exploitation *and* e-safety trainers because the online spaces where children are groomed need *both* these skills and knowledge. Contextual safeguarding as it is called needs contextual knowledge of the online spaces because people behave differently in contextually different spaces, even though the grooming process remains the same, i.e. Reddit clientele are different from Fortnite players.

I am here to educate you, the reader, in what children tell me, what has been written by children and young people about their experiences, and to consider the nuances of technology and what this means for us as practitioners in listening out for, working with and helping educate around these processes, using lived experience, research and a good deal of human behaviour knowledge. We need to educate children about early warning feelings and what they can do with these, and knowing that children with trauma may not be so in tune with these feelings leaves us with a cohort of children who need more than the 'here are the signs' education. We need to go into neurobiology and that sense of intuition that children are much more in touch with (more than many adults to be honest) and we need to use what we call the 'oh-oh' feeling.

Now, if you have read my previous book you may recall that I talked about the 30–40 cm distance between the screen and the eyes (Knibbs, 2022). You may recall that I talked about the false safety zone. You may recall that in this false safety zone there are fewer cues about a person and their body language, tone of voice and facial cues and this can lead us to make incorrect judgements about whom we are talking to. If they use trickster or con artist engineering, then this is even more difficult for children to work with and do something with. Education about time and space can help them create the (cognitive) space with which to critically appraise and analyse. When it matches their bodily awareness, it can empower them and for children to master this we need to go back to the chapter on consent.

If we educate about those often short, cliché aspects given to the students about 'you don't know who you are talking to' or 'know who you are speaking with', along with the advice about not talking to strangers or randomers (a word to mean a random person), then we miss the most primitive sense of *trust and safety* that can alert them to *a conversation with ill intent*. And the gaming spaces are full of strangers who often do not mean to cause any harm of this type. In the words of one of my clients,

> 'so which one is it; don't ever talk to strangers (so I can never play online) or we can if it's gaming and how do I make friends if I never speak to anyone that I don't know, that's stupid like saying ignore everyone at the skatepark 'cos they're you know; strangers till I get to call them my mates?'

Online safety and the false zone of safety

Discussions with children about online safety or being online never seem to go quite far enough in how to recognise what is going on in your body when you are talking to people online via text, chat (voice over internet protocol) or video calls. And therefore, I feel much of the education system needs the neurobiological angle that I suggest throughout this book. Our early warning signals are different when using technology and this is a factor that needs synthesising into education about online activity. It is no longer viable to see communication and interactions as text-based activities, or voice when using gaming examples, though this is much easier to detect because of the way our ears can pick up communication messages. And again, this is different for children with autism and middle ear complications (Porges 2011, 2017). When we can tap into a deep sense of ourselves, we can notice those moments that don't feel okay, and this can provide us and our children with the knowledge they need to speak to someone about what's going on.

When I speak with clients aged five and upwards in therapy, we often talk about how the body feels in varying situations. I work with them on their neuroceptive danger signals and many children will tell me that their bodies felt wobbly, icky, weird, funny or numb when a traumatic event was happening. Children seem to *know* this stuff inherently, most are experts in this field and yet we talk to them as though we are the guardians of expertise rather than listening to them, who are the actual experts, with less of the resistance, defences and filters that we adults have.

To make this readable, digestible and the most important outcome related to your work as a practitioner, and one that is needed when you work with the families, I hoped when writing this that I would be able to give you tools to educate and work with. If this heinous crime occurs to a child you are working with, the first tool or piece of advice I give practitioners is to take the responsibility away from the child as a priority, as this is necessary and an obligation to the mental and emotional well-being of the child.

To do this and provide you with the background information, I want to share what might be occurring in the mind of a perpetrator so that you can understand how the children become a commodity for their intended outcomes. This may be difficult for some people to read and as I write this, I am aware this can be traumatising and anger-inducing, and may result in some very disturbing feelings for you.

The caveat, time out and trauma support: Please take time for yourself, read at your own pace and take breaks where necessary. Please seek out help from a professional if you feel this section of the book has affected you in any way that you feel you cannot manage and of course cannot 'get it out of your head'. Please take care of yourself.

What would perpetrators hope to gain? Why would they do it? What is the function?

This section contains reflections about the abuse of children from the perspective of a hypothetical child groomer, based on several conversations in therapy with victims and those who may also be classified as perpetrators. I have also been privy to some online grooming conversations from an academic (as far back as 2013) who asked me not to share the details (personal communication). Those conversations were difficult to read and herein I will be as gentle as possible about what I learned. Identities have been stripped away and in some cases, the sex/gender is non-identifiable, also to protect the children and young people I have worked with.

Children and young people talking to me in therapy have included: pre-court processes, post-court, no further actions taken on the case (Child Protection Services decision, as often there is not enough evidence to charge or take the case any further), where no offence was ever recorded further than a referral to Social Care, or the child told somebody in settings such as residential care or foster carers, and this was documented as 'slander, false allegations and making a fuss' (yes these words have been used). I have seen forms from services that have discussed pubescent children as 'attending sex parties' and 'consenting under the duress of having a weapon placed against them', reports that denote 'rude behaviour' by the perpetrators rather than its actuality, which is *illegal*. We *must* do better for these young people when we speak about them or write reports and referrals. However, I am digressing a little here.

What would a perpetrator hope to gain? Simply put: compliance. Why would they or do they do it? Because they can, and due to many other factors around power dynamics, philia disorders and sextortion outcomes. What is the function? To gain something for one's self (which includes self-gratification of the kind I probably don't need to explain in depth), and for the functionality of trading, manipulation (to recruit others) or sextortion (blackmail for monetary gain).

How it can occur: what they said they said

'He said it was just a picture, and that real abuse is when you hurt someone. He didn't actually touch me, so he didn't do anything wrong?' (Girl 14)

'They asked me to shove it in my front bum [a pencil]. I thought they were joking but they were gonna send my parents my other pic.' (Child under 12)

The other picture referred to another graphic image that the child had previously created.

'He said bend over and touch my toes without my pants. He asked me nicely and then said to turn round if I could, which of course I could cos I am stretchy!' (Child, aged 8)

This child did not understand what was being asked of them, or why, which was to have the child's face in the picture on the sexual image.

> 'They wanted a picture of all of me, cos obvs they wanted to see my, you know, bits, to see if I had done anything with them yet. So I said, just my chest, so they could see that I was serious! I keep getting it (chest binder) taken off me, and like I don't give a fuck what my parents say, they don't get this process and I'll just get another.'
>
> (Transgender child, 14 receiving and buying chest binders)

> 'They jus' wanna talk, never asked me to do owt without clothes, they were proper nice, but I did feel myself up like they said, and it was good. They were my friend and they just 'got me', you know like when ya mates do in school but like they jus' don't ever talk like this and its probs 'cos I'm not a popular.'
>
> (Girl, 15 Never specifying whom they (male/female) were talking to)

Images here were created with underwear *on* and what we worked out together to be a request for sexually created poses akin to posters of the 1980s and 1990s (commonly called 'Page 3' and *Playboy*). No further action was taken as the images were deleted from the phone with no idea to whom they were sent.

Grooming as a profession: isn't this the same but different?

This is another contentious aspect I am going to bring to your awareness, and I have been met so many times with the latter part of that phrase, 'what we do is different, Cath'! The intent of the perpetrator is clearly to make friends and to 'get' the young person so they feel felt, a term from Dan Siegel that explains just how important interconnectedness and attachment processes are (Siegel, 2010). This allows the perpetrator to ally with them. This method or recipe follows the literature around grooming, but I was curious about the online settings with the children as to how they know these people were friends, 'got them' and understood their plights. For example, in my therapy room, rapport, listening, reflecting, co-created relationships and the therapeutic alliance all make for a space where children can talk to me openly and I can help them open up.

Sometimes they reflect that I 'get them' and of course, I should because this is what I trained to be able to do! I can empathise well with children and young people as I remember vividly my childhood and teenage years and the trials of growing up. I trained and learned about co-creation in interpersonal relationships, building and maintaining an alliance, and how to question, support and listen to a child without causing trauma or further trauma which involves lots of skills I was examined for during my training. I learned these skills deeply and profoundly to work with children and young people to ensure I was good enough at my job. My training courses included teachers and many peers 'learning the ropes', so to speak, and helping each other along the way so that we developed and mastered skills that help us connect with vulnerable people interpersonal skills that look on paper similar to grooming. Imagine what the professions of police officers, barristers and social workers look like on paper in this context. But they *are* different. And the intent is not to use those power dynamics for ill intent, but to give the client space to work through their trauma, for post-trauma growth and healing. This is why it can be so easy to cause harm if the intent is good but the process of trauma and this issue of exploitation, grooming and abuse is not fully understood by the practitioner.

So why wouldn't a perpetrator follow this kind of education-based model and learn from other experts in their field? When you can switch your thinking to consider that many of the perpetrators of crimes against children are skilled communicators, or perhaps skilled students learning from their mentors and *some (not all)* are previous abusers, you can begin to see how they carry out their charm and enticement upon their victims. Perhaps some of them possess the same skills as a therapist, coach or social worker and have studied these spaces to be able to have conversations with vulnerable children, to create the environment in which they can pursue their goals. After all, don't we see many professions such as teaching, coaching and youth groups as having the perpetrators within them? Therefore we vet potential professionals and have the Disclosure and Barring Service in place (UK regulations) to reduce as much of this as possible.

Conversations

If you looked at the conversations that perpetrators of crimes against children have with young people, it is fairly obvious to the outside world and adults that the groomer is attempting to 'befriend' the child on many occasions. I'm not going to show those conversations here as I don't know who is reading this book, who may read it and how those conversations will be understood/ shared or whether they could cause trauma. Also, I have been directly asked not to share them by the academic who shared these with me.

In the above examples of the children's recollections, the intent with many of the crimes committed was to get one, or a subsequent picture created by the child. I use these examples above as these were young people in my clinic who told me they provided only one or two images (which is one or two too many of course). The devastation they felt was incredible and many of these images were provided in less than a few hours or days of knowing these strangers.

Given that children spend a few hours online per day according to almost any parents, online safety reports or mainstream media, it's unlikely that the entirety of that online time was with these perpetrators, and so this gives an insight into just how little contact time was needed to elicit the images. Moreover, the perpetrators seemed to frequent the spaces where the children played games, talked on chat, and had other group chat spaces. They did not 'just' befriend the child but appeared as a 'squad' member in many of those spaces for a while before approaching the children. When I spoke with the clients, they were not alerted to the behaviour of the one squad member by the others in the group as it seemed an innocuous, banter or sexual type conversation that 'everyone' engaged in, so there was no out-of-the-ordinary or 'creepy' conversation at this stage. No direct contact took place in these settings, this was the space where everyone chatted with each other. The direct contact came later and via other platforms, apps or spaces after they had 'gotten to know' the groomer, who by the standards of grooming education was now no longer a stranger or someone they didn't know.

What was a curiosity with these children in therapy conversations, though, was the acceptance of what seven- and eight-year-olds are now calling 'dirty-minded' jokes by '*the other children*', who was the groomer and employed this as a tactic to move the conversation towards sex and parts of bodies so that when the direct singular conversations took place the 'scene' was already set in motion; words and images had been googled so now the children felt they were 'in the know'. This made it easier to continue the conversation 'in private' about 'privates'. This is how con artists layer in social engineering tricks to scam adults. Making the talk familiar before moving in to strike.

This is why these children, in the examples above, were unaware of the classic signs, because all of their friends (already known in real life, for example via school), were engaging in that very behaviour *together as a team* and so this was a normalised environment of 'tit talk' as one 13-year-old client called it, where the groomers also lurked. They did not buy them gifts, or ask them to meet in the real world, but 'bantered along' and got to know the children as masquerading squad members. They had insider information before striking with their request. They were familiar.

The grooming process is the same as Finkelhor's (1984) model; however, in this format the sheer number of children present in a game, squad chat or platform now allows for the offender to include those other children as *their team members*, who are unaware of the intent of this squad member or player using them to recruit others to help set the scene. Players can come and go and the sheer number present at any one time makes it easy for a wolf to hide in sheep's clothing. And there are always so many gaming and social media spaces to choose from that if one child smells a wolf they can go elsewhere. The actual chances of being known as a wolf beforehand in the new game spaces are often beyond slim. For example, on average there are 45 million users per day on a well-known platform, Roblox (www.pcgamer.com/if-robloxs-daily-users-were-a-country-it-would-be-bigger-than-canada/), and Fortnite stands at 83 million per day with 3 million on at any one time (www.gamesradar.com/how-many-people-play-fortnite/).

This *never* happens in the real world as groups of this size and frequency of meeting don't exist. For example, football, rugby, netball, hockey teams etc. don't meet as often and other team members, plus families, plus dogs only total *a few hundred*, at most, for children's grassroots teams and max out at 150,000 at a major premiership stadium. Actual contact time is limited to perhaps once or twice a week. And a clear, real-life presentation issue is that predators are not able to pretend they are children because this would be easily spotted.

Are you shocked by the figures for gaming platforms?

Assessing risk, questions to ask and tools to think with

So let's go slowly and consider that online life can be approached like offline life by first assessing risks and dangers and creating a plan of safe communication, without terrifying the life out of the adults or children. This empowers parents and carers and the child and, of course, allows for the space to have daily conversations regarding the child's online life. As a practitioner, you can use the above to think about how you would chat to a person about the conversations they have online, as often this can be a good temperature check of the people they converse with.

Thinking about this, what kinds of questions would you ask? How would you explore whether sexualised language was being used, whether there was 'dirty minded' banter and chat and how would a child know if they or their squad peers were being funnelled towards direct messages and intimate chat conversations? Asking these questions outright can be shaming and can cause shutdown or aversive answers, and yet not asking direct questions may create confusion, as 'indirect' questions may not be understood. This is the balance needed by you as a professional and one that certainly requires a depth of interpersonal connection to the child, as well as a framework of the gaming and social media space beyond what you read on a newsfeed. Head to www. taminggaming.com to learn more about the games and their contents, and have a go in those spaces to feel and notice what's going on there. This is one of the best lessons you can learn experientially.

How can a stranger elicit this kind of behaviour in a child?

To go through the points above I will address how children end up in a digital space where grooming happens. Backed up by research, child development and the broader theories of 'being human'.

This is not easy to explain without causing a feeling of shame in the adults who are likely to read this. It is not my intent to shame anyone; however, this is my succinct meta-perspective based on the answers the children have given me over a decade. This is the process of development: the process of becoming a thinking, speaking and full of feelings small person in a world where rules exist. Some feelings and expressions of thoughts are accepted and others not.

The process by which perpetrators manipulate children is all about how we raise them. It's called socialisation, manners, 'Ps and Qs', 'don't say no to me', adapted behaviours, good behaviours, authoritarianism, lack of anatomical body part naming, taboo subject avoidance, embarrassment and the lack of autonomy of children to be able to say no to something they don't want or like. And consent.

In transactional analysis there is a great explanation of how a child learns to exist and live in a family dynamic, the village or environment in which they are raised. Larger than this is the world in which those families and societies are living. This process is how a child develops an 'adapted' part of themselves. This is taught very early in life. For example, with infants where we as adults pass something to them and say (usually in an extended motherese voice) 'taaaaaa' (to be fair even dogs are taught something akin to this). This process goes on until the child makes a sound that is like, if not actually the word 'Ta', and then we smile broadly and exclaim how good the baby is for conforming: 'good job!'

The baby learns that this 'trick' or making a noise like 'tah', 'dah' or 'mah' gets them smiles, attention, love and praise. It must feel great. I cannot remember my early infancy in this way, but based on child development theories, we know that these moments, called contingent moments, are what connection, communication and being seen are all about (Fonagy, 2001; Gerhardt, 2014).

Self-disclosure: I did this too and my children 'learned their manners' in this way because I was not a therapist then, nor did I know what I know today. And, we need social norms and manners for a well-functioning society, so please don't think I am advocating for no manners – far from it!

It's what we do as parents. We create the child who adapts to our wants and needs because somewhere along the line not saying thank you is considered 'rude!' and as I am in England as I write this, it is very British to have manners and not be considered rude. So we teach our children to obey commands, laws and social norms to have a cohesive and functioning society. And in doing so we teach them they must not answer back to adults, they must respect their elders, they must do their work diligently, they must not question, they must stand up, sit down, talk, be silent, say something, say nothing, be kind always, be respectful, answer questions when asked and the most difficult (to talk about if we don't know) is we create rules around body safety that violates the neuroceptive warning cues (see Chapter 6 on consent).

We ask or demand children to kiss, cuddle or hug other people even when they don't want to because at that moment in time it is about us and our feelings, so our children comply with a rule so that we don't look like 'bad' parents.

Now if you are still reading this and have not thrown the book down … I wonder what feelings you currently have coursing around your body and what thoughts you have about your early childhood. *Are you angry with me for writing this*? Do you feel like a rubbish parent, betrayed child, irked at the societal ways in which we create this world for children or perhaps you think I'm talking rubbish because of course manners are not the sole reason a child can be groomed? Are they?

Truthfully, no, this is not the sole cause, and again, with a research hat on, I say we have no other causal factor than the perpetrator makes it so. However, it goes a long way toward understanding the explanations children give in therapy when exploring the underlying mechanisms. And so does this mean as a society we now stop teaching manners? No, we do not, otherwise we will likely repeat *Lord of the Flies* I suspect. If Covid-19 taught us anything, it is we often look out for ourselves first and others can 'jog on'. Remember the toilet roll crisis of 2020? (Forever something that your children will be associated with in historical texts by the way. Way to go adults.)

In summary, I could say go back and read Chapter 6 on consent, as this will give us a perspective to think about and provide children with that sense of autonomy and ability to say no; but also we need to create conversations *with* children that allow us to convey that talking about body parts *is* part of childhood and, yes, 'toilet humour' is a thing, and by the time they start getting to approximately seven years of age and above, this being the age that many children begin to play games online with peers (Robertson, 2021), we should have conversations with children about this toilet humour and 'dirty-minded' conversations. Swear words and toilet humour are very similar in many gaming environments and parents should sit with their children to learn about the space by listening to the conversations taking place between those present (listening to begin with, and only acting where it crosses the line of sexual, inappropriate or safeguarding issues) and taking that conversation into the family space at a later stage in the day to critically analyse it.

As practitioners, you may be treading a fine line between advising parents and being seen as attacking them, a killjoy or over-sensationalising the prevalence of grooming. If you give them an idea of the numbers of gamers online, with an unknown number of potential groomers, you could certainly be dealing with this reflection from parents and carers; however, there are increasing numbers of both adults and children using these spaces and this does need highlighting. Education about language and behaviour is a nuanced space requiring, at times, ninja level skills to navigate. Children need to be free enough to experience and explore conditions of normalcy among peers; however, they need support to develop their 'spidey senses' in being able to detect when someone is asking them for those images or videos, or engaging in those types of conversations, and, most importantly, an open space with which to discuss these environments and who it is they are speaking to. You may well be talking to parents and guardians after the fact and so keeping these facts and figures in mind may help you direct your conversation away from an 'I told you so' or 'you should have known' approach.

And it is likely this idea of parents and carers not talking to children is because of the embarrassment and shame that the predators use to prey upon children, because shame and secrecy is the 'weapon of choice' with perpetrators of crimes against children. Coercion and blackmail are the use of those weapons. Having open, non-shaming conversations with children is our defence against these villains. We are not asking the children to defend themselves because this may not be possible and so our position as practitioners is to listen for the unspoken, tap into our superhero neuroception and transference (for those who are therapists) and heighten our detectors of 'oddness, inappropriateness and beyond toilet humour' in the conversations we have with children. Helping parents develop these tools can also be a part of our work and getting parents to take a vested interest in their child's digital behaviours, gaming and online time is how we fight this crime in this landscape.

Tech solutions and assistance?

So what else can we do, and can technology help, given that figures relating to child sexual abuse are always best guesses, since many crimes go unreported for many reasons and many cases are not prosecuted? Sometimes people only report when they are an adult and if you are looking at cases right now, ones reported in the future about this time are not there. Do we know how many young people are providing images or are groomed to provide them and how technology can help? This is likely a no, but when you see the figures shared by the organisations named below, it is staggering to think that recent figures suggest 80 million websites are reported and each of those websites hosts hundreds or thousands of images per site, many of which are historic images.

Some organisations are tracking and removing a lot of these images, such as the Internet Watch Foundation (IWF), INHOPE, the National Centre for Missing and Exploited Children, the International Centre for Missing & Exploited Children and even sites like the Revenge Porn helpline (see the helplines section at the end of the book also); these are the superhero services dedicated to removing these images, but they can only work with reported sites, images and videos. Their tireless and dedicated services prevent ordinary people from happening upon these images and reduce the impact on victims, but this is like walking in sand, given the sheer number of people, devices and storage capacities where the images can be housed for many years, by many people and sites.

We know that technology can trace these images (using hash technology) if they are reported using the functions on the websites and reported to local police services when they are discovered. And we may not be able to prevent all images from being taken, shared or captured, as young children often take their devices to the toilet, bedrooms and other locations where they are not monitored (see Chapter 10). Older children may send images to their peers and some may go astray or be sent to groomers. When and if we discover these images we can take the actions above and help slow down the trading and sharing of the images, which is in all likelihood what you will be engaged in as the practitioner.

Neither I nor others have a solitary answer to how to prevent this issue, as we need to understand that teaching about consent is like teaching quantum physics to younger children unless we can simplify it without it being all about sex. And so returning to the Polyvagal theory I referred to in my previous book (Knibbs, 2022), we need to consider that teaching about 'oh-oh' feelings, 'WTF' moments and 'erm …' thinking/feelings are our body's way of communicating that we don't feel safe and this is an occasion to tell a trusted adult.

Repeatedly, I say we are complicated, and we need to learn complexity, nuances and personal approaches to how we understand the world and how we can protect our children, who may not be able to protect themselves. They should not have to, yet they are often advised about doing so. And as such, we need to have continuous deep, but not pathologising or victim-blaming, conversations as parents, professionals and politicians about these issues. Creating technology to prevent these instances is great; however, humans with ill intent adapt, circumnavigate, cheat and lie, and technology will not solve a human issue. It facilitates the perpetrator's modus operandi more often and so our way to achieve this is to be realistic about the responsibility we put upon children to prevent this. We need to educate and prevent adults from committing these crimes or wanting to, and the best approach to this I have seen so far is the Stop It Now service (www.stopitnow.org.uk) – an organisation dedicated to preventing adults with a sexual interest in children from following their desires and acting upon these. However, to make a comparison to serial killers again, we haven't eradicated the human drive to harm others, and the drive to have sex (or mating as it is proffered in anthropological terms) is stronger in terms of reproduction and propagation of the species (Buss, 2016, 2021; Geher & Kaufman, 2013), even if this is skewed in the direction of young children by those with a philia for children.

We need a 360-degree approach to this issue and, as a therapist, I say learning about ourselves is the biggest portion of that 360-degree circle. I suspect we need to go beyond social and emotional learning packages in schools and have a curriculum that educates about bodily safety, cues of threat (Polyvagal theory driven) and how to recognise these when using technology (Knibbs, 2022).

And lastly, we need to ensure that our children have open communication channels with us, about any topic, no matter how embarrassed, taboo, or silly we feel as adults. If we wish to prevent the issues discussed here we need to step up as adults. This requires us to sometimes move out of our comfort zones and change the narrative landscape, especially now that the Internet is here, is evolving and our children are part of its development.

Capes at the ready

When one child grooms, recruits or manipulates another, and the linkage with online grooming, is now being referred to as child-on-child abuse.

The child who grooms another child is often a victim themselves of this crime, or perhaps they are a young person asking for nudes or, as you can read in the previous chapter, they lack comprehension and understanding about sexualised language and what they are asking of another child. There will always be cases of a child who is completely aware that they are asking for images and have a sexual intent behind this, although we tend to see that in the ages of pubescent children (and upwards) as having sexualised feelings about the images. Many of the children and young people I work with explain that they ask, coerce or blackmail for images because of envy, peer pressure, power, curiosity, happenstance or blackmail by their perpetrators. Often these requests are driven by those needs to be seen, safe and secure. Some younger in chronology and development may not understand the intent of what they are doing because sexual activity and its meaning is often for these children a concept that is not understood in the same way as by a child over 12, 14 or 18. However, what is of importance before finishing this chapter is to highlight the two flowing concepts and reasons that need holding in mind when looking at child grooming.

1. Children who have been sexually abused in the real world (contact abuse) are often sexually more developed than their peers and have been exposed to language and behaviours that their peers may not understand, find exciting or enticing. They can be having text-based conversations that lead towards the exchange of images and the abused child may use this in the same way that their abuser behaved towards them. They may be asking for images. They get a sexual thrill from them as they engage in solo sexual activity because their bodies feel to peers of their age who have not been abused sexually.
2. Children who have social, social learning or mental health difficulties that include language, comprehension and intelligence aspects may be engaging in the talk they have seen or heard elsewhere without understanding the sexual overtones, or the abusive or sexist nature. Depending on the spaces they visit online, or what others tell them is acceptable in this space, this may influence how they speak to their peers and in turn, perceive asking for images, perhaps to feel included.

References

American Psychiatric Association. (2013). *Diagnostic and statistical manual of mental disorders* (5th ed.). APA.

Buss, D. (2016). *The evolution of desire: Strategies of human mating.* Basic Books.

Buss, D. (2021). *Bad men: The hidden roots of sexual deception, harassment and assault.* Robinson.

Finkelhor, D. (1984). *Child sexual abuse: New theory and research.* Macmillan.

Fonagy, P. (2001). *Attachment theory and psychoanalysis.* Routledge.

Geher, G., & Kaufman, S. (2013). *Mating intelligence unleashed: The role of the mind in sex, dating and love.* Oxford University Press.

Gerhardt, S. (2014). *Why love matters: How affection shapes a baby's brain.* Routledge.

Knibbs, C. (2018). *Presenters, Media and Conferences. Cybertrauma by the experts.* Accessed online at https://childrenandtech.co.uk/2021/05/21/presenters-media-and-conferences-cybertrauma-by-experts-the-shock-factor/.

Knibbs, C. (2022). *Children, technology, and healthy development.* Routledge.

Porges, S. (2011). *The polyvagal theory: Neurophysiological foundations of emotions, attachment, communication and self-regulation.* W.W. Norton.

Porges, S. (2017). Polyvagal theory in practice: 2-day seminar. Breath of Life Conference, London.

Robertson, A. (2021). *Taming gaming: Guide your child to healthy video game habits.* Blackwells.

Siegel, D. (2010). *The mindful therapist: A clinician's guide to mindsight and neural integration.* W.W. Norton.

9 Coerced and sexually explicit content produced by children and young people

I am hopping over the real depth of these issues due to word limitations and a need to communicate the harm in a way that minimises harm to you the reader. This a difficult line to hold when writing about this topic, and others in the book as I am aware that people with a history of sexual assault and abuse may find these chapters uncomfortable, as can people without histories of sexual abuse and assault.

This chapter primarily addresses pubescent and post-pubescent adolescents, though there is a section on younger children. However, younger children who produce these images are mainly discussed in the next chapter.

'Self' and the generation of content and images

Self-generated content as a term *could be seen to be victim blaming*; however, when compared to computer-generated content versus person-generated content you can see why the term exists. Would we have been better saying *'child-user'* or *'child-generated'* content (which is likely an academic term in the waiting if not already written somewhere)? And there is a proposal for the use of 'first person produced'. How can we avoid what looks like (on the surface), a statement that says you *chose* to generate a said image, placing the blame on a conscious decision?

To go back to my point in Chapter 8 on grooming, we do like our catchy terminology outside of academic settings. So let's take a quick look at the current (and past) terminology associated with this topic: indecent images, self-produced content, self-produced imagery, youth produced imagery (content), sexting, child sexual abuse imagery, coerced and or underage sexually explicit selfies and finally images that are nudes, which may be half naked images but still are called nudes (meaning genitalia and breast images usually).

To understand the process and production of the images (including videos), their intended outcome and why this feels like normalised and often accepted behaviour to young people, we need to begin by looking at the child and sexual development. This topic has been written about extensively in a recent

DOI: 10.4324/9781003364177-10

handbook (Lamb & Gilbert, 2019). What is noteworthy in the chapter on the use of technology and sexual development is it is geared towards social media's influence on sexuality, and studies are taken from queer, gender, anthropology, pedagogy, sociology and media studies. Many of the studies and conversations look to adolescents, and the research is dated to approximately 2015 as the most recently cited, suggesting we have much more research to do in this domain (or the chapter was written some time ago), and this would be enhanced by using front-line practitioners working with these issues at the coal face. I wonder how many social workers, therapists and youth workers have anecdotal case studies and examples that they could bring forward to help us understand this issue on a larger scale? I am also aware not every practitioner likes research (with many loathing it to be honest), but it's needed now more than ever in this space.

'Sex'-ting? Why are gender and age important here?

When is this issue about normative sexual development and/or curiosity about what one's own and others' bodies look like abnormal, when does it consist of perverse, ill or macabre sexual intent, when is it coercive, when is it exploration about relational needs, when is it a mistake and when is it sinister?

Atop the title of this chapter is the necessary thinking around this issue from a child development perspective because often this issue is seen from a 'teen' development aspect as that's the age at which we expect it to happen, or around about this age. I am not just talking about sexualised images for sexualised intent in this chapter, I will be talking about all things genitalia and breasts and the capturing of these images.

This broad topic requires the practitioner to know and understand that background knowledge of sexual development, attachment and identity are the processes that underpin this issue, alongside the considerations of gender. This topic is not 'just' a heteronormative only issue and can be complicated by identity issues overlapping and becoming aligned or muddled with trends, pressure or coercion. This may take a practitioner time to unravel with a young person and answers may not be immediate and may be frustrating for those involved or experiencing this. The story behind the capture and sending of this content is highly important.

Now if I tangent off for just a moment, you may have heard the term self-generated (sexual) content. This is where a person, in this case, a young person creates an image of themselves via a camera or video-enabled device and sends this via an internet-ready or online-enabled device. It doesn't matter if this is 3/4/5G or on a Wi-Fi network, it's still classified as internet-ready. In this chapter, we will mostly look at adolescents as the sender and/or the receiver, not sending this content to adults (see the last chapter for that issue); examples are mostly given using child-to-child or adolescent-to-adolescent when this is discussed.

Innocent and normalised pictures: how the baseline is created by the adults?

Many children send 'everyday' images to each other, dance with their relatives and friends on camera for social media, and send photos or videos to geographically far-away relatives, usually of how they are growing up, changing and what they are doing this week. Yet, often we do not question the types of poses, clothing or otherwise in everyday 'normal' image-based communications. It is a 'normal' part of people's lives now to grab a quick selfie, send Grandma an image of you playing on the swing or trampoline and a quick text to Dad before you say goodnight. Or popping a photo onto social media of little Lucy at gymnastics as she wins the local gala, or Bobbie at the grassroots football match who is now running around the pitch with their top-off, emulating their favourite player from the premiership. This is *our* everyday behaviour, isn't it?

Examples from therapy

All the images discussed above have been sent by children to other children or posted on social media channels by parents or guardians. These are everyday examples discussed in therapy and each of these images could have been classified as a sexual image, based on the lack of clothing, knickers showing, or in one case none being worn. They are examples of *innocence without thinking* and, of course, these moments bring that ugly feeling when you think they could have been sent to or collected by a perpetrator. I once contacted a professional from my field about the images of his children playing naked in the paddling pool that he had posted on Facebook (when it was called this) in the early 2010s. That professional was not aware that images could be seen by 'friends of friends'. Do you remember that setting (no longer an option thank goodness) when it allowed images to be seen and captured by others? And do you really know the sexual preferences of all your online friends?

And what about what young people post?

So let's start with the idea of non-sexual 'sexting' so we can begin to understand how sending images can become a normative part of an adolescent's life with digital technology. And consider that concept of, it's only 'sexy' when it involves sexuality, sex, and sexting; or is it? If we teach this as a rule, then the following should not be an issue, right?

Feeties?

(I'm making this word up but it looks good as a potential for descriptive aspects to follow.) '*Some people like candy floss and lollipops, others like feet*'. That sentence may have conjured up some feelings for you about the idea of people enjoying anything other than 'normal' (whatever this really means). But, if a young person took a selfie holding a lollipop in their mouth we would immediately be able to see the sexual connotations connected to the mouth and lollipop. These kinds of images have been in our peripheral and central vision for many years with the sexualised and objectified versions of 'sexy' poses on magazines, posters and TV.

However, what would you do if you found images of a child's foot, hand or knee on their phone? This does not immediately suggest the idea of sexual gratification, kink or even grooming. It does not indicate self-produced sexual imagery, does it? And if you are thinking no, allow me to elaborate.

It may not even bring to mind the idea of making money. And mostly the idea of having images of someone's hand or foot on a digital device can be flurried away with simple dismissive statements such as, 'oh that, it was sent to me by Lilly as a laugh and dunno why I still have it on there, lol', or 'oh that … I was taking a picture of my feet as I thought they looked different/out of shape, weird etc.' And so, many of the children I have spoken to regarding issues like this will tell me some of the following reasons for having, taking and sending images that might be this easily dismissible and not create any kind of questioning, suspicion or a need to think about safeguarding, when in fact they are sending images with the same intent as genitalia in self-produced content.

Over the last few years, I have met with mostly young females discussing this issue (who identify as female, and often identify as lesbian or bisexual which may or may not be relevant), who have told me about their peers 'loving their hands' and 'thinking they are sexy with the veins showing' (alongside ears, neck, feet and elbows as an object to photo and be enthralled by). Yes, these are all bodily areas which young females are beginning to explore as erogenous zones. Now, there's a word you don't see that often anymore, especially on magazine covers! Females who then 'trade' images of feet and hands with each other and who have also sent them to people online who have 'feet fetishes', and in the case of the site 'Only Fans' have made money out of this, have spoken with me about these transactions. The clients' responses so far have been:

'Its only feet innit, so it's not like a pic of my tits.'
'I don't get it, but if some paedo wants to pay for my hand/feet images and knock one, get on
    mate.'
'What's the problem? Sexting is my breasts and I know they are collectables, and this is just
    for my friends. No one will know or even think it's weird because it's just my hands.'
'Oh yeah, I know he's 50 something. But he wouldn't be able to tell whether they are mine or
    not, and it's dead funny as I sent him ******, and she thought it was proper funny too,
    unless he knows about my scar he'll never know the difference.'

In short, these females are aware of the images', 'usage' and 'outcomes' and seem to not care, because this is not what they perceive as sexting or revenge porn, nor do many practitioners. They know that feet are almost always unidentifiable, not a fact I want to correct them on, given the biometric data issues we have going on right now and that, yes, they *could* be identified.[1]

Feet: unrecognisable to most, 'except by your mam'

A fact I hadn't considered till a client and I were discussing feet and they said feet were 'only really recognised by ya mam as they always have socks or shoes on!' (The joys of working with young people are moments like this when they say something both outrageously funny and mind-blowingly accurate too). Had you ever thought about your feet in this way before?

This client had learned to disconnect from the, as she called it, 'weird bloke clearly on something'; but for all intents and purposes, was this a man requesting these images – how could she tell? She had learned (from the Internet) that this was not illegal, could make her money, and of course, could not be 'sexting' because – it's not. Is it?

And herein lies one of the issues with the creation of self-produced content, selfies and images taken of young people:

(a)   in school uniform (or PE kit), fully clothed
(b)   body parts other than those categorised as sexual
(c)   images that are in poses or using 'props' that have been requested
(d)   images in bed attire or in bed (covered to the face).

The images here don't meet the criteria for 'sexualised' by having genitalia, semi or full nakedness on show, and of course who is to say what one person 'gets off on?' How would we know what image is being sent to another person for that feeling? And do we need to consider all images that are sent to peers (older or younger) or other adults may well be kept for nefarious sexual solo time?

Yes, I went 'there', discussing masturbation, because this is the reality about the conversations I have spent many hours having with young people, who have then discovered that the other person (the stranger or friend) whom they sent the images to, only wanted them for the reasons mentioned at the start of this subsection.

Practitioner's pause for reflection

So as a reflection to you, the practitioner, whilst self-generated content is referring to images that are sexualised in some way, other images may also be used and traded in this manner, but not worth as much or known to be wanted for reasons other than everyday communication.

So how do we look at this issue, define and measure and of course criminalise, prosecute, or speak and work with the young people engaging in the sharing of images when we can or cannot say with clarity they are sexualised in some way, and without scaring them and you into thinking no one can ever share an image, ever again?

What about gender and sexual identity?

If there is genitalia showing then this is most definitely an offence. If there is an image that has skin showing between the waist and face and is tantamount to upper body nakedness, and if the nipples of a female on the image are showing, this is certainly classified as sexualised content. Now to throw a spanner into the works. But not if the image is of a *male* torso? And who decides who is male in these images?

The issue of chest, breasts and gender

Consider this: a bare chest image sent by a designated female at birth yet who identifies as a trans male. Prosecutable or not? And why? Is this sexualised content being shared in the same manner as a female sharing a naked chest image to excite the recipient who may also be female or male, or is a trans child sharing an image of their pre-binding procedures? Have we asked? Have we even considered this issue yet? Does this count in the same way? Are we going to prosecute female breast owners only or female chest owners and is this only after puberty, so at what moment in early breast budding do we hold the line?

And, what if this was reversed with males identifying as female and sharing an image discussing their intent to change their breasts through surgery or hormones and are in the process of this, so budding nipples are showing for example? What about an image of gynecomastia (budding nipples often seen on pubescent male or breast cancer patients)? Prosecutable or not? And why?

And as I ask these questions, I am aware that breasts that '*belong to a female body*' are the ones that are continuously removed from social media accounts for going against community standards (which include post-surgery breast removal images). So where are we on this issue alone? This is before we consider gender and genitalia and we are struggling to define the breast or chest issue accurately.

Practitioner's pause for reflection

Sex, gender and identity formation are complicated. Consider your assumptions about how you see these issues, and the complication I have mentioned here and you will see the content and imagery issue is also context-dependent. We must have open minds to explore these issues with young people before heading down the low road of panic, prosecution and pathology. The road ahead is loaded with many concepts that you as a practitioner need to consider and so we continue our journey on this topic.

Are we past the bumps in the road?

Once we see that an image is identifiable as sexualised imagery (as much as we can), we can see how these are the images criminalised, but when it comes to the gender discussion what do we currently have in place? What do you do as a practitioner if the child in the images identifies as anything other than female in the waist-up images? For example, what would you do and how would you work with a non-binary child? Would you report to the police and authorities and what if the child only identified as male until 'you went away'?

Where do we draw the line, where do police forces prosecute and why, and where do we have legal and safeguarding policies in place for this? Do we treat 'all chests the same' in which case would this have an impact on males being 'bare chested' in images, on the sports field or in the street? And what would suffice as a guideline in light of the arguments of biases towards one sex, equal rights and gender orientation of these issues?

And this question is only addressing breasts. Imagine the thinking that organisations now must put into place for the gender orientations that exist and the issue of sharing of images that could be classified as 'sexting' or youth-produced imagery or self-produced sexual content or whatever we call it. Who decides what is sexual or not if this falls out of the currently designated categories? Is this going to be based on factors such as, say percentage of skin showing?

When gender is seen in the same way as sex (differences), then the classification of these images becomes easier for the professionals involved; however, this is not how the world is today. I am not saying that where we are is the end of this discussion, either.

It is also a discussion and broader thinking that we need to apply to child sexual abuse imagery, self-generated content and the sharing of such images between children.

We need to put the language and legal processes in place to cover this appropriately and with a broader brush than currently exists, because the identity politics conversation is going to make this issue more complicated than it already is when this is then used in defence and perhaps taken up under the human rights banner.

Family snaps, school promotions and the perpetrator's catalogue

I'm going to be contentious for a few moments here. What about those images that are captured by the family, for example on holiday when children are in bikinis, shorts, swimwear and clothes that are suitable for sunshine and sea, and may be see-through, partially revealing, capture a moment of a child jumping into a pool with legs wide open, eating candy floss or ice cream lollipops directly facing the camera. Are they sexualised and if not, why not? I was careful not to say how old the children were in these examples. I suspect most readers will have considered young children as these images are so widely captured by us as parents on our jollies and the older teens tend to shy away from allowing these images to be taken. These are not 'self'-generated; can and does a child consent to them being taken in this way, even though they are not being taken for the same underlying reasons – I hope, but they are utilised by perpetrators of crimes against children in the same way. If we are going to prosecute and educate children on how they should not share images like this with each other, do we have a right or need to do this for the adults sharing these images? Is this one rule for young people and one for adults? This is an exact comparison given to me by a 14-year-old victim of sexual abuse who wanted to know why her parents could take bikini photos of her on holiday, but she was berated for sending the same ones to her groomer. I applaud her logic and so I am sharing this here for you to consider too.

So when is it sexting or self-produced content if one image is sent to peers directly and another image is posted online on social media, especially with parental consent?

Now I'm not talking here about the adults sharing these images, but what if a child shares them on their social media account or sends them to a friend or cousin for example? How do we police these images and what do we classify as sexualised when it is peer-to-peer, child-to-child or adolescent-to-adolescent? What if a child took a picture in the hotel bathroom and posted it to social media? Is this an issue for the parents or would we say this was the same as above? What about the people who would like to keep these images private in the family; for example, Karen, age 13, takes a picture of her and her cousin Naomi, age 15, on holiday, and both are posing in skimpy, almost translucent bikinis. Is this self or other produced imagery if Naomi sends this to Liam, who is 17?

This thinking is what we need to consider and employ when we think about the images young people take and share between themselves, as part of their sexual identity and gender explorations; which of course has an unconscious bias here towards adolescents, as this means we can say 'it's about sex', because (said tongue-in-cheek) all adolescents are taking and sending images as part of their sexual development, no? So why is this our silent and unchallenged assumption?

So what age can and does self-generated content begin?

If you speak to almost any parent who has given their young child, approximately 4–7 years of age, a camera phone, then you are likely to discover that at some point the child took this to the bathroom and filmed themselves 'having a wee' (or poo), or their genitals, because they wanted to know what it looked like.

Young children have discovered that filming themselves can give them a different point of view, a selfie of discovery about who am I to others. They can see the me, the self, the I, 'in there' and study it to learn more about the 'me out here'. Never before has the human race been able to do this with such regularity, and discovering what genitals looked like has usually involved awkward poses and mirrors.

How wonderful is it, that this camera on the front of this thing, allows for the perspective of 'a film producer' to record and watch (after the fact) their bodies by dancing in the room, gymnastics, pulling faces with Dad and seeing the filters, filming the dog, oh and toileting!

And of course, having a wee in general means that you cannot see the process in its entirety without having to contort between your legs where your genitals are, so this thing can do it for you and you can watch it back, more than once. How marvellous! the child declares.

And they could, can and some have forwarded these images on to their friends, relatives or even to the numbers contained in the phone if it belongs to Mum, Dad, carer, friend or sibling. After all, they are just numbers and perhaps they don't know what they are doing, or perhaps they do if they have been instructed on how to or watched how Mum, Dad or sibling clicks on the photo and voilà, 'send to all' is but a mere few button presses away. But back to this chapter's remit.

You see we often think of 'sexting' and self-produced content as adolescents purposively sending images of naked and semi-naked bodies to each other. But this issue begins with the smaller children who can use a phone and press record.

And how easy is this to do when the manufacturers place the camera right on the home screen, no actual technology talent is required and no depth of understanding about video/image capture technology is required either? Just click and GO!

In 2018 I went to the Internet Watch Foundation (IWF) research presentation about the prevalence of children producing sexually explicit images. Some of the images that were discussed in the report were ones taken in the bathrooms and bedrooms, with children displaying their bodies for others as well as engaging in coerced sexual acts.

The facts were not that astonishing if you know much about children and their fascination with bodies, technology and of course the family dynamics of 'buzz off to your room' or the capacity of children who have been given these devices for precognitive thinking and critical appraisal skills as discussed in my earlier book (Knibbs, 2022). But having somewhere private to explore their privates, well, that is perhaps the most prolific message we give children; for example, we say: go to your room (punishment), buzz off (annoyance), go to your room if you want to explore yourself like that (positive parenting about masturbation in public settings), I don't want to see that (parenting around nakedness), and *this is the space in which perpetrators exploit that privacy* (IWF, 2018, www.iwf.org.uk/media/tthh3woi/once-upon-a-year-iwf-annual-report-2018.pdf; *please be aware this report contains descriptive case studies of sexual behaviours and abuse*).

For much of the audience, I think they found the stats shocking, with many of the press reporting 'children under 11 as sexting' (what a blame-based phrase or naivety). Year upon year the figures grow rapidly, and concernedly, which is terrible, and the education we need is (respectfully) better aimed at informing parents how to protect their children, rather than the children themselves. However, we do need some psychoeducation for children that explains their images are not for everyone and, certainly, genitalia is to be kept private, for sure (see the caveat and confusion on GP/health issues below).

Dunbar's 150 and too many to think about if you're less than nine years of age

Imagine you are back in primary school aged seven: can you tell me, accurately or by guessing how many pupils there are in the hall for assembly? (hint: use your seven-year-old brain and not the logic you have now about the pupil numbers at that school). This is not easy, is it?

Consider the concept of 'everyone' or 'outside the family', 'lots of people' or 'all of the school' and this becomes a problem for pre-pubescent children, especially if we consider the added difficulties of brain development and trauma having an impact on the ability to think like this. Children do not have the capacity to think about longer-term consequences (their brains are not evolved or mature enough to manage these linear time frames) of images being shared with 'everyone' (or other concepts of large bodies of people). Numbers outside of their small circle of family or perhaps classrooms are often impossible to calculate until they develop what Piaget calls concrete and operational thinking (Piaget, 1969). And to give you an example of how difficult this concept is, imagine how many people you can fit inside your house or garden to the nearest five.

And, family means different things to each child, given that some of these young children live in residential care settings, in a foster family or with kinship carers so we cannot really use terms like this when educating children, as the numbers in these families will vary and can be confusing for children in care systems.

We need numbers they can comprehend; we need to explain what sharing via technology means and what it can result in, in ways that children's brains and underdeveloped cortexes (due to trauma, social or learning difficulties) can understand, and we need to check in with the children to see if they do. Often the children can tell you where the limit of their imagination lies and perhaps we need to accommodate their communication and brain development into our teaching.

Early years, middle childhood and messages to parents

The ages that are quite important for this chapter are 0–5 which we call early years, 5–9 which we call middle childhood and 9+ where we will say, children and young people. Most of the education we need for parents is for early years and middle childhood. This is the age at which innocence and exploration take place, with the middle childhood cohort being the ones most at risk of toilet or 'what's yours like?' type explorations, be this alone or with others.

This is also sadly the age at which increased coerced images and sibling abuse are on the increase in the IWF's research reports. This education should be informative, but not terrifying. I work with too many parents who tell their children strangers will steal them (in real-world settings).

An example of 'tell them off?'

I once worked with a single parent in therapy where we talked about what they called a 'wee wee video' taken by their child, a boy using their phone, without their knowledge. They wanted me to chastise the child (aged six) as the professional who would not condone the behaviour (so they didn't have to be the 'baddie', as there were already tensions with the absent parent and they didn't want to always be the critical parent). It turns out the child wanted to know where urine came from, and so had borrowed Mum's phone. She was horrified as she hadn't seen the phone taken, nor did she have any idea that this had been filmed until the child asked to watch the 'wee wee video'. The Mum was initially thinking the child had been on YouTube watching videos and was devastated to find a video like this. This ultimately led us to have a conversation about unsupervised times on devices rather than talking to the child about this one video event. However, imagine if this parent's phone was confiscated, found or somehow someone else saw the video or the child told someone else. Imagine the shame, horror and judgement that would follow, and imagine the safeguarding process or prosecution that might follow a scenario like this.

What do you think most parents or professionals do in this situation? Should, could and do we have a surge in safeguarding calls because the child is taking images of their genitals or do we brush it off as non-sexual because they are five or seven or even nine or maybe put it down to exploratory behaviour? Are we saying to children this is silly or rude behaviour rather than sitting down and having deeper conversations? What about if they send it to friends? I'm afraid I must share with you that these videos are indeed the type asked for, among others, and a child can be asked to do this and send it, so you can see why we need to discuss these images too in our 'self-generated content' chapter (Chapter 10) and education settings.

So who you gonna call and who has the training to deliver the interventions?

Privacy, private and or privates are words that get confused by many adults, never mind children or young people. Explaining to children, we want them to understand that keeping their identity and their data history private as well as their private's private means that we may need to rethink our language about 'privates', privacy *and* privacy. Confused? I often find this needs a better format, and given the common words used with children for genitalia are privates then perhaps we are stuck in a muddle until we can think of another way to educate about this.

For children and young people, this becomes an issue when they do keep their genitals to themselves (shame, fear, embarrassment etc.) yet some are expected to get changed or shower communally with their peers in sports, education and even some family settings. Confused? I'm sure young people are too.

Messages about technology

Is 'keep your privates private' adequate as a message to children and young people? Or would we be better off saying keep your genitals private? Does this really sound any different and how many parents will allow that message to be educated in schools if the word genitalia is used? Or, what about being open and direct and saying, 'we don't share images of our, or anyone else's penis, vulva or anus with other people[2] and this includes via technology'? Who is going to let the adults teach this as a message in settings where parents have a say about how their children are educated?

Who is responsible?

We often create messages that are confusing and hypocritical and that put the onus on children to protect their bodies from perpetrators in much the same way as we give people messages about not becoming a victim of 'mugging'. The children I speak to get differing messages based on the family dynamics and use of language in those homes, schools or even organisations that make resources for children to help them understand that they should be protecting their bodies. They are confused and this is often how they are exploited. Someone tells them it's okay because it's not *that, in this instance.* Or is it?

In fact, there is a framing of this education called 'body safety' or protective-based education. It's aimed to make children aware of and carry out behaviours to prevent sexual abuse, with phrases being used such as good touch and bad touch (which have religious overtones and 'shameful' language associated with them), and the courses can be delivered differently by the professionals based in the use of Sex-Ed language and what they believe is 'right and true' and how they perceive victims and the age of a child.

Again I am not saying this education should not take place, and recent research has found that parenting, and perhaps the messages shared there have more impact when delivered by parents and carers than outside of the home, for example in education settings, with the report suggesting this, 'So, in our study, it was parenting rather than CSA education that was related to decreased experiences of CSA' (Rudolph et al., 2022). Furthermore, children exposed to trauma, adverse childhood experiences and issues such as previous online grooming need a different approach to this topic as their knowledge and stored threat detection and historic feelings may get muddled, so to speak, when approached by groomers. That is to say, they may have great detectors for noticing this kind of person, but conversely, this may be a blind spot so to speak. The issue we have about these messages of body safety and protective education for children, when it comes to technology, is not necessarily the professionals delivering this material, but the material itself, if we consider the research about protective education perhaps?

Given that e-safety professionals working in this role often give the 'don't share' message based on this protective education perspective and paradigm, using examples such as family and friends, how do we help them as educators understand child development, children in care settings and how to talk to the children to elaborate on messages about family and the wider settings of society? Their job is to teach e-safety after all, and this is to educate about risks, dangers and pitfalls. Often, they, like the Sex-Ed professionals in their fields, are not trained in child development, neuroscience or relational theories and so are doing their job by teaching the content.

How does a professional, not versed in or having deep knowledge about the impact on children who live in single-parent, acrimonious separation families, in care, or with blended families, or are fostered or adopted by special guardianship families, have a depth of knowledge about trauma, poverty and sexual abuse and how this affects behavioural choices, and how are they able to deliver these messages in educative settings? Does this now mean e-safety as a sector needs a broader scope of involvement from professionals working in care-based settings such as social workers, therapists and youth workers, more than is currently happening? And conversely, do these professionals know the online world enough to consult, guide or deliver this with enough depth either? I am very privileged to have a foot in each sector and have been attempting to educate both of these worlds in the necessary basics so that we can have a trauma-applied work base. However, it has been highlighted for over a decade what is missing from both professional environments and why children are still missing this in their world when these professionals appear in it. We cannot teach children in isolation about sharing self-generated images when we do not have the context to be able to speak to children about their behaviour if we do not understand attachment, family dynamics and child development models.

Does e-safety, cyber safety and digital spaces education need a facelift? Do we need to synthesise the digital citizenship and media literacy programmes as being about life *and* life online as:

A biological, social, emotional, psychological, developmental, trauma-informed, political and (linear) time-specific model?

Yes, yes it does and we do, and hopefully, these books are the steppingstone between ideas for this.

Body image and shame versus no shame

A further difficulty in this educative space is the personal, religious, societal, geographical, cultural and familial levels of knowledge, comprehension and acceptance of the issues that sharing images of bodies can create. This is crystal clear in the messages we see on billboards, TV and social media (there will be more on this in the section on bodies in Knibbs, forthcoming). There is, for example, a movement called body positivity that has adults sharing semi, if not fully naked images of themselves online in the guise of body acceptance and reverence with slogans such as: 'No fat shaming here with this chunky funky body positive person!'

Let us lead by example ...

'Just say no' to bodies on show?

To be clear, this is never going to work. Media is dependent upon the visual images of bodies in scripts, plays, dramas and documentaries about health, sex, romance, murder, religion, politics, crime, comedy and war. TV, film and cinema ratings classify this media with age ratings and one of the categories pertains to nakedness, sex and harm to bodies; this is so ubiquitous to the industry that we are not going to change the human race so to speak when it comes to bodies on show. Added to this, the inventions of advertising and social media have brought the sharing of bodily images, which are often skewed to the sexual domain of voyeurism and it is almost hypocritical to say to young people *just say no to bodies on show*, because the adults are doing this very thing right in front of them.

Adolescent victim-blaming messages, on the whole, are very prevalent when it comes to substance use, sex and bodies. Youth or young people are often demonised by the media, adults and the older section of our society. Regarding bodies on show, especially 'teens', we have a taboo, horrified and abstinence-based narrative from parents and carers, some education settings, organisations and the upper levels of government who deem that we need to follow the approach of the war on drugs and 'just say no' without embracing the complexities of our messages.

And so, by the time children become adolescents and begin exploring their bodies, sexuality, or gender (and coming out if they are on the continuum of non-heterosexual), they are often secretive or ashamed and can also become highly rebellious in nature because of the messages we the adults have given them. This can also be encouraged by those influencers online suggesting they have rights to 'do whatever the f★★★ they want' and young people can move into a space of the 'Screw you, I can send or post the images of barely covered sexual organs, and you can't stop me!' This is a time when adolescence and social media become a volatile compound akin to explosives, that can be lit by one moment in family, school or peer dynamics in a time when what their peers deem important overwhelms the values of the individual. A moment of non-thinking, limbically hijacked adolescent brain-based behaviour. I am sure from the conversations I have with these young people that they already have the guilt and regret, which lies heavily on their minds and souls, and they do not need that atlas stone of shame adding to it as well.

Change the narrative, change the behaviour?

What would change with self-generated content if we created compassionate and empathic parent groups, or training, or where we discussed these issues with parents and helped them create boundaries with and for technology? If we had non-shaming language and discussions about the sharing of images that could be used by others for sexual gratification, without causing parents or children distress? How can we talk about sharing 'nudes' when the first generation to engage in this is probably the younger parents now being educated about how dangerous it is? Think of the reflections and historic behaviours they engaged in now being demonised and how they would feel about that.

The adults, and not just parents, need the education, not to scare but to inform and many of the adults I work with (parents and professionals) do not want to hear or think about the sexual kinks, desires, likings and philias that other people can have at the expense of a child, especially their child. It makes many people feel physically sick. So we often omit this aspect from training and perhaps say something like, 'the image can end up anywhere' or 'perpetrators keep and share these images', or we make documentaries with the outlier examples to horrify, shock and clickbait people into watching, with no real advice about protection or *why* children engage in self-generated content.

The *why*?

And so, as a young person approaches the fifth trimester of life (post the fourth which is childhood outside of the womb and this is only a way to understand the life cycle, not an actual trimester!), the pineal gland signals now is the time to change from child to adult, signified by pubescent changes (damage or tumours to this area can result in early puberty called precocious puberty). This is the time when sexual desire is said to begin (Nelson & Kriegsfeld, 2022). Some research and writings show that sexual desire is driven by hormones (the endocrine model) and some writing shows this is a coordinated system of nervous system activation, thoughts, accumulated signals from the other person and hormones together (the sexuality model) but I am not going into depth here in this book about this.

This is the time when young people often begin to make associative networks in their brains about how sexual and romantic relationships work in comparison to friendship. They are learning about what can make people look at them and pay attention sexually (not the attention-seeking type of attention, or the attention economy model). At this stage, I want to highlight the 'relational needs approach' of attachment from my earlier book (Knibbs, 2022) and what Panksepp calls the seeking system (Panksepp, 2004).

As they progress through adolescence and mature, peers and those in the peer group who may be a few years older or younger become the focus of their world and of course the two processes of puberty *and* adolescence signal the body's opportunity to be able to procreate, engage in sexual behaviours and to find others sexually exciting, enticing and attractive; for the most famous of the theorists on this we need only look towards the writings about childhood sexuality in Freud's theories as discussed by Sugarman (2016), or even trace back through the volumes, of which there are many written by Freud that are still contended today. I am not citing directly from his works as the disciplines of Psychoanalysis and Psychodynamics can provoke those not versed in his teachings as the language can be difficult and intense. They are very emotive ideas for many people (and technically cannot be researched, and certainly not ethically).

Moreover, of course, not all young people go through this sexual attraction phase and shortly I will discuss the issues my clients have faced who are neurodivergent and what this brings up for them during this stage in life and the actions of sending sexual images.

Sexual Development 101: a crash course

To give you the reader a crash course in the sexual development of young people it is necessary to explain the changes in the adolescent brain in terms of social connections and what this means for the exploration of their identity, which in this case includes sexual identity. And so around the ages of eight to eleven puberty can begin, and yes, this lower age bracket is because there have been noticeable changes throughout the world to the onset of puberty as low as eight or nine (deemed to be due to lifestyles of parents, changes in water supplies, exotoxins and, would you believe, exposure to sexual material online, but I'm not sure whether some of those references are at the far end of quackery or have real substance and so have left them out, but do take a look at the bibliography for further reading).

Note: Puberty is different to adolescence as puberty is about the body (proper) changes, and adolescence is about brain changes. Puberty lasts for about eight years on average and adolescence can be up to 13 or 14 years (and more in some cases). These are slow processes relative to the early development of an infant or indeed the quick development of the brain architecture in the first few years of life.

As a child enters puberty the sexual glands begin to move into a getting ready, get set, go! space and time, for the experiences they will encounter related to procreation. No matter what gender a person identifies as, the function of sexual glands is to produce either sperm or ovum known as eggs; even in intersex humans this biological process takes place (Nelson & Kriegsfeld, 2022). Obviously, with those children who take hormone blockers, this may not occur at all, or in this time frame. This is not a discussion for this book though.

Once the developmental phase is fully completed, these organs are said to be 'adult'; for example, breast or penis size and reproductive capabilities, even though the affective process that accompanies this stage is often controlled by the brain architecture and hormones (Panksepp, 2004). These may still be surging throughout a body that is still maturing. However, children may develop body parts faster than the rest of their maturational process; for example, a young female may have well-developed breasts by the age of 13 and yet this is so far away from the other end of the spectrum of adolescence (and brain maturation), which occurs around the age of 25–28.

What we know about this phase of life is the body seems to almost have a mind of its own, with the penis randomly now being able to 'practise' and become erect at any time, without being provoked by thoughts or images or being attracted to another person (directly). These 'random' erections are often discussed as being the most embarrassing thing because they can sometimes hurt and ache, feel like they are cramping and debilitating for the person who is experiencing this, and of course, they are often very obvious to the people who are around them.

Some of my clients discuss the randomness of the hard-ons and how shaming it is when someone else notices, or how misunderstood the process of waking up with 'morning wood' is. The males in my therapy office often say it's not fair because you can't tell that females have issues like this to contend with. This is also a misunderstood issue, but nonetheless, yes, one that is not so 'obvious'.

Then there is the ever-present sexual 'liquids' of wet dreams and pre-come for the penis owners and the lubricant, and cervical mucus for the people with functioning cervixes in their vaginas (not vulva and this for once is the correct term in the correct location of education). This can feel 'icky', as though one has urinated, and for those children who have been sexually abused these liquids can create all sorts of sensations of terror, fight and flight and shut down when they are noticed (due to the association with the sexual abuse).

Atop of all this, these organs create feelings of sexualised somatic (bodily) responses, and this can be confusing to developing bodies and brains. The very fact that a developing body can suddenly become preoccupied with the sensations of wanting to touch themselves, looking at other people and fantasising about them touching them, wanting to not touch themselves or others, wanting it to go away and stop being in the forefront of their mind; comparisons to others, questions like 'am I normal' for feeling this, having pulse-type sensations and heat in their genitals and not being able to speak to anyone really about it beng confusing, to say the least. And, what about the fact that many young people can find themselves, at times, attracted to the same sex, whilst not being gay? Or perhaps find themselves looking at other people's bodies (as incognito as possible or perhaps even blatantly) as they discover what they find attractive? And to quote a male client:

'When does it become gay, if I think David Beckham is good-looking? Is it when I think this, or if I get a hard-on thinking about the fact I think he's good-looking, or seeing an image of him, and is it really a hard-on for him or just a randomon?'

I had no answer; well I did and it was: 'I dunno, what's your thoughts on it?'

So what do you do when confused about something? Well in normal cases you google it! But ... the young people, ah, they know not to google 'this stuff' and so they look elsewhere. Cue the pornography sites, Instagram and Snapchat gurus, and go underground so to speak to find out the answers. Or they send images to each other in the hope they can get a baseline schema (predictable outcomes) in the same way the baby learns about their attachment bond schedule with their caregivers in the first few weeks and months of life. Brains really are good at learning associative processes and why would this be any different?

From text to sext, to immersive tech

The sending of these images to each other has become a normalised part of 'growing up' and sexual exploration if we consider the term 'sexting' and its origins via text and how this has developed into images with or without accompanying text. Again, this means we have to time travel back a little and go back to the time when phones were of the block-like types and could not display images. Or when we advanced and levelled up and could send grainy, tiny megapixel images on screens that were the size of a basic stamp. To send an MMS (multimedia message), would cost a lot of money and so the origin of sexting began based on language accompanied by emotes created with text characters. This was before emoticons. This cohort of 'sextors' are now young adults in their twenties and beyond and, in many a peer-to-peer conversation growing up, this was their 'normal' part of flirting, courting and experimentation.

Nowadays the conversations around sexual behaviours in the real world have been synthesised into the space of text and imagery. This is a logical step that technology has facilitated, without the deeper knowledge of how young people utilise, adapt and embrace technology and the dangers, risks and pitfalls it presents when you consider the content of the images.

Imagine how the next step in technology is going to provide haptic feedback (sensory touch type suits and clothing, external devices that can be worn externally and internally) and that element of touch and how this will be utilised for this phase of maturation, sexual development and identity. Imagine how immersive technology is going to change the landscape of sex, relationships, gender, exploration, abuse, violence and harassment and how we may not see the impact till it is too late.

We already have gaming suits that allow for a more immersive experience, so imagine the full body suit with extra, 'items' and, for now, I will close this chapter before I go into too much depth on a subject matter that you may need a few more cups of coffee to sit down with and read.

Notes

1 That would be giving out worrying information that is unnecessary at this stage in therapy, though where possible I always share concerns about data and how it can be identified, that is another book though and is many sessions later with clients.

2 Until of course there is a lockdown, and you have an infection and you can't physically get to your GP or health setting and may need to send an image or stand naked in front of a camera if you have an illness/issue with your genitals. I honestly do not know how many times this happened during Covid-19, but it's a guess that somewhere someone had to do this. And where are those images stored I wonder and who has access? In 2022 a father was flagged for doing this exact thing: www.nytimes.com/2022/08/21/technology/google-surveillance-toddler-photo.html.

References

Knibbs, C. (2022). *Children, technology and healthy development*. Routledge.

Knibbs, C. (forthcoming). *Online harms and cybertrauma: Legal and harmful issues with children and young people*. Routledge.

Lamb, S., & Gilbert, J. (2019). *The Cambridge handbook of sexual development: Childhood and adolescence*. Cambridge University Press.

Nelson, R., & Kriegsfeld, L. (2022). *An introduction to behavioral endocrinology* (6th ed.). Oxford University Press.

New York Times. (2022). *A dad took photos of his naked toddler for the doctor. Google flagged him as a criminal*. www.nytimes.com/2022/08/21/technology/google-surveillance-toddler-photo.html.

Panksepp, J. (2004). *Affective neuroscience: The foundations of human and animal emotions*. Oxford University Press.

Piaget, J. (1969). *The psychology of the child*. Presses universitaire de France. Translated to English: Perseus Books.

Rudolph, J., Zimmer-Gembeck, M., & Walsh, K. (2022). *Recall of sexual abuse prevention education at school and home: Associations with sexual abuse experience, disclosure, protective parenting, and knowledge*. Child Abuse and Neglect, *129*. https://doi.org/10.1016/j.chiabu.2022.105680.

Sugarman, S. (2016). *Beyond the pleasure principle: Beyond the pleasure principle (1920)*. In *What Freud really meant: A chronological reconstruction of his theory of the mind* (pp. 87–104). Cambridge University Press.

The Internet Watch Foundation. (2018). *Once upon a year*, annual report. www.iwf.org.uk/media/tthh3woi/once-upon-a-year-iwf-annual-report-2018.pdf.

10 Child sexual abuse and exploitation material

I am hopping over the real depth of these issues due to word limitations and a need to communicate the harm in a way that minimises harm to you the reader. This a difficult line to hold when writing about this topic, and others in the book as I am aware that people with a history of sexual assault and abuse may find these chapters uncomfortable, as can people without histories of sexual abuse and assault.

Child sexual abuse and exploitation material (CSAEM)

To quote a campaign by the IWF – there's no such thing as child pornography. I fear this phrasing will be used for many years to come because it's often used within legal settings and the precedent for this language was set some time ago, and I think the most difficult space to change language in is that of the legal sectors. From here on in, I will use the acronym CSAEM.

This chapter contains conversations about child sexual abuse. This is not a trigger warning which may put you on edge or is intended to scare, it is a factual statement about the chapter's content. Too often trigger warnings can put a nervous system on 'high alert' and, whilst intended to help, can harm by bringing a dysregulated nervous system to the words on the page. It is not my intent to do this; however, in this book, this chapter is the one that people may find disturbing. *I do not share intimate details of the abuse.*

For the sake of readers who may not have the capacity to stomach the deep and dark contents of this subject matter without wanting to vomit, scream or even faint, I am going to attempt to explain the conversations *without* gory details. I am not sorry to those who are here as voyeurs, this is not the book for you.

I have no power over your own imagination for filling in the details. If you feel queasy, outraged, in disbelief or any other overwhelming emotion please take a break from reading and come back to this chapter when you are regulated.

A global crisis: and no, this is not an exaggeration

This is not to scare you, it is the conversation that has and is creating the most passion and drive in organisations dedicated to protecting children, creating

DOI: 10.4324/9781003364177-11

change and making a difference to children of all ages whenever their crime is shared online. This topic is also the one that creates the most anger in my trainees (or readers) that this happens to children. I have seen therapists react, cry and ask me not to speak of the ills in this online space when I begin to describe for example how live-streaming perpetrators are behaving and operating. What bothers me on a professional level is that, as the adults, *we* need to listen, hear and be able to contain this level of trauma for these children. It is *our* real duty of care to make room in our hearts and minds, as well as in our rooms, for this issue. It is painful, yes, and this book is hoping to bring ways of helping the therapist to be that individual for these children, as this issue is not going away; in fact, and the reality is, it's becoming more prevalent.

As much as we campaign and start conversations about this issue, the perpetrators are many; they are tech-savvy and they exploit that chasm of ignorance around tech; they exploit the shame and avoidance that many adults have in their psyche regarding not wanting to hear about or acknowledge this issue. Because of the incredulous shame, secrecy and silence that often surrounds CSAEM for the children, they are more often than not unable to speak about it. When professionals stop listening because it's difficult, then children suffer, and so this chapter is your moment to open up wholeheartedly for these children. *They need you to.*

Courage is your superpower here

I once heard a practitioner say at a conference 'I'm afraid where there are adults and children there will always be child sexual abuse'. Perhaps it would be wiser to say, 'wherever there is technology, perpetrators of crimes against children exist', and there will be sexual abuse of children using this technology (which can spread far and wide for an unspecified amount of time). This statement is quite terrifying to write as well as read. Yet, it is true since adults have always abused children – only now with technology at their fingertips this facilitates that abuse on a larger and speedier scale.

The difference between the real-world cases (often called contact abuse) and those that have appeared since the invention of the type of technology that allows for images to be recorded, saved and shared is: *those images can last beyond the lifetime of the child*, and in turn, the impact of knowing this as the victim is why working with this as a practitioner is a reason this chapter exists.

That reflection is perhaps one of the most distressing within this book. Child sexual abuse that lasts beyond the lifetime of a child. Surely not?

A little background

When I was first meandering through my definition and understanding of trauma through and with technology, at the end of the first decade into the 2000s, I began to receive my first cases from the police of children who had been groomed online and had provided images to the perpetrators.

In working with the children, I realised they were violated as victims of both the creation of child sexual abuse material through coercive tactics and manipulation, *and* the CSAEM material that 'explains to them what to do' (and of course to shock the children, so that blackmail could now occur, given they had opened and viewed file contents containing these images).

At the time I called this virtual trauma, and then Cybertrauma, and presented on this at a national conference where lots of discussions were taking place about children who had been abused online and about how Cybertrauma affected the children. I was explaining how this affected recovery processes when primary school-aged children were not able to understand the long-term implications (those under 12 years of age on average, due to brain development). I am now writing here about children of all ages.

I am not entirely sure whether I spoke too soon on the framing of trauma in this space, or the audience was not ready to hear about Cybertrauma because my statements were perhaps too soft at the time as I didn't want to traumatise the audience. My compassion silenced my outrage rather than fuelling it in a compassionate and empathic manner. By trying to contain the audience I feel my message did not land.

I now say it here and, whilst the words are not full of anger or activism, the message is as clear as I can be as a trauma therapist; this is *the* most pernicious long-term trauma to date in the existence of our species. And I still stand by this proposition.

I really do mean that this trauma is the most pernicious in terms of its effects and how victims are going to manage this issue compared with historical theories of trauma, the way our brains manage memories and process trauma. I am not making a trauma hierarchy here and saying this is worse than that. *I am proposing that this is a trauma that will and does repeat, like no other type of trauma that theories or research can attest to at this point in time.* We have never faced this before and I am angry on behalf of the children that I cannot find robust trauma theories on this subject matter, even though I have been working on it for over a decade.

What is interesting at the time of writing this book is that almost all of the trauma congresses, conferences and conversations in the fields of psychotherapy, counselling and social work are not discussing this issue with practitioners at the 'high end of the table'. This issue of taking images and sharing them has been going on since before the Internet existed, but most certainly has been speeding up over the last decade or so with the availability and presence of internet-connected devices (and increased hugely during lockdown). It is sadly left down to organisations such as IWF and Marie Collins who are working in this field and tend to have conferences with lots of law enforcement staff, who already work in this field, in attendance. There is (at this point in time) a disparity between this information being in the hands of qualified and trainee clinical professionals and those in other fields.

Whenever I educate therapists, safeguarding staff, teachers, social workers or indeed some police, local authorities and other professions, there is often peripheral knowledge of child sexual abuse online, without the deeper knowledge of this trauma that occurs, and what needs to be considered as a practitioner is how you would work with this issue. Sometimes I find that knowledge about where to seek support for the child and family is missing, although some attendees do know about the National Crime Agencies Child Exploitation & Online Protection service or the National Society for the Protection of Children. Mostly that knowledge is being aware of how or where to report this issue. How to support children post-CSAEM is sadly missing at the level I hoped we would be at 27 years after the Internet began and these images started circulating. There are some smaller organisations and individuals talking about the issues of child sexual exploitation (CSE) as this has been a focus of large media campaigns and these have overlapping elements in this space, but often I see a void, a gap and a deficit in some post-event treatment, interventions and support spaces lacking the depth of knowledge needed for the younger victims. I hope by the time the book is in your hands this will be changing.

Where has this deeper conversation been for therapists, social workers, residential staff, adopters, foster carers and other professionals or hobbyists volunteering with children, such as grassroots sports? The answer is very likely tucked away under many *other things we need to know and do first in the line of safeguarding.* I get it we are all busy and this subject matter is so difficult that it is covered in an overarching knowledge of sexting, self-produced content and sexual abuse conversations. This issue can be glossed over with a one-size-fits-all approach to 'self-generated content' perhaps, rather than the understanding of why children are creating content and how this is happening so often to children under ten years of age, with an increase in siblings appearing in and for these images. And so this chapter is here to explain why this is an issue of great importance to you as a practitioner (or trainer, if you are going to explain this to some other professionals).

Beginning with the practitioner at the coal face, we need to (where necessary) get comfortable with being uncomfortable around this issue for the sake of the children.

Children under the age of adolescence

Much of this section is framed around the primary school child, late-to-middle childhood or early adolescence as there are writings around the topic of CSE that often allude to the child who is pubescent and, in that world of coerced sexual imagery, self-produced content. The emerging trends in the research by IWF suggest that younger children are being targeted and so I want practitioners to read the following sections with a tech-enabled four- or five-year-old up to perhaps a 12- to 13-year-old in mind.

Non-verbal trauma and young people aged 25 and under

As a therapist working with children, adolescents and adults I am trained to work with nonverbal and pre-verbal trauma. This has included working with adults and adolescents and children on issues they encountered before they could talk; for example, in my previous book (Knibbs, 2022), I talk about Michael who is involved in a car crash around 18 months of age, which his body remembers and stores, but his verbal recall is not present at this age. We know that car crashes are traumatic at times (obviously depending on the severity) and we know that adults can often tell us what happened because more often than not it is the adults that are driving.

But what about those children, under three years of age, with little or no language skills or accurate memory recall, called 'pre-verbal'? What do you as the practitioner reading this know about that? I have attended training on trauma and sexual trauma concerning adults; however, there are many years of working with young children that do not present in the same way that I was educated in using these models. These children do not 'show up' in the ways that adult training describes, and this was my biggest learning lesson working in the sexual abuse recovery settings many years ago. We need education about children from practitioners who work with those children, rather than using literature and research to talk about this from the coal face, and this is why I say that education is missing as I am not entirely sure anyone is asking the questions of themselves, indirectly, or has knowledge about pre-verbal CSAEM when they work with children or adults.

I was lucky enough to work with a fantastic team many years ago that educated professionals about the aftermath of sexual abuse and this is where our knowledge of this issue needs to evolve from. Tiny children do not 'do' what the middle childhood and adolescents 'do' and this makes for a controversial point here in this book as many of the current educators in this sector are adult practitioners. Pre-verbal CSAEM is a thing: it is in our society much more than people want to imagine, notice or talk about. We must as practitioners begin to think about the prevalence of CSAEM in children and young people under the age of 25, given the Internet is 27 years of age, and so we have a cohort of adults among us, some of whom are victims of childhood CSAEM. In neuroscience terms of brain maturation, we are looking at almost anyone who has grown up with the Internet potentially being subjected to this event. Now that's a difficult pill to swallow for many as that suggests that we have not been looking, noticing or hearing this crime in spaces outside of law, order and crime.

When I am working with a client of any age, and children or adolescents that have encountered domestic, physical or sexual abuse under the age of about four, I am always struck by the deep work that we do, the non-verbal 'record' that the body and mind have of this event and how this plays out in the creative work and, more so, the presentations and release in the somatic (body and nervous system). In the words and books aptly named from Babbitt Rothschild (2003): 'The body remembers', or Bessel van der Kolk (1994), 'the body keeps the score' and children are not that far away in linear terms from the abuse and trauma as it took place.

Images, pre-verbal or barely verbal

The children abused under the age of perhaps five or six may not have a good recollection of images (photos or videos) being taken, but their bodies and psyche will. Are there enough therapists, social workers and coaches trained to 'look for' this issue if they are unaware that this exists online in the manner it does? Young people under the age of 25 have been around since the Internet became the beast that it is today. Are practitioners looking for this in their clients and patients under the age of 25? And how would you explore, inquire, or even consider this if until now you hadn't conceived that the adolescent you work with could have, might have or was a victim of this crime?

And so I want to introduce you to the dark world of the issue in this chapter. We know for a fact that perpetrators sexually abuse children, physically in the real world (often called contact abuse), and for many years have also recorded, stored and shared images of the abuse. We have a name for the sexual abuse of children in the real world and we have words to define the specific age ranges of the perpetrator's interests or 'paraphilia' (which is a dysfunctional attraction to something sexually), as it is called in academic language taken from the *Diagnostic Statistical Manual of Mental Health Disorders* (DSM-V, APA, 2013). However, the volume I have quoted has not included the issues relating to this form of sexual interest in children and adolescents using technology as we are still in the early stages of understanding and researching this issue when it includes children under adolescent ages.

However, many books on sexual offenders against children discuss the philias contained in this book. In this chapter, the attraction being discussed is that of children aged from birth to 18, where legal aspects would say that children become adults at age 18. I am not discussing here for word count reasons the adolescents that are vulnerable beyond the age of 18.

Nor am I going to discuss the fact that the DSM-V suggests 16 years or older is necessary for this category of paedophilia and that the perpetrator needs to be five years older than the child; yet they also state that older adolescents having an ongoing relationship with a 12- or 13-year-old are not to be included in the paedophilic category. Given my understanding of adolescence being a process that can take a person up to the age of 25 years, I am refraining from discussing the above criteria because that is almost too difficult to write about in this context, without my opinions becoming overt and clouding the chapter. Safe to say, I do not agree with the manual's approach at all. Furthermore, the digital space has moved so fast that even the updated version of this manual is missing the CSAEM of children under the age of 13 and we are about to head into immersive technology!

For the sake of clarity, the often broad-brush insult used for any person with an interest in sexually abusing children – 'paedo' – will not be used unless it is a quote from a child discussing this type of person. I am also not referring to the new labelling of minor-attracted people, because this is not an official label; however, this is also a phrase to be aware of and the political undercurrent it carries. As a practitioner, you need to know what is legal terminology; if, for example, you see these words on intake or assessment forms it can provide you with the language to be used surrounding these crimes. You can read around these issues and the terminology if you wish and I would suggest books about offending and how this can tie into digital technologies is the best place to start (e.g. Greenberg et al., 2000; Davidson & Gottschalk, 2011; Pearce, 2019, among many others). These are separated into age categories, as follows: infantophilia (infants and toddlers), paedophilia (prepubescence) and hebephile (post-pubescence). This language was also missing from the Sex-Ed service I worked for in their teaching. When I used the correct terminology with the children, many secondary school children referred to 'paedos' as a broad-brush label and insult and did not know that there were other words to describe the crime, and why would they? Mainstream media uses the insult, and we often don't want to categorise here because it makes us think about the younger children by default.

Breathe

Waff it away, it's awful!

We are often horrified to think that sexual abuse occurs to children, particularly those who are under maybe eight or nine and try to 'waff it away' like an annoying wasp in our ear: and, as one attendee said at my training, 'Don't make me think about it, Cath, and don't make me think about the babies and toddlers ewww'.

Adolescents are not seen in the same way

We somehow find a way to rectify in our mind that child sexual abuse by hebephiles against young people aged maybe 13–16 is 'less traumatic', as practitioners often begin to use language like young lady or man for this age group. The understanding of sexuality (having been a young person ourselves) can often mean we see the young person as nearing the age of consent rather than the child that they are. There is an implicit stereotype, and as soon as their physical bodies begin to mature through puberty, then this seems to change a practitioner's viewpoint about consent, abuse, coercion, trauma and the impact, with many victim blaming statements still in use today in 2022. These victims are still children in law, being under 18, and developmentally in terms of brain and child development theories. What are your assumptions, biases and blind spots here?

I find the responses from professionals often echo this, with many feeling more anger and compassion (and sometimes pity) toward the youngest, smaller framed and female victims versus the older adolescent, much bigger-framed child and those who are male as receiving less empathy, concern and professional care. We do have to change this; however, this is much bigger than this chapter or book – this is a societal issue writ large.

We all view the world through our lens of what it is to be mature and grown up; and to provide a reflection for those who refer to children and young people as children who make 'choices' about their behaviour (which of course a trauma-embodied practitioner will realise is not ever a choice in these circumstances). However, my point here is CSAEM affects each one of these victims. On a case-by-case basis, it is parallel and at times deeper in psychological, emotional and physical ways due to the nature of permanent data. As the practitioner reading this, consider your own biases and opinions about victims, given the age, sex and gender of the child you work with. Consider what you may need to rectify to work with these children equally and fairly and why this type of Cybertrauma may need to become a focus as a major part of the case.

The unthinkable

Mostly, we don't want to think about this topic. It's abhorrent and it's happening, and we have to make a difference and we have to talk about this issue. Perpetrators abuse children of all ages, including as early as infancy to just before they lawfully become adults aged 18. These children can be familial or friends' children (groomed for this purpose). And in the real corporeal world, we have many psychological theories about how and when and where this happens (Finkelhor, 1984; Goodyear-Brown, 2012). Children are groomed, exploited and used for the pleasure of the perpetrator and in the real world. We have lots of safeguarding training to recognise this issue, *in the real world*. We even know that showing children sexual material, *in the real world*, often thought of as magazines, and pornography on videos or DVDs is also sexual abuse. Because much of this *real-world* safeguarding training was designed pre-Internet. Once we knew that pornography was available on the Internet this was included in the training. Often skewed in the direction of adults, or older children such as teens showing children these images. *And beyond that: who is doing the 'showing' and where and how?*

What is sadly missing in much of the training to date (unless you bring in specialist companies like Lucy Faithfull or Marie Collins, organisations providing some training around child sexual abuse and exploitation and digitally facilitated abuse) is how to recognise whether a child is being sexually abused online, or encountering these images and being a victim of Cybertrauma. This kind of trauma involves being asked to provide images of self, and or other children (often siblings), being shown pornographic images, images of other children being abused or indeed animal sexual abuse (explained as falling under the IWF categories of A, B or C). So, imagine you are Tiny Tim aged seven and doing your homework alone in your bedroom. You know how to click on messages in, let's say, a social media account that you or your parents installed. You get sent a video link by your friend from this social media account (this could be one you added or a school friend). Being seven, of course, you don't know how to critically think about what you have been sent because it's 'from your friend', but you do know how to use the 'play' icon, as it's designed to be understood by all users.

Who sent the video becomes less of an issue here for the child, and so ... 'click'.

Child sexual abuse material that is shown to children can be sent by other children and sometimes this happens through direct messages (DMs) and other platforms that children are using. This child sexual abuse material can be of any child or children, from anywhere in the world and at anytime. Because much of this material is like the 'evergreen' content you can find in training, on social media and anywhere else for that matter it is timeless and re-sharable many many times. This material is 'reusable' by anyone who can find it, has it, gets sent it, uploads it, time and time again, and can be sent to more than one child (or person) at any time and sent repeatedly.

So how are you being educated about this issue in safeguarding training? As the practitioner, do you know where or how to begin with safeguarding children from this material, what to do or where to go if and when you find out the child has seen, been sent, sent on, uploaded, downloaded this material or otherwise?

Notwithstanding this, each video or photo is a child being abused, each time this is viewed this child is effectively abused again and again and again. This trauma can go on indefinitely, or for as long as data exists. It can be downloaded, uploaded, sent, deleted, retrieved, watched, rewatched and printed.

This data is permanent trauma like no other that has ever existed for these children. And this is not new behaviour. This has been going on for just over a quarter of a century already.

Removing CSAEM

There is a battle going on that you are probably not aware of on a moment-by-moment, hourly and daily basis with organisations around the world, such as (and please bear with me as I use their acronyms, explained in the helplines and bibliography sections) IWF, ICMEC, NCMEC, INHOPE and Interpol ... and many more crime-based services or tech industry applications or services and developmental areas such as WeProtect. They are trawling the Internet and removing as much of this content as possible, microsecond by microsecond, using amazing technological advances like hashing and lists of restricted, unsafe and recently removed sites that are shared across the globe. There is loads and loads and loads of material on these sites (see the reports by these organisations cited in the Bibliography). More than you could probably comprehend.

This chapter is potentially bringing a tsunami of possibilities and horrid thoughts or images into your awareness and you may be feeling overwhelmed as a practitioner and as a parent if you are one too. This is one of those *pause-and-breathe moments.*

This material also exists in places that make it nigh on impossible to remove, such as in the dark net. I won't get technical and go on to explain how the organisations work in removing the images, but safe to say there are many layers to the digital space and some are impossible to reach for law enforcement, so like a deep dive swimmer, the images can resurface onto and into those internet spaces where the above organisations can do their thing and remove them as quickly as possible.

They are fighting a battle that is growing in size and speed. Moreover, the need to identify children in those images is perhaps the most important aspect of this role. (I am not entirely sure that all images get reported by services, schools or parents, making this what is referred to as an infinitesimal loop in computing and systems designs). This, though, is the next step in education and change in policing, reporting, social work and practitioner front-line practice. We must identify these children to identify their images and prevent Cybertrauma from occurring repeatedly.

The speed of the Internet, the transmission of data and the rise and fall of images and videos into the space where law enforcement exists is like watching a race between a land speed record car and a human being running, where one is way in front of the other and seems impossible to catch. *It doesn't mean we shouldn't try though!*

And so these images are zooming around the world, at lightning speed landing in front of the eyes of children and adults, who, when they encounter them, can have a myriad of trauma responses. These images stick in the mind of the viewer because they are incomprehensible, abhorrent and shocking, bringing to life a dark side of human behaviour, depravity and the recognition that innocence has been stolen like the voice of Ariel in the film, *The Little Mermaid*, and this hits hard, no matter who the viewer is. (Obviously, those excited by these images are a different type of person to those I am discussing here.) Moreover, the feelings we adults get about this issue drive behaviours of wanting to bring down the perpetrator, akin to the mob mentality. This has also led to 'vigilantism' groups appearing. It is the feeling of parental angst and outcry and I suspect some readers will be feeling this throughout this chapter. *Again, pause and breathe.*

Culture, Westernised theory and images of children

Of course, the crime here under discussion is looked upon differently in cultures around the world when we start discussing the age of consent in these countries. Given this book is being written in the United Kingdom, I am discussing UK law, child development and neuroscience; however, some of these images may be of children in other countries and unless there is a passport image next to the child we can never assume to know anything about that child in the image other than they are a child being abused in a way that bodies remember, regardless of the culture. Those viewing these images are affected because it is a child.

Child marriage, what are your thoughts?

For example, imagine seeing a scene where a family is getting married, the man is in his late forties and the young girl is about ten. What does this conjure up for you? How outraged are you that this girl will lose her virginity in this way, in a culture that believes in this marriage format? How about we consider that there may be images of this event or marriage ceremony? Would we put this wedding image into our bank of CSAEM training, open it up for discussion in schools and education with children and would this allow us the opportunity to discuss consent, underage sex and images that are classified as CSAEM?

If children see in religious studies or history lessons that cultures around the world marry off children as an okay behaviour, then how do we educate them that an adult looking to talk to them online, about sex and relationships is likely doing so to groom them? Is this something to be considerate of, especially if they are non-native to England? For example, given the sharp rise of refugees over the last few decades and even the last year or so (as this book goes to press, the Russian invasion of Ukraine is occurring), there are likely going to be more children in education settings with differing religious and cultural values, beliefs and traditions. Not all children will be Westernised and they, along with their families, may think differently about the current messages we portray in our education settings. What will they do if images of children being abused end up in their inbox? How, as the practitioner, are you going to address this and work with children if we don't have the education in place and we only get the 'case' after the event has occurred? We are not investigative officers, journalists or intrusive parents but practitioners who need to be aware of this issue so we can appropriately deal with it in practice. How do you have conversations about CSAEM with children who are culturally raised with arranged marriages, which may include underage sex, and does this count as CSAEM for them in the same way we see it legally, morally and ethically? However, images in this country (the UK) need to follow the safeguarding processes of illegal images and this is a thought experiment for you, not advice.

Giggity, Giggity

The topic of sex becomes a quagmire of stuck-ness when we consider religious, societal and cultural beliefs and practices. And how interesting that the US TV cartoon *Family Guy* used the name Quagmire to refer to the 'sex pest' in the cartoon – the 'dirty-minded' man who makes inappropriate references to sex with young women (and often underage females). Whilst this was originally aired after 'the watershed', access to this program for young children has brought the 'dark comedy' element to the therapy room on many occasions. As the child quotes the 'Giggity Giggity' aspect of the Quagmire character or makes reference to the clips they watch on YouTube, as said in other chapters, the phrase 'dirty-minded' is now being used by seven- and eight-year-olds, who can tell me with clarity and accuracy that Quagmire is 'dirty-minded too' and that dirty-minded is discussing, referencing sex or indeed is a sexual swear word. When did this phrase become an everyday part of childhood and how long has this taken? Do you hear children around you using this kind of language and lexicon? Certainly, in my secondary school experience, the first year of being there (Year 7, aged 11–12 for non-UK readers) was full of innuendos, references to sex, masturbation and 'getting it off' at the back of the bus or behind the bike sheds (even though our school didn't have these sheds, but you know what I mean). And there was no Google, so we either played clever and said we knew what this meant, or we waited to hear an explanation from our peers (or went to a library, read magazines or asked adults; and these results could be just as skewed too).

As practitioners I ask that you think about this language being used by children; is this coming from the yard or playground, TV, video, on-demand services, real-world abuse, families' language or potential online groomers and images of CSAEM – and how would you know?

DMs, Discord and dark nets: e2ee and CSAEM

The app is not the issue. However, the name Discord is perfect to describe the feelings that arise when educating about the issues in this chapter. Firstly, do not rush to remove the app 'Discord' from children just because I have it in the subtitle here in this chapter. It is a metaphor and fitted nicely with the flow of words as well as being the name of a file-sharing app, just like File Transfer Protocol sites and LimeWire were used many years ago. As discussed earlier, many children are sent videos and images of CSAEM or their images are sent and shared using social media apps.

Cue the most asked question I hear: 'So, Cath which one should I not let the children on, be wary of, or tell parents about as a practitioner?' Well, it's not the app, it's how it is used and who uses it for ill intent. All these apps have the potential to be a place where these images can be sent, shared, taken or discussed – even ones that have great security, privacy and age verification, until verifying a child on these platforms is 100% sorted.

Currently, there is no app that cannot be used for ill intent if someone so wished it. There is the possibility adults appear as children in these spaces and vice versa. You see the Internet helped create spaces where both adults and children would be; some of these spaces are labelled for children only. Perhaps with obvious names like: 'Playground app for 3–7-year-olds' and 'Social media space for teens' versus those spaces created for adults: 'Dating site extraordinaire' or 'over 18s Gambling and Sex Casino, no children allowed!' And of course, in the time frame I write this in, the year 2022, where there are children online, adults are pretending to be children, and where there are adults online children are pretending to be adults.

Who's checking and how?

The online safety bill, currently at a stage of development still (at the time of writing) is now going to include age assurance processes and age verification and is hopefully going to address this issue somewhat. However, this may only apply to some but not all the platforms and spaces. What will be addressed initially are sites that, after the children's code was brought into being, have adult sexual material and/or gambling, and sites where children's data is processed (Information Commissioners Office, 2020).

Until then …

On the apps, children tell me they get sent messages by their friends, randomers, friends' friends, family members and of course 'professionals' (more on this in the chapter on harms professionals in Knibbs (forthcoming)). These apps are often used with the additional layer of DMs being a part of the app, if not an offshoot of it for that very purpose. Think of Instant Messenger, WhatsApp and Discord as messenger-type apps. Each of these and many of the other apps allow for text, image and video to be sent, or indeed providie the ability to have a live video call, and at the moment.

When these platforms create a direct and often secret or unseen space, this is like the metaphor of 'a direct channel into your child's bedroom' (and mind), as has been portrayed in educational videos online and TV adverts. This means that often parents and professionals have no idea what appears on the screen facing the child because you would have to be sat at the side of them to read or see it. This differs in so many ways compared to TV because in the 'living rooms' of families we are all watching the same thing on the big screen, and so parents can, at the drop of a hat change the channel, press pause (a new variation since Live TV became a thing) or turn the TV off should a child be present during content we think they should not be exposed to.

So unless the parents are sitting at the side of the child for the entirety of the time they have a device or console, then the same goes for how we would safeguard our children in the real world by considering the spaces they can visit. Would you allow a child to go on the bus, into town and round to friends without checking these spaces for stranger danger, safety and of course trustworthy adults in those places? How can you see all they see without having a mirroring process going on, or being present for every moment on screen?

What children get 'sent' by their peers varies on a day-to-day basis, dependent upon the viral trends, hoaxes and memes circulating at that time. Often it is YouTube or TikTok videos of 'funny stuff' which generally goes along the lines of songs, pop music, silly behaviours from their peers such as dancing around or pulling faces and of course the filming of their families. It's a shared experience of *look what makes me laugh, look at what my dad, uncle or mum is doing, look at me with my dance group, look at what interests me and of course,* *look at what *this* influencer is sharing.* It is a normative aspect of peer relationships about likes, dislikes and changing hobbies, interests and new learnings.

However, there have been cases reported in the media, via research and those I hear about in therapy, of children receiving videos and still images of cartoons of children being abused, commonly known as lolly porn, actual images and videos of children being sexually abused, or they have joined a platform where they are exposed to live streams of children being sexually abused (apps such as Chatroulette, Omegle and many others). This is not adult pornography, these are images of children being subjected to varying degrees of sexual abuse at varying ages, including infants. Notwithstanding this, adults have been sent or happened upon and seen these kinds of images too, or been session hacked.

Breathe

Imagine being that child who sees this. Imagine what sense they make of these images or videos and how their worldview can change in an instant. Imagine, if they have been abused, what this does in terms of revisiting their trauma? Imagine what they do with this video or image and whom they tell. I can say that many of the children who say they see 'weird stuff' online might just be talking about this kind of material (and lots of other weird stuff too), and they don't have the language to explain it because it's not something they understand.

Some children have been able to say exactly what was happening on the video, but many do not (usually these are my clients who have been subjected to their sexual abuse and as part of that process have been shown this kind of image). Imagine how many children have or will see these kinds of images and as a practitioner how do you even begin to address this issue when you are likely feeling overwhelmed at the prospect of this?

This is indeed the reason why large organisations want this material off the Internet. It causes undue damage and harm to the victims in the images and to those who view them. Writing this chapter meant I had to take regular breaks because I could feel myself hacking at the keyboard in rage, despair and at times contempt for the lack of broad and focused education that we (practitioners) have about these subject matters because they are distressing and people do not want to look.

And of course, we don't; it's horrifying and I suspect you may have felt this as you read the above paragraphs.

I'm not sure anyone who has seen these images ever gets over it. The adults who have been exposed to this issue through social media pranks and targeted attacks explain: it replays in their minds, it made them feel sick, they cried, they couldn't sleep, they couldn't save the child, they reported it, they would never know if the child was safe, they were angry for weeks, they had intrusive thoughts and got the shakes. They were often unable to go near their device for ages, would never go back onto some of the platforms, stopped using technology as they thought they would be arrested and charged. They panicked about their professions 'finding out', needed to find a therapist who understood this issue (they often say that they struggled to find anyone), became overprotective of their child and wanted to bury the PC or smash it up. And most of all they were angered that people do 'this' (carrying out the abuse and sending it to others) The people I speak to who have their own children imagined that it could happen to their child and they were sickened by it.

Breathe

Empathy: walk in my shoes and see through my eyes

And so we need to think, when working with children, about what their experience is. They may struggle to articulate what they saw, may not even understand it and certainly will have a deep knowledge of the harm, pain and 'wrongness' of this activity. (Even young children know that this behaviour is wrong as the body is wise even before we can speak.) The recollections about any of this kind of material in my therapy clinic have revealed the confusion and anger about why someone does that to a child, baby or anyone!

I am always open to children in therapy about all issues, and yes, it means that at any time I can be subjected to the horrors of abuse and trauma, and if this topic arises, the conversations and processing of this 'yukkiness' are mostly experienced by children with no knowledge of sex. Those who are versed in the language of 'shagging' and 'fucking' due to family behaviours, language or sexual abuse still find it yukky (which has included four- and five-year-olds knowing these words). But they also have a broader knowledge of a knowing (in their unconscious mind) that this is an intimate act. The children who have been sexually abused find this the most distressing type of YUK.

So imagine the complexities of children being exposed to this material and how they make sense of it in a world where swear words are rife, gender and sex-based narratives are beginning to infiltrate the classrooms as we make way for all manner of inclusivity and the ever-growing world of gender affirmative language. We have varying words for sexual activity and genitalia ranging from the more modest and simple to the vulgar.

Imagine as a practitioner how you will work with this issue going forward, 'now you know more' And imagine this chapter being in the heads and awareness of many more adults through education and bringing it to their attention – would this change things? Would we see the outrage and change to our children being 'online' and would we want changes to the regulation of this space? Would we support the move to encrypt everything at the bequest of Meta, the privacy advocates and those who want to harm children?

E2EE: silent, secret and sacrosanct

Once we create a system where end-to-end encryption (e2ee) takes place and is protected from law enforcement and child protection services, with more adults being able to navigate, prevent and check for sexual abuse images of children, we create a silent and 'secret garden' of Eden where images and videos can be traded, shared and created without the person who protects children being alerted.

Such a space can give the perpetrators a haven to discuss, plan and carry out those crimes. And who and how are the children protected in this space? Spoiler: they won't be. Not unless we make child protection *the* priority by creating systems that can check for this material. And tech would allow for this to be assessed without breaking the rights and freedoms of the individuals, unless, of course, we are standing up for the rights and freedoms of infantophiles, paedophiles and hebephiles? Is their privacy worth more than anyone else's or are the children more important, given they have no voice in this space, and no power to stop or prevent these crimes? *Whose welfare is sacrosanct and matters most?* The answer is complicated and more than this chapter can get its teeth into and so I am highlighting the issue at hand.

Recollections in the therapy room: first-, second- and third-hand pain

Children have told me that these CSAEM videos (or sometimes the comments) contain dirty words and 'people making funny faces' (they are often referring to the face at the point of orgasm but don't know this is what this is). They tell me that the children in the videos are not looked at by the children watching the videos, because the children often seem fascinated with the adults in the images (I could speculate that this is about an attempt to understand what is going on, who the adult is, how they can assimilate this information about grown-ups and '*grownups who do this*' into their worldview etc.).

This is a topic matter we can NEVER research ethically; moments like these are the most harrowing that I have encountered in therapy and will never leave me because of the sheer confusion and Cybertrauma the child feels (its transferential, heart-breaking and confusing beyond any other feelings I have ever experienced *with* children who are sexually abused). I wonder how many therapy rooms and professionals are not open to hearing this kind of conversation and unconsciously communicate this in varying ways. It is the most difficult of pains to witness and feel with a child (of any age). And so children exposed to this material may *never* speak of it, to it, or process it comprehensively if we do not allow the space for it to be spoken about. I feel the pain of my clients and feel the pain they feel for the victim, I feel the pain for the victim, somewhere out there in the world; never knowing how long ago this event occurred and whether that child got the help they needed.

Perhaps the recollections of these children are an attempt to make sense of the size difference or understand why adults hurt children. I have never been able to answer this question for those children. I don't think I ever will. It feels glib and cliché to say that some people do things that we don't understand; humans who do not do this cannot comprehend it themselves.

You must be courageous to listen and a gladiator to hear

What does this viewing do to their sense of belonging in the world and how, where or when can they ever trust some adults? In the words of Erikson (1998), 'Trust versus Mistrust occurs in early development'. But would this issue rubber band you back to that stage, would you now mistrust the world? Once you have seen horror you can never unsee it.

Reflections

As a point to note, I think research *and* conversations need to be had about this space and how we could possibly ever gather the data about it ethically and morally. I am curious as to the children's recollections and why they report watching the adults and not the children. Apart from guesswork here, such as, perhaps they glance at the child and are confronted by a face of fear, deadened by drugs, perhaps there is an unconscious parallel to the age of the victim and what this does internally to the child's psyche. Though this issue can never be researched ethically, we have to consider what this is doing to them and how it affects them and, hopefully, the book here is giving you space and time to think about this.

A reflection point for practitioners about language with children

We need to also consider, when we talk to children about these videos or sexual abuse in any way, that we should not use words like 'rude', even though some of my clients have been told to do so by other professionals who are struggling with the issue. It is not rude, it is *illegal* and it is abuse. Nothing about this is rude, or naughty. Please do not use this language with children. Shutting the door in someone's face, or sticking your tongue out at someone is rude. Think what a child may feel if, for example, a teacher says 'that's rude' as a child blows a raspberry to another student for a laugh, and how those words can be associated with sexual abuse. 'Rude' is a language from the eras from the 1950s to the 1980s. Correct language is helpful when we make the uncomfortable comfortable and not the palatable 'othering'.

Again, breathe

And so moving on to the 'permanent record' idea of CSAEM

We can begin to see that each image, each video and each sharing of these creates a vortex of foreverness that means, 'the digital and real crime scene' is forever captured, forever recorded and forever shared, until it is hashed and removed. This sentence can terrorise some people because I have inserted the word 'forever'. I have been asked on occasions not to say this (by friends and colleagues) when speaking at conferences, and certainly not to utter it to professionals who are just learning about this world, because 'they would lose all hope of being able to help a child in these situations. People say, 'these images are easy to delete because you just remove them from the phone or website, no?'

Sadly, no. Those who are not versed in the world of binary or computer language find digital data and the entry into the cybersphere difficult to comprehend and so the word 'forever' confuses and dismays and it obliterates hope for many. And this is the truest part. This is the most difficult perspective to wrap one's head around.

Cybertrauma: so far from the cutting room floor

Images in memory are concealed from the creator by the inability to recall or compartmentalise, or they are forgotten to conscious processes dependent upon the image, context and emotional valence dedicated to that image (Baddely, 2007). Sensations in the body are often held until they are worked through (Levine, 2005, 2008) and all that is known about trauma has yet to produce books and literature on this subject matter specifically. However, I will say that we mostly have this topic covered by the greats in the field of trauma; it is perhaps just that aspect about repeatedly repeating that is missing from the literature, because as I said earlier this has never happened to our species in this manner before. Memories of our trauma, yes; actually seeing it on a screen online many times or receiving emails from organisations to say it's been taken down, again, and again and again; or receiving contact from random people to say they have it, have seen it and have passed it on. Wondering who has seen it every time you go towards your computer or device and wondering if today is the day your image will be finally deleted? I don't think I can find anything about that in the books or research articles.

To bring the idea of camera film encased in its housing (like the cameras of the old days), well, they rot and are aged by light and time. But digital images are so very different in the way that they are utilised, and can be copied many times, sent and redistributed; and of course, in the world we live in with worldwide connections, uploaded and downloaded many times, giving others the options to do the very same with the data. This is not a film 'recorded on a negative that will fade over time', this data can be edited and used by many people for many different ills and gains.

It is the data hidden on a hard drive and hidden away from prying eyes? The spaces where the films are 'traded' may seem to conjure up images of seedy, dingy clubs filled with smoke and whiskey bottles, but these spaces are often just out of plain sight to the unknowing. These spaces have the door supervisors on call 24/7/365 and if your name ain't down you ain't getting in, so to speak.

DIY shops

These spaces are filled with like-minded people of all ages, sizes, genders, races, cultures, languages and sexualities; though the main interest to them all is children. Trade secrets are shared about the how to, when to, where to and what to. Advice about keeping items stored out of sight is in top tip guides. Think of your local DIY shop that has an expert on every type of tool, screw, wood, glue and plant. Handy pamphlets dotted around everywhere to help you get the best out of your house and garden, such as 'How to cultivate and propagate your plants'. Like many of these guides you find in your local DIY store, there is always a person happy to hold a webinar giving you information. Gosh, they can even show you the process in real-time so you can get it just right and cultivate the process.

And, no, I'm not talking about plants or shelves here.

Live streaming: the ever-growing problem, the ever-moving target

Simon Bailey, chief of Norfolk Police and lead on this topic for many years in the UK has spoken at a few conferences over several years. In itself, it is so brilliant to see that this topic is on the agenda so often, and yet, what is heart-breaking is the fact I have heard him say (paraphrasing here) for almost seven years now, live streaming is the most concerning aspect of CSAEM, as these events take place, often without warning, booked up in advance like a webinar, on platforms that are used for the duration of the event and then gone again.

It is nigh on impossible to keep up to date or ahead of these events in real-time, as that would require some seriously heavy-duty technology to pick up these events and trace who, what, where and how. Some of these events are the streaming of historic child sexual abuse, some are live, some have a few viewers, and others are like a conference. Some, many and most of these events disguise where they are being 'held' through the use of technological advances like virtual proxy networks or are out of the country and we may not be able to tell which is which.

Furthermore, these events often have children from other poorer countries, where payment is about staying alive for that family and sacrificing a child in this way means there's food on the table. Perhaps the thinking goes: as long as the child isn't killed in the process this could mean the difference between life and death for more people in one family than that one child, *a sacrificial lamb*. So children are becoming a fiscal commodity for the live streams, to ensure that families stricken by poverty and famine can survive, like the rest of us are allowed to. Our Western privilege seems moot in comparison, does it not? Money that we might throw into a pot for a well-known coffee house tip could keep some families in bread and milk for a day or two and, for that, children may well be the tradable item. No haggling.

And the most difficult aspect of this issue is: due to policing laws and criminal justice processes, the events can never be captured by legal teams (i.e. recorded) because to do so is an offence, and so, how does one collect evidence for prosecution when you cannot screengrab or record the perpetrators in real-time?

Perpetrators like Pokémon; 'we gotta catch 'em all!' *We have a lot of work to do here.* And unto the void, the criminals and villains go till they feel it is safe to surface again.

You are now educated in this and cannot ever unthink the terrible here, so go forth and tell people about this issue. These children deserve our action, and we must start somewhere, so conversations are often the start of that action.

Breathe

Motives: mine for writing this book

Every time I write and talk about this chapter, I become more passionate about and driven to shout about this topic so that you know, like really know, why we *must* start talking about this. Why as practitioners you *must* understand this, regardless of how much this makes you feel angry or sickened. It is not my intent to traumatise people here and long conversations were had with the publisher regarding talking about this topic in a way that was unambiguous, gave enough information and kept the horrors out, and this chapter is likely the one that has indeed created trauma for some people. My motive? Imagine the children to whom this happens and how they feel.

If we really want to play the comparison card here we are not the children in the images, and if we were, then you know you would want to do and say everything in your power to prevent it from happening to another child. And of course, as I do explain this topic here and in training, I want to cry for the children in these videos and images.

Why this can sometimes feel futile for many people in this space is that the topic is cowered away from (by people engaging in what I call ostrich syndrome and sticking their heads in the sand and fingers in their ears), because who wants to hear, see, read or know about this? I want you to know that these children *could* be the next person you work with, now or in the future and of course how would you know? This is not something they may remember if they were drugged or preverbal when it occurred. Therefore, the trauma spaces *need to have this conversation in every conference*, continuing professional development space and in training institutes from now on.

We *must* begin to talk about the last 25 years or so where this technology has facilitated this kind of abuse and this topic is not, as far as I can see (at the time of writing), on the agenda with the experts at conferences who work *with and for traumatised* clients and individuals. I do not understand why this is missing, still, and professionally I am pretty much speechless as to why.

Reflection for the practitioner

Adults are walking among us who were subjected to this kind of abuse when the Internet began, and of course, some were abused before this technological age, with images from that time now uploaded and stored and shared like the ones since internet connections enabled this. What is this like to think of, as you now reflect over the last 25 years of practice, or growing up and who could be one of those children that you know? How many children are you seeing in the spaces of education, after-school clubs, youth settings and beyond who may have been subjected to this kind of abuse? What did you or are you learning in your training? And how are you feeling now, knowing these images have been traded for a quarter of a century already?

A lifelong Cybertrauma?

And what about the children who are sent these types of images via DM (not many children use email in the same way we working adults do but it is not to say this couldn't be emailed either), ones that happen upon it accidentally or purposefully via a live streaming service, or even are the children later identified in the images and notified by services that *their image* has been identified? How do you as the practitioner open your mind to the impact of any one of those spaces and how do you work with a child or young person to whom this happens? How do you put your feelings aside to be able to hear the unspoken, the sometimes unknown and, of course, the unthinkable?

Breathe

Virtual is as impacting as corporeal!

Let's have a thought experiment break. For a moment I want to invite you to think about a very hot sunny day (few and far between in the UK but play along!). The sun is shining, and you are thirsty. You head to the fridge and grab a lemon and the cold bottle of spring water off the shelf. As you walk to where you keep your glasses there is a droplet of water forming on the outside of the bottle. It is cold and the bottle feels wet on the outside. You pour the liquid into the glass and it's cold to the touch. You reach for the knife and as you cut the lemon open the droplets of juice squirt out onto your hand. You can see the shapes of the little segments (endocarp) and the droplets of lemon juice pushing out eager to mix with the water. You drop the lemon into the water. You lift the drink to your mouth.

Have you noticed that you are likely experiencing more saliva in your mouth right now? How is this happening and what magic is this?

Our brains are very good at not being able to distinguish what we are doing and what we are thinking because, as described in Knibbs (2022) and through neuroscience, our brains only need to receive the stimulus of an event, and this can be driven internally like the thought experiment above.

This is how anxiety works for many people. As mentioned previously, have a look at Joseph Le Doux (2015) and his writing around anxiety to understand these mechanisms (as I describe in Knibbs (2022)). The magic is in the mind!

The zone of false safety and how images are understood by the 'watching brain'

A quick and very brief description of our eyes and how they work is as follows. Our brains, namely our optical systems, take information from external light sources and recreate them into an image using the 'inner eye' mechanisms created in the occipital lobe. This system has a high priority for movement as a survival mechanism (Gregory, 1997; Livingstone, 2002).

Now, given that these images appear on the child's device screen, held at that false safety distance (discussed at length in my previous book (Knibbs, 2022)), I am suggesting that the body and brain of the viewer react in a visceral way with an added impact through the mediation of mirror neurons (Ferrari & Coudé, 2018). They experience shock, trauma, disgust, curiosity, disbelief and confusion in a matter of milliseconds.

The eyes cannot turn away as the survival systems scan the environment (the image) for '*anything that could be a threat to me, and whilst you're at it I'll just activate these empathy circuits, so you parallel what's occurring in the image. That way you know what to look out for in future!*' And this takes place in a matter of milliseconds and for however long the image or video is viewed.

If the child experiencing this viewing is also a previous or current victim of sexual abuse, those circuits that are already superhighways of familiarity will be working at supersonic speeds. Those children who are not previous abuse victims will see something that will, in an instant, delete the innocence we romantically hold dear for children. They will see something that will resonate in ways we do not fully understand because we cannot research these using ethical methods. And so, for the next 25 years or so, whilst these children mature and begin to explore this experience with practitioners and tell their stories, we will only have the best guesses and generalising from adult models to children. We often do this with adult theories of trauma, but the children we work with are not adults and so do not necessarily follow this theoretical patterning.

I am suggesting here that we may not know for decades what the level of trauma may turn out to be if we don't start discussing and enquiring about this issue now. And that, dear reader, is not good enough. We are already 28 years into the digital space of CSAEM and two more decades would effectively take us to the 50-year point before we have an answer.

The 25-year legacy, the police officers, the moderators

We don't have 25 years to wait. We must begin to act now, acknowledge and speak out about these issues. We must provide in our sense of self, a space in which children and those who have already reached the ages of adulthood (the age of the Internet) can speak freely and openly and work through what must have been thousands of times of this material being seen by the number we cannot know until adults talk to us about it also. This material is being seen by an unknown and incomprehensible amount of other people including children, adolescents and adults. We really don't have another 25 years of waiting.

Moderators and policing

We know that those who work in the field of child sexual abuse imagery moderation and content analysis undergo rigorous training and psychological support to be able to carry out these roles of viewing, categorising and dealing with these images. General, on-the-beat policing does not seem to have the same level of training and psychological support, as part of the everyday job they undertake. Viewing these images may be a small part of their role, if ever they have to sadly deal with this as a case. What I can tell you about attending spaces such as conferences and training where these officers have previously seen these types of images and are now in the front seat, driving the message about e-safety and CSAEM, is they are all in some way once removed emotionally and psychologically from those images, the children and the events. They can suffer with post-traumatic stress or be seemingly 'not bothered'. It is traumatising work to see children being abused, and this is a trauma reaction. These professions are included in the DSM-V for this reason.

These professions often need to be removed in some way, to work with this issue, and I cannot imagine what it is like to see one of these images first-hand and have that feeling of powerlessness of not being able to prevent the crime and of course protect the children in the images. The ex-police officers that work in e-safety tell me that they are hardened to and disconnected from these images, and not many of the news reports or learning about these issues phase them anymore. Because they have seen the levels of depravity of human beings, as a way to manage that deep compassion, they detach cognitively. They tell me the images become akin to the way a surgeon works with a body on the table and not a person they are caring for – it's less, well, personal.

The way that the human mind can do this is both fascinating and troublesome when we want to address this subject matter. We must care enough to do our jobs and protect children, but we need to ensure we don't become overwhelmed with that care, resulting in burnout and compassion fatigue, or compassion disconnection.

It has been very difficult to write this chapter because I wanted to allow the children's voice to be heard, I wanted the facts to be clear and I wanted to do this compassionately but fiercely.

I wanted to hide away some of the abhorrent nature of this to protect you but found my advocacy for the children who have already won a battle by speaking out. In doing so, I have fought here to bring their wounds, traumas and abuse to the centre stage because it is needed in the world of child protection, child therapy, social work, teaching, nursing and policing, and for anyone else who has a child, or knows one or works with one. I am aware that this chapter, along with the others, will be hard-hitting and you may react to this long after you put the book down.

If you are outraged, then join the movement bringing this issue to the minds of us all. Let's not keep failing children and, where I have spoken honestly, openly and frankly here I don't want to apologise on behalf of the children, but I do want to say sorry for this opening of your eyes if this hurt you in any way. I want to see this being talked about at trauma conferences and what has been a delay of over 25 years leaves me writing this here as a statement of need.

As I once said to a colleague, and this became the name of our research[1] at the time: 'If not now, when?'

Note

1 That research missed this issue for ethical reasons.

References

American Psychiatric Association. (2013). *Diagnostic and statistical manual of mental disorders* (5th ed.). APA.

Baddeley, A. (2007). *Working memory thought and action.* Oxford University Press.

Davidson J., & Gottschalk, P. (2011). *Internet child sexual abuse: Current research and policy.* Routledge.

Erikson, E. (1998). *The life cycle completed: The extended version.* W.W. Norton.

Ferrari, P. F., & Coudé, G. (2018). *Mirror neurons, embodied emotions, and empathy.* In K. Meyza & E. Knapska (Eds.), *Neuronal correlates of empathy* (pp. 67–77). Elsevier.

Finkelhor, D. (1984). *Child sexual abuse: New theory and research.* Macmillan.

Goodyear-Brown, P. (2012). *The handbook of child sexual abuse: Identification, assessment and treatment.* John Wiley & Sons.

Greenberg, D. M., Firestone, P., Bradford, J. M., & Broom, I. (2000). *Infantophiles.* In L. B. Schlesinger (Ed.), *Serial offenders: Current thoughts, recent findings.* CRC Press.

Gregory, R. (1997). *Eye and brain: The psychology of seeing* (5th ed.). Princeton University Press.

Information Commissioners Office. (2020). *The children's code of practice.* https://ico.org.uk/about-the-ico/media-centre/news-and-blogs/2020/01/ico-publishes-code-of-practice-to-protect-children-s-privacy-online/.

Knibbs, C. (2022). *Children, technology, and healthy behaviour: How to help children thrive online.* Routledge.

Knibbs, C. (forthcoming). *Online harms and cybertrauma: Legal and harmful issues with children and young people.* Routledge.

Le Doux, J. (2015). *Anxious: The modern mind In the age of anxiety.* Oneworld.

Levine, P. (2005). *Healing trauma: Restoring the wisdom of your body.* Sounds True.

Levine P. (2008). *Healing trauma: A pioneering program for restoring the wisdom of your body.* Sounds True.

Livingstone, M. (2002). *Vision and art: The biology of seeing.* Harry N. Abrahams.

Pearce, J. (2019). *Child sexual exploitation: Why theory matters.* Policy Press.

Rothschild, B. (2003). *The body remembers casebook: Unifying methods and models in the treatment of trauma and PTSD.* W.W. Norton.

Van der Kolk, B. (1994). *The body keeps the score: Memory and the evolving psychobiology of post-traumatic stress.* Harvard Review of Psychiatry, *1(5)*, 253–265.

11 Revenge-based sharing of intimate imagery and abuse

This chapter looks to non-consensual intimate image abuse and revenge porn as the overarching subject matter; however, the chapter looks to the acts carried out by spurned lovers, gender outings and secretive filming of images and how they can be shared online without the knowledge of the person in the images. Relational factors are discussed as to why a young person may carry out this behaviour and violence against women and girls in the male and female aggression framework.

I am hopping over the real depth of these issues due to word limitations and a need to communicate the harm in a way that minimises harm to you the reader. This a difficult line to hold when writing about this topic, and others in the book as I am aware that people with a history of sexual assault and abuse may find these chapters uncomfortable, as can people without histories of sexual abuse and assault.

Revenge porn

To clarify before we begin this chapter:

> Section 33 of the Criminal Justice and Courts Act 2015 creates an offence of disclosing private sexual photographs or films without the consent of an individual who appears in them and with intent to cause that individual distress.
>
> (CPS, 2017)

> The South West Grid for Learning hosts the Revenge Porn helpline and considers this term as non-consensual intimate image abuse.
>
> (SWGfL, 2015)

For those who are reading this book and have realised I am talking about children, this chapter is not about children per se. Well, it is, but not in the sense of the crime attributed to the adult population. That is because the title of the chapter pertains to the legal issue of revenge porn, and whilst I hear this phrase used to describe the sending on of images and videos of children

DOI: 10.4324/9781003364177-12

and young people engaging in relationships and sexual imagery produced in those relationships, this is not revenge porn. The crime of revenge porn (RP) is only applicable to those *aged 18 and over* in the United Kingdom, so all other material that has been discussed so far is CSAEM and remains so for anyone who is not of the legal voting age. And for those of you who have grasped the concept of what it is to be a child, and have some understanding of adolescence and brain development, 18 years of age does not denote full maturational capacity, nor would learning or social difficulties mean that a person over the age of 18 years is 'an adult' and can make those decisions, or understand the world in an adult manner. *Chronology does not necessarily mean capacity or maturity.*

This chapter is about the revenge that hurt, dismayed and insecurely attached people take. It is about how adults in relationships find themselves engaging in this behaviour, and of course children may engage in capturing these images and/or may be very close to the age of legal adulthood when engaging in image-based recordings, then sharing them once they have reached 18 years of age.

RP is an interesting concept, given the word pornography tends to conjure up the idea of consent. I mean that's exactly what we were covering in the chapter on viewing this material and the assumptions made about the videos and images that appear there (unless you are looking at channels where it is clear this is not the case). So let's start with acknowledging that RP is currently classified as an act that affects the over-eighteens only. On porn sites it 'looks' like in most cases that the person, or persons are consenting to take part in a recorded and uploaded sexual act, from masturbation to group sex and acts of bondage, simulated torture and fetishes. And so the word porn is associated with this prospect by default. It conveys consent and therefore this chapter has been left until you have read about consent, porn viewing, sexting and CSAEM. The nuances and assumptions we have matter.

Shots snapped to snapshot

Not only can a child and young person get themselves into a tangled web of deceit, bravado and coercion in this domain, but these sexual images and video-based conversations are also used and abused by adults too. The cameras of old, the Polaroid camera, for example, made for an instantaneous moment between sexual partners. It was and still is a thing; however, this particular piece of equipment has a slight advantage over the technology of today in that it only ever produced one image. This does not mean that in today's technological world this image cannot be copied, scanned or even photographed itself; however, many years before the Internet, this was a more secure way to have only one copy and for this to be kept 'between' partners.

We have the ability to take, and record images on a device which may be a professional camera or handheld smartphone or device. Once captured, the images and videos can be uploaded to the Internet, usually onto a website aimed at pornographic material or it can be one designed specifically for this RP purpose (and through the years there have been a number of these). You only have to watch documentaries about this, for example on Netflix (e.g. *The most hated man on the internet*, www.netflix.com/gb/title/81387065, 2022). These images are used to hurt or get revenge upon one another, or are uploaded (or recorded) secretly. This can cause lifelong trauma to the one upon whom the revenge is carried out, resulting in a lack of trust in any sexual partners going forward.

Now to give a little relationship theory and what happens when interpersonal relationships break, become banal and boring, lose their novelty and adoration processes, and are threatened by others in the form of adultery, extramarital flings and all the other phrases we use to explain a betrayal of the monogamous exclusivity we 'expect' as a society, this is an adult-based narrative surrounding adult relationships of monogamy. There is an acceptance in some spaces and places about polyamory or 'open' relationships, but on the whole, we are like prairie dogs and mate for life (see the work of Sue Carter (Carter & Getz, 1993) on this topic, who is the wife of Stephen Porges (2021) who writes about our nervous systems in response to other people). You can also listen to Ester Perel who is a leading relationships therapist, podcaster and influencer (see www.estherperel.com/).

This is not necessarily how it is for young people who are seemingly, according to the Internet and ever-changing relational, sexual and gender landscapes, *not tied down to one person or sexual partner at any one time*. This is where and why the Internet has changed (and is constantly changing) the expected relationship dynamics of the young people who live in that space. It is like trying to plait fog at times, keeping up with all of the changes. For example, from the 1970s to the 1990s young people would 'ask each other out' on dates, and words like boyfriend and girlfriend would seem appropriate when dating. These words would denote to others that this person was dating or 'courting' you and not others.

However, over the last few decades, as gender and sexuality processes have been changing, the way in which young people identify in relationships has also been changing. This is important when it comes to RP as a category of criminality for adolescents, because sometimes this is about gender revenge, gender outing, revenge for non-exclusivity, disclosure of sexual assault or abuse, and more. This differs somewhat from hurtful revenge on a sexual partner in the 'old-fashioned sense' that is often assumed for this crime. There is a saying that *hurt people hurt people* (allegedly attributed to Charles Eads, a speaker during a parents and teachers meeting in 1959, and also psychologist Helen Boyd in 1980 and Will Bowen a public speaker in 2009 (see https://quoteinvestigator.com/2019/09/15/hurt/).

RP is certainly one way in which we see hurt people hurting others in action.

Example from therapy (vignette for confidentiality purposes)

Zoe was 14 when she decided that she no longer identified as female (correct pronoun use as Zoe is now referring to herself as she/her). At this stage in our conversations (the early sessions), she hadn't labelled what or who she was, just that she no longer wanted to be seen as female. She also explained to me at this stage that her partner, another 'non-gendered, non-binary person born as female' (her words) wanted to date her 'exclusively' and this is the common term to mean that monogamy was the way in which they would conduct their relationship with each other.

However, Zoe at the time wanted an open relationship and to be polyamorous (a word she had learned online and wanted to try out as a way of sexual exploration) as this afforded her more scope to find out who she was sexually, and this was how her mates were dating:

> "'cos didn't you know Cath, the world has changed and people are just not tied down to one person anymore, because openness to other experiences means that people could see you weren't closed down. If I date ★★★★ then people will think I'm this or that, straight when I could be bi, or whatevs, but you know I want to try it all out first to know what I really am. Do you get me? It's like *how do I know*?' [emphasis added]

Zoe told me she had been sending images to her partner that were about her development (of breasts she hated), and what were going to be in the future chest-binding photos to compare with. She doctored her images (using an app) showing that she could look as though she did not have breasts and some of these images went to other people (she tells me she sent them on to others). We discussed the permanence of these images and what might happen to them, and Zoe said they had already been shared in her year, as this was, 'how we communicate to each other' and this was 'normal' for her and her peers. She didn't care about the ramifications, because in her eyes 'the breasts would be removed and if people wanted to keep them they could', she added and explained, 'We trust each other and this is about support for our sexuality'.

What may have been a good relationship for Zoe and her partner soon turned sour due to the way in which Zoe wanted openness and polyamory versus her partner's wants for exclusivity. Upon the 'fallout' they argued over whether Zoe was 'ever really non-binary' or was doing this to date her partner to try out lesbianism.

What may now be a common practice in young people that we need to be aware of in our work with young people is: Zoe's now ex-partner shared her images in an online group of *'never really were non-binary in the first place'*, where taunts of not 'doing' the non-binary process properly were the theme (as per the manual for 'how to be non-binary' which doesn't exist by the way … I'm being ironic).

She was outed into a group by name way before the images were shared and so the space of deadnaming and 'doxxing' (outing personal and identifiable details) now involves the element of sharing of sexual images, taking us right back into the chapters you have already read.

Revenge sharing now includes elements of the emerging identities around gender and sexuality for young people and this layer of complication makes this crime much more pernicious for young people, who may be outed at a later date in their life.

The problem with classification

What is apparent very quickly is that this form of sharing images may not fall under the remit of how we see the classic RP crime committed by adults. This act is about shaming and of course, through the uploading of sexual acts, also for the sexual pleasures of other people. The sharing of self-produced imagery known as sexting may not be the correct terminology here either, because this *intent and modus operandi* may not be about sexual behaviours but rather about gender and sexual identity shaming. The sharing of the images in Zoe's case in revenge for the breakup was an attack on that presentation and not the sharing of sexual-based images about sexual behaviour.

We need to choose our language and descriptions carefully and, of course, the legalities around crime may well still call it RP or CSAEM for a long time under sexual offences acts.

Intent

We must, as practitioners look behind the image or crime as it presents, and what was the intent behind the sharing of the image. Furthermore, revenge in young people is and overlaps with bullying and so we need to ascertain what was the story behind the act and who was involved and what for. RP in adults is about one person hurting their now or previous sexual partners, recording images of sexual acts without their knowledge, ratting out an adulterous or 'cheating' partner and is often just about those people in that relationship.

When it comes to revengeful acts by children and young people, it can be done to humiliate friends, humiliate sexuality, humiliate gender, humiliate ex-partners, bully others, share without consent and also share without knowing, understanding or comprehending the long-term impacts (alongside the sharing of an image of someone they do not even know as can happen in groups akin to the websites that traffic and trade).

Our way of understanding what is going on underneath these issues is the skill we bring to the table with these crimes and presentations. Using all that you have read so far in the book should help you approach and face these cases with more understanding, compassion and an awareness that what something is called under legal proceedings may not be the full picture of the case you are dealing with.

Playground to online

Playground issues as a metaphor for jumping ship and the change in the adult space?

When one young person, perhaps, say a boy in primary school aged about nine, finds out in playground gossip that their friend has 'jumped ship' to play a different sport or listen to another band to the one he likes, he can become enraged. They have lost their friend to something or someone else. They might be seen to punch, kick and wrestle the 'traitor' to the ground and perhaps even twist their arm to persuade them to come back into the fold of 'our' friendship. I am sure you will have seen these moments in your childhood and understood them for what they were (and are).

This behaviour can carry on throughout adolescence in terms of friendships and other forms of aggression. When this behaviour in later years (in the teens or older, perhaps) is viewed through the lens of sex- and relationship-related behaviours, we expect to see males physically harming others in this rageful place, because the media often tells us about how aggressive this sex is. I am sure you have seen males physically fighting over partners or ex-partners or read in romance novels about the man who went to war, had duels or fisticuffs to save the woman they loved (I don't read romance novels so am basing this on my early recollections of the books I had to read in my school days).

Yet in the world of RP, as it exists, it is seemingly mostly males who share these images for other males to attack through comments and 'rip a new one' and 'roast' the female. This seems counter to the literature about aggression in young children where females are often seen as the verbally aggressive sex towards each other (Owens et al., 2000), but certainly fits with the violence against women literature and narrative (for more information see the UK government programme to investigate, research and tackle (VAWG, 2013–to date)).

And further still, this language of tearing down the sexual practices and habits of women is the same as seen in the pornography sites discussed earlier in the book. When it comes to sex and aggression, we certainly need to look at an overlap of theory and behaviour from physical fights with other males to the compadre-based approach that RP seems to take in its misogynist framing. I have not looked in enough depth at stats or research about gay males and their 'taking down' of each other and whether this is also a parallel, and so have refrained from commenting on that here in terms of RP. However, RP is often about relationships, and gay men, non-binary and other groups of non-heteronormative sexualities are likely to behave in the same way as any other hurt human being and so the motives are likely to be similar. This was not the remit of the book and that's another area to discover and research for future updates.

A reflection

And, yet, I wonder about the space of the female, who in childhood and adolescence laughs, humiliates and is (in the tradition of labelling of behaviour) catty, manipulative, secretive, bitchy and can effectively carry out revenge through insults and derogatory language, and whether this is also creating the same kind of RP space online to humiliate males in this way, which according to de Becker (de Becker, 1997) would be the most damaging to the sense of safety that men feel. A thought to think about. And indeed, if females are gossiping, bitching and slating other females in this space, then the behaviours of spitefulness, revenge and humiliation will continue.

We need to educate all sexes about revenge and not just the males as so often is seen in the approach to violence and RP. If the females lay the foundation of hatred against each other in the sexual (behaviour) spaces, then what changes can we make in other spaces? How as a practitioner will you address this issue?

References

American Psychiatric Association. (2013). *Diagnostic and statistical manual of mental disorders* (5th ed.). APA.

Baddeley, A. (2007). *Working memory thought and action*. Oxford University Press.

Davidson J., & Gottschalk, P. (2011). *Internet child sexual abuse: Current research and policy*. Routledge.

Erikson, E. (1998). *The life cycle completed: The extended version*. W.W. Norton.

Ferrari, P. F., & Coudé, G. (2018). *Mirror neurons, embodied emotions, and empathy*. In K. Meyza & E. Knapska (Eds.), *Neuronal correlates of empathy* (pp. 67–77). Elsevier.

Finkelhor, D. (1984). *Child sexual abuse: New theory and research*. Macmillan.

Goodyear-Brown, P. (2012). *The handbook of child sexual abuse: Identification, assessment and treatment*. John Wiley & Sons.

Greenberg, D. M., Firestone, P., Bradford, J. M., & Broom, I. (2000). Infantophiles. In L. B. Schlesinger (Ed.), *Serial offenders: Current thoughts, recent findings*. CRC Press.

Gregory, R. (1997). *Eye and brain: The psychology of seeing* (5th ed.). Princeton University Press.

Information Commissioners Office. (2020). *The children's code of practice*. https://ico.org.uk/about-the-ico/media-centre/news-and-blogs/2020/01/ico-publishes-code-of-practice-to-protect-children-s-privacy-online/.

Knibbs, C. (2022). *Children, technology, and healthy behaviour: How to help children thrive online*. Routledge.

Knibbs, C. (forthcoming). *Online harms and cybertrauma: Legal and harmful issues with children and young people*. Routledge.

Le Doux, J. (2015). *Anxious: The modern mind In the age of anxiety*. Oneworld.

Levine, P. (2005). *Healing trauma: Restoring the wisdom of your body*. Sounds True.

Levine P. (2008). *Healing trauma: A pioneering program for restoring the wisdom of your body*. Sounds True.

Livingstone, M. (2002). *Vision and art: The biology of seeing*. Harry N. Abrahams.

Pearce, J. (2019). *Child sexual exploitation: Why theory matters*. Policy Press.

Rothschild, B. (2003). *The body remembers casebook: Unifying methods and models in the treatment of trauma and PTSD*. W.W. Norton.

Van der Kolk, B. (1994). *The body keeps the score: Memory and the evolving psychobiology of post-traumatic stress*. Harvard Review of Psychiatry, 1(5), 253–265.

12 Autism, vulnerabilities and sexual issues

Vulnerabilities, how do they make a difference in this space?

For clarity: autistic spectrum disorder, neurodiversity and even the label Asperger's (still being used to date) are what I am discussing in this chapter based on several clients over the last decade or so. It contains a vignette of clients to begin a conversation with practitioners.

This is not a diagnostic or pathological chapter but one in which I am bringing curiosity to the reader and exploring the findings; it is *anecdotal* in the framing, but *not evidence-based*. Again, we are going to be struck by the *ethical constraints* of working with some of these client presentations and we need to have robust methods in place for researching this issue and how it ties to sexual identity, gender and maturation.

ASD, mental health support and gender

Bear with me as I tie together a perspective of synthesising of an issue I have noticed. I am not entirely sure that the need to ask about gender in every supportive setting that exists for children is helpful, aside from the pursuit of data collection. For what purposes do we need this information and how does this relate to the issues contained in this book? For example, I am aware that some helplines for children are collecting data about gender when children initially contact them and this means that in today's society children seeking help for mental health issues are aware they need to have their pronouns ready, just as you have your national insurance number ready when calling a governmental helpline, or your personally identifiable information ready when you call the bank.

What does this do in terms of special needs and the constant need to know 'what', 'who' and 'which' you are, so you can be typed or classified and how does this issue impact a child who is exposed to the sexual harms online discussed in this book? Take for example Joe, who is ten, is neurodivergent and is also identifying as bisexual (yes, children as young as five and six have

DOI: 10.4324/9781003364177-13

gender and sexuality identities and have discussed these in primary school settings); he goes online into a space where he can and does announce his pronouns, as he believes it is necessary, given the pressure from social media spaces and his peers, to name your pronouns and sexuality as a norm. What will he be exposed to, given that about five years ago the online space was not as busy or prevalent with the announcing, debating and vitriolic hatred of pronouns, sexuality or gender? This question is simply reframed as: what has the normative practice of pronouns created for children who were naive about and absent from this information, and how has it or is it shaping their experience of the online world?

We have inadvertently, through a change in our expectations in society, set the stage for the constant awareness of sex (biology), sex (the act) and sex(uality) for young children by continuous awareness campaigns, asking questions of children or the social media space and the polarised landscape of having to declare who you are. Innocence is afforded to those too young to comprehend the world and is more complex and confusing to those who have learning and social difficulties. I suspect it is confusing to children who are cognizant too and I for one am often perplexed as to the shape, progress and direction of our species at the moment; I can't imagine what a child must be going through.

Trauma applied to practice: what's missing from the current landscape?

Children, developmental processes and questions about sexual orientations

What I have seen in terms of the current education around some of the topics of sexual harm discussed in this book and how this is applied to special education needs (SEND), neurodiversity and social learning issues is the approach of rushing in, asking questions without due diligence or trauma-applied practice and deep knowledge about child development. Children with the kinds of vulnerabilities in this specific chapter often have support groups in the real world.

Some are faced with 'expert parent groups' online who do not fully understand the consequences of asking children about sexual issues, orientation, gender or who they are (self-representations) and can be operated by well-meaning individuals with a case history of one child or one family as the foundation for their expertise.

Or there are overarching assumptions that a broad-brush approach is helpful for all children with x diagnosis. Child development as a theory encompasses the growth and development of the psyche, unconscious processes, and the development of the self in many aspects and there are some professions and groups who have this as their foundational approach; however, I am often struck by the online space and the lack of this knowledge as the underpinning synthesis and integration for these support groups handing out advice to the parents who join them in the groups or follow them (this is also prevalent in other issues discussed in Knibbs (forthcoming)).

Writers and researchers who have studied child development in depth provide us with a wealth of knowledge from this discipline, and, as I mentioned briefly in the earlier chapters, we cannot wholly rely on retrospective theories or adult educators regarding children. We need to look at people in this field and there are so many who have brought to life the mind, brain and body connection *with and from* the eyes of those children.

We cannot utilise a broad brush or speculative approach with children, and the difficulty arises in how we can research and find the answers without traumatising children and young people, which I feel is the unintended outcome of the current climate in the fields of sexual and gender development research and education with children. This requires conversations at a much higher level than we currently seem to be employing and as a result children are exposed to harm by professionals and adults, which is further exacerbated by the online space, especially for those with vulnerabilities.

Child practitioners need a whole-istic education in this paradigm as the highest priority, and this requires deep knowledge of many areas. Peripheral understanding of the issues in this book has resulted in some child clients attending my clinic for post-trauma therapy that resulted from well-intended child therapists and practitioners with little or no knowledge of how a child develops using a coherent model such as interpersonal neurobiology. This approach synthesises neuroscience, biology, psychology, sociology, spirituality, epigenetics and the cognitive, moral, sexual and emotional aspects of a person. It includes trauma, mental health pathologies and safeguarding issues. It cannot be learned in a weekend or short course and we must look to educate those who work with children to understand and embody this knowledge. We owe it to the children to be excellent practitioners when working with their development. We know implicitly and explicitly that adults often seek to repair that which was missing, denied or screwed up in childhood.

For some excellent reads on child development in this paradigm see the Bibliography.

Vulnerabilities

Herein this word is applied to diagnoses given to children, such as autism and/ or neurodiversity (newer language changes have placed these terms together in recent years), SEND, psychological and pathological diagnoses, living in care settings and all forms of developmental, attachment and interpersonal trauma.

As I have previously said, 'vulnerable' is a noun and a verb when it comes to online spaces (Knibbs, 2022). However, when we add in vulnerabilities such as those mentioned here, we find that sexual issues can be fraught with multifactorial and layered complexities in this space. And human beings are complex.

I am going to discuss some anecdotal findings and conversations I have encountered over a decade with children in this area. You may find as a practitioner this is not your direct experience of how children have opened up about their use and confusion around these subject matters. However, I suspect most of the children and young people you work with around sexual issues in, of and from digital spaces are labelled with one of these 'diagnoses'. Furthermore, I think we are currently doing a disservice to children, pathologising them and using legal terminology reserved for adults who appear in the criminal justice system when engaging in sexually related behaviour and the online space, as their motives, intent and actual behaviours do not have the same level of developmental maturity as an adult.

To take a few of the mental health diagnoses and issues as they appear in the diagnostic manuals, they are often on referral forms, in conversations and meetings when the issue is related to sexual behaviours and online, and these are: attentional disorders, emotional regulation disorders, learning disorders, attachment disorders and social disorders alongside the setting in which the child or young person resides, such as residential, foster care, adoptive homes and kinship care. Pretty much in each case that I deal with, the entire spectrum of trauma or adverse experiences is also mentioned.

Given what was discussed in my previous book (Knibbs 2022), you can see that unmet relational needs in the corporeal world may well lead to the yearning and searching for these to be met by the other in the online spaces. This will likely lead to some, most or all of the issues named in this volume, and for children looking to be loved, sexual issues often have an affiliation with that feeling because often someone tells them they love them in this process. Why wouldn't they believe this if they have no real baseline with which to measure it, especially if someone tells them that 'this' is love?

Autism, neurodivergent thinking and confusion about sexual issues

When it comes to ASD in particular, I have noticed a frequent theme, confusion and use of the online space to navigate social issues such as sex, gender and identity in what can only be described as an attempt to reconcile and understand what is misunderstood. The many discussions I have had with my ASD-diagnosed clients around consent, sexting, appropriate sexual language, dating and approaching someone for a relationship, and the many confusions around pornography and content created by the client have been as follows (all identifying features removed):

Consent

17-YEAR-OLD CLIENT: I don't get it, you have to ask repeatedly, like keep asking for them to say yes? But isn't that annoying?

ME: Hmm, this seems to be a common question, and I think that you mean you would need them to clarify this with you with words?

CLIENT: Yeah because I couldn't be sure if they didn't say so, I just don't get the feeling part of it. So like how would I *know*? It's like a dream without borders.

ME: What a metaphor!

CLIENT AGED 16: So you would just ask them and then you would have s e x? [spells this out for me]

ME: Well, I don't think it's as simple as two steps like that as there are lots of mini or micro-steps along the way, but in principle, that's how it would work. Perhaps not directly asking someone to have sex with you without a warning, what we adults say is 'out of the blue'. So what do you think would be the steps to start this process and what would be the steps in between? Let's start with when you would ask someone for sex?

CLIENT: Well you know I said that I was going out with XXXX and they said that we needed to seal the deal, but I don't know what that means, but XXXX told me it meant I had to shag them and I am horrified about that. I mean do I just ask and see if they say yes and if they do what the hell do I do about it? What's the procedure?

ME: Ah, I think you might be looking for the social rules here and perhaps a road map so to speak of the what to do's? And I'm kind of wondering why this is so urgent as you spoke about this in the last few sessions. So maybe the consent lies with you to begin with, as this feels like the pressure you are under and discomfort about that?

CLIENT: Yeah, cos I have to seal the deal and do ... [makes vomiting noise]

ME: Ahh, I see. This 'stuff' is something you don't want to do and so this seems a great time to talk about you making choices that you are comfortable with and how you can express that to XXXXX because this does not feel like you are consenting. How about we look at that this session?

For the rest of the session the client and I discussed autonomy and being able to say no as a right, and peer pressure from a partner to 'seal the deal' and how this was causing distress, and this underpinned the lack of consent. We looked at ways that they could say no without feeling under duress, and so their partner would understand it didn't mean they were dumping them (though we discussed the outcome of not having sex may mean their partner could dump them).

CLIENT AGED 13 (PREVIOUSLY SEXUALLY ABUSED BY FATHER): So we were making out and I was like I don't wanna shag you. And he said it's not like you haven't done it before so you know what to do and probably would be good at it. We had been texting about this and I'd said this was something I wanted and that I had done it before. So I told him, no, and then like he said that he just wanted to see what it was like to go down on me [meaning oral sex] and that I didn't have to. But it was okay as his mum came back early so I just said I had to go home. I mean if I had then it wouldn't have been proper shagging if he went down on me and I am glad that XXXX came back. I'll make him wait. Can we make some moon dough? I don't wanna talk about this anymore.

With many of the clients who have an ASD diagnosis and a history of abuse behind them, they can often be confused as to what 'proper' sex is, given they may have been told lies and untruths by the perpetrator. Or in education about the reality of the online world, sex or relationships. Or they may not understand this on a cognitive level, which is often an issue for children with ASD. For example, they may not consider oral sex as being sex because their understanding is that vaginal penetrative sex is sex. It is also common for them to be in a different intelligence, social and emotional space from their peers around sex and sexual activity after exposure to it as it becomes a conversation they repeat in inappropriate settings or times (rather like echolalic repetitions). This can mean they do not seem to 'fit' with their peers as their comments are not understood by their peers and are considered disgusting, shameful or abusive and this is the reaction they often receive. If a child is a victim of contact abuse they can often talk in ways that mirror the perpetrator and this can be confusing for their peers (who do not necessarily know what they are talking about and have no experience with this type of language). Often, I find these clients when aged over 12–13 engaging in sexual activity of some description with older peers and most often this is sex talk (dirty talk as they often call it) in the online space.

This client in this example was in their words 'dating' an older person (who turned out to be another 13-year-old and not an adult masquerading as a child) and during our conversations, you can see that the topic about sex was changed once the client had said their piece. Often this is the case with shame, trauma, grief and sex-based topics and the pace is set by the clients in therapy, leaving an unspoken fear about 'when to approach the subject again'. The fear they tell me is that it will result in another safeguarding referral as they may be discussing further sexual abuse.

When it goes awry and ruptures occur, because I 'did my job'

I asked this client more questions about dating and sex for safeguarding reasons and, unfortunately, my timing was off in our therapeutic relationship, resulting in a breakdown of the session and the client having a 'meltdown' (her words) and then needing to speak with Mum and social care after the meeting to put safeguards in place. The client's response the week after was: 'I'm not fucking talking to you, you're just like them', as the client had her devices taken away (often a punitive measure) and the issue was escalated to services for grooming and sexual abuse.

It took many weeks of allying and pacing on my account to repair this and, to be truthful, I'm not sure I ever fully did. We live in a world where therapeutic alliances are teetering on the cliff edge so often with sexual issues and the online space.

Practitioner's pause for reflection

How do you explain consent as a concept when it is surrounding sexual activity to a child or young person too young to engage in sexual activity? And how do you explain consent to a young person who is 16 or above and may struggle with the concept and process if they have learning or social difficulties? And to posit a question to you, does this mean that young people old enough chronologically cannot engage in sexual activity if they cannot understand consent because of learning and social difficulties?

Do you think we need to change the current Sex-Ed approaches to include those with SEND beginning much earlier in life, given the contents of this book and the harms they can be exposed to at an earlier age, and how do we include gender, sex and identity, given the points above?

Porn viewing

CLIENT AGED 16 MALE, CONSIDERING THEY MIGHT BE TRANS, OR GAY: But I was told to look at it [porn] on a forum and they [forum members] said if I got a hard-on then that was because I must be gay at the least. I didn't but then I found myself looking at the weird stuff and now I don't have a clue. Sometimes I get a hard-on and the gay porn seems boring and sometimes I get a hard-on looking at the other stuff. Help me Cath, am I gay or trans?

CLIENT AGED 14: Well I saw it on Snap and of course, I was looking at the language and so I just googled it. But I know that rankings are paid for so I would have to likely subscribe to those so I just used a Reddit link to follow and I was on a less popular site but FML the stuff on there is weird, like with straps and these things that gag people. It was like one of them horror movies, you know hostel and when they stop them scream-ing. And who would want to do that? Do I have to do that 'cos some of my mates are cosplaying and on those forums so that means they do? It's all weird and I don't know what I'm supposed to like but I do use it for wanking. Mostly wanking as I don't have an imagination and I can't snap people for this stuff as that's illegal.

CLIENT AGED 18: I use Discord and Pornhub, but it's okay as XXXX [foster carer] doesn't know it's on my phone, I just don't use it on the computer and then she doesn't know. I do delete my history too just in case she checks my phone and I always search for something about art in case she thinks I don't use the internet. [laughs]

But I did want to ask, is the stuff in the bedrooms real Cath, that's normal sex? So those people are okay with people like me watching because they are doing it for us to watch? I mean my boyfriend sends me links all the time on discord and they [the boyfriend] watch porn too, the real stuff, so it's real people and not the ones who get paid in Lamborghinis as that's acting isn't it?

ME: Yup, it's all real, it's a professional recording studio and equipment for that purpose. As you say, paid in Lamborghinis, that makes me think you know about the stars of porn, and you consider them to be rich? But it is all real, it's people having sex in lots of different ways for sure but it's most certainly real. I wonder if you mean real like 'scripted' versus unscripted like a play or a film?

CLIENT: maybe, I just got told by XXXX that porn is not real and I should not be taken in by it; I've got to learn it though because that's not what people do is it and what happens when I get into a real relationship? But there are real people on there.

This client also was the first to explain lolly porn many years ago, a term I had not heard about but a few weeks later another two clients mentioned it. It seems that clients tend to discuss the same trends at the same time and so this was more than interesting as to why this term and style of porn was becoming a part of my therapy room 'newsfeed'. This resulted in a blog about this issue, which is to discuss the content of cartoonised porn, including child sexual abuse.

Practitioner's pause for reflection

This real versus not real argument is often given to children and young people with SEND and ASD diagnoses, from a well-intended place, about content on the Internet and especially regarding pornography.

This following statement is to clarify why we must be truthful: *it is very real*, it may be professionally recorded or not, but the actions that the people are engaging in are real and those people on the videos have likely discussed, consented, agreed or otherwise to the set of behaviours they will engage in. Some of the sites have videos where people have not consented or agreed to this, and you cannot always tell whether the people on the videos have or have not agreed. Either way, the behaviour is real and the acts are indeed real. The child could be watching a rape or sexual assault, or they could be watching a consensual process. There's no contract showing, no consenting process that's recorded pre-sexual activity and even if there was a scene showing conversation, contract signing and agreement before the main act of the sex scenes, would it be true consent?

This is why pornography is at times not a good decision to watch because it could be a crime. It is, however, real in every sense. This may change shortly with Deepfakes and so that is when we can attend to this real versus not real debate.

Children and young people with ASD may not be able to tell whether the people in the videos are of age, underage or close to the legal age if we don't prepare them for this fact too. I would also lean on the fact that many adults cannot tell the age of some younger adults in these films and so conversations about crime and consent may form a better discussion about this content than 'don't do it' or 'oh darling that stuffs not real'.

ASD and online grooming

Many of the clients I have worked with who have been groomed online have fallen under the diagnostic criteria of ASD and ADHD alongside other vulnerabilities such as living in a residential setting, adopted or foster care settings. That is not to say children outside of this cohort do not get groomed online but it is certainly a major factor in all the clients I have seen over the last decade. Those subtleties in communication are often missed by children with ASD diagnoses, akin to not quite getting the sarcastic tone or element of a conversation. The need to be seen, soothed, safe and secure form the primary goal, approach and connection model being manipulated by the perpetrators. And where they may need to do less 'trickster' work in using subtle approaches and can give more direct commands that are followed without questions or unease by the child, it makes the process much easier for the perpetrators.

Moreover, the skills required to notice subliminal, gentle coercion, grooming and manipulation are the very ones often difficult for this cohort of clients to understand, due to the subtleties of this kind of social communication. This skill could be taught in many ways in the earlier years; however, this is often missing, omitted or impossible due to the chaos in the home and education settings that surround children with vulnerabilities.

And so, we face a catch-22 situation when we consider the fact these children need education in the grooming process and how they can notice it and ask for help, given the difficulties they have with learning those very skills. Often they struggle with peer relationships and so developing those skills in action is difficult. Sadly the adults in those settings are not always present, are busy, are struggling to manage many children (e.g. teachers) and cannot spend enough time with those children to help them learn social skills beyond the basics. *Groomers rely on this fact* and hence this is an area for us to work on in online safety, citizenship and media literacy and one size does not fit all with this cohort of children.

CLIENT AGED 13: [this client sent an image of themselves in cosplay to another child and groups online and the language they used with the image was explicit which is how and why they were brought to me.] He said he was my friend Cath, and he didn't buy me gifts which the teacher told me was what groomers do. We learned that in class, and he just talked to me so how was I supposed to know? He was into the same things, like Witcher and XXXXX [removed as this could identify the client as it is a niche area] and we both liked Marvel better than DC so that's what we talked about. He was kind to me and helped me with my friends at school and that meant I could have mates over for tea like the other kids. I didn't sense anything wrong or anything like that stuff they say on the videos, and anyway it's not sex like they taught because I didn't ever meet him. I don't understand what I did wrong or why I got done as I did?

['getting done' is a Yorkshire term for getting into trouble]

CLIENT 8: They just asked where mum and dad were and told me which buttons to press to make it go off-screen. I told them mum and dad were in the garden and they showed me some other children they were talking to just like me. They were my friends. They showed me how to create a profile on dating apps and how to talk to grownups.

(This client was recruiting other children via DM and asking adults if they liked sex. This child provided over a hundred images over a few months to unknown perpetrators.)

CLIENT 13: It's just funny innit and I don't care. I fucking hate my parents, I hate my dad and he can fuck off, this is my boyfriend and I'm gonna be a boy so it doesn't matter. My mate says this is okay because they do it and they are a boy now so that's what I'm going to do. I play role-play with them on XXXXX and that's how we became friends. They are my age so I don't care. I like them and this is funny. Even when they send the lezza porn to show me why being a boy is better and it's just funny.

CLIENT 15: It's not how it happens, I could have screamed as we were all watching *Corrie* [*Coronation Street*] and they just did that story. My parents think that's how it happened to me, but I dint 'cos they were my age and we talked about it loads in school. I got told it was consent 'cos I said yes because they said it was a sex party and I'm almost old enough. I thought it was okay 'cos I had some booze with the others, but I didn't like the taste of it. And I've been back to that place loads of times now. I even looked at it on google earth cos I think someone could have seen it. They took pictures too but I don't know which ones were sent. They just kept talking to me on DM and no one would believe me!

Many soap operas have tried to address grooming plots; however, they had not covered online grooming, and this client was angry at this fact, due to the difficulty in not being able to generalise the storyline to her experience of online grooming, which then transitioned to the real world sexual offences that took place, and was filmed. She struggled with the narrative in the soap opera because it wasn't like her story, and the educational difficulties she was diagnosed with made for a lengthy explanation about stories being used as an example and not a person's direct experience. Generalising from the grooming story to hers was our process for a long time. Her confusion around consent and the grooming was more difficult as the groomers were peers her age and younger, adding to the complexity of lessons she had received about groomers being adults.

A further issue that we faced involved the professionals who had initially seen this girl telling her she had consented, because she said yes (under duress) and that she was attending sex parties as that was the focus of the behaviour after consuming alcohol.

Back to consent

The main conversation I have with ASD-diagnosed clients and this issue here is what constitutes consent and how the groomer persuades them they 'gave consent', or are manipulated into believing that what they are doing is okay because it's not penetrative acts carried out by the perpetrator and therefore doesn't match the education they have received about sex. This does not mean they have not received this education, far from it, but it does seem that ASD-diagnosed children and young people need a high-end explanation and perhaps even definitions through conversations to help them understand the grooming process.

Perpetrators are very excelled at the art of 'this is not that' and so the children and young people I work with can justify their actions as being okay, when in fact they are often the ones who can be easily manipulated by the 'confidence' of the trickster. Absolutes help them feel safe and if the perpetrators can say it is so then this can often mean for them it is safe to do and engage in the behaviour when in reality it is unsafe.

Moreover, ASD-diagnosed clients struggle with sarcasm, and nuances of intent and so may miss the 'signs' often taught in PSHE programmes around grooming. They likely share more personal information with perpetrators as I often find in practice that ASD-diagnosed clients speak out and 'tell the truth' with no filters of shame, embarrassment or applicability to a situation. For example, they will tell you how itchy their bottom is when they are in the reception area and surrounded by other people as there is often a lack of situational awareness or appropriateness. And if your bum is itchy, why not tell people so they know?

Practitioner's pause for reflection

Imagine having to explain how a perpetrator operates in detail to a child with ASD or SEND. Now imagine visiting that child in an education setting and telling them to accompany you on their own to a room where you can speak with them alone so you can carry out your assessment. But this situation is okay because you are one of the 'good professionals'. Irony in action?

It is imperative that we discern for them the good versus bad analogy, and allow children to say no to us, the professionals – for them to be able to say this to another adult or peer (see Chapter 6 on consent). Professionals groom and abuse too, and children need empowerment to be able to say no, even if it means we can't do our job at that moment or on that day.

Social appropriateness

ASD and text, sext and sexual imagery of self and other

1. Show me your tits LOL
2. I would wanna rape you like …
3. I just want to know how you taste

These are texts some of my ASD-diagnosed clients have sent and here was their understanding of what they meant, or what they thought would happen.

CLIENT 1 AGED 12: I thought they would poke them out like this [puffs out chest] I didn't know it meant boobs without a bra!

CLIENT 2 AGED 9: I was copying what I heard on COD and I don't know what it means. I thought it was like a no-scope headshot. I don't know why they blocked me. What does it mean anyway?

CLIENT 3 AGED 13: I thought it meant to kiss them and you can taste their dinner. I didn't know it was rude!

For many of us, we have learned this sexual language, and at school its use is often as rife as it is online. However, my ASD-diagnosed clients struggle with this language, are often overly fascinated by it more so than my non-ASD-diagnosed clients and seem to spend an inordinate amount of time in my clinic asking questions about or searching the Internet about these words and their meanings.

Sexual language is loaded with innuendo, hidden psychological messages piggybacking on the social message we use; for example, 'would you like to come in for coffee' does not always mean that! This type of artistic semantics confuses them, they don't understand what it is they are being asked, and if they can use the language and are not rebuffed by the ones they send it to then they develop a way to integrate this into their development, as do other children, and this is how we learn when and where sexual language is appropriate. However, they can and do send a message loaded with sexual inferences and it is offensive, out of the blue and can be harmful if it is aggressive or sexist in nature.

Clear, unambiguous and explicit

Hints are not necessarily understood and so open dialogue with children and young people with ASD means we have to be unambiguous, transparent and explicit (not swearing but clear) when we discuss these topics with them.

Many children and young people are entering into a space where they are trying out new language in online spaces that often result in rejection, cajoling and being reported for harassment. There is a rise in children and young people in my clinic 'not getting it' and finding other hidden channels in which to explore (not described here) and this worries me as those spaces can be dark in nature and unhelpful to socially desirable behaviours and may result in many more children being criminalised as I suspect is happening with sexually harmful behaviours being carried out by children. Some will be criminalised for 'being' a child *with* ASD or SEND and repeating words, phrases or behaviours they have seen online, particularly in unregulated spaces that also have polarised or racist, gender/homophobic, sexist and sexual content (this also applies to radicalisation and Incel material).

Often ASD-diagnosed children think along the lines that 'rude' is when it comes to toilet humour and not sexual abuse or violence unless someone tells them this. Often sexual imagery that is sent (via text messages for example) is seen in this way too; it isn't cared about by the child in the same way as a child who sees the consequences; for example, my ASD-diagnosed clients often say in the sessions they don't care if a police officer sees it, or if someone shares it, and they often have less bodily shame (which may or may not be due to ASD). Asking or sending nudes is seen as a normality for many young people and intent to harm, shock or otherwise would have to be discussed and talked through. This is often logical in nature, too, with my clients when we talk, without the understanding of harm to others, which of course requires a theory of mind, empathy and mentalisation capacities which are often the issue with ASD diagnoses.

Reflection for practitioners

ASD and sexual activity are complicated enough on their own, and you will need to assess the level of comprehension in a child about sex, sexual activity, harm, intent, causation and outcomes on a case by case basis. You may need to consider gender and sexual identity as part of this process and of course the influences surrounding the child who may be struggling with the social intelligence aspect of our mating rituals as adolescents and adults.

For me, this is the most complicated chapter and one that I take on a case-by-case basis. Given the prevalence of what used to be called peer-to-peer and child-to-child abuse, we are looking at sexually harmful behaviour (a term that is still disputed and difficult to define as this is based on the victim and legal framing), which is on the increase and, of course, the causality of this may be pointed towards porn, the Internet or gaming. However, I ask you to notice how many more children (and adults) have a diagnosis of ASD in today's society. Moreover, do notice how many more TV and film productions show more sexually explicit content before the watershed and, of course, the reality TV shows aired that are all about 'love' but mean sex and mating. What about music videos and songs that are explicit and do not fall privy to the same ratings as TV, film and cinema? And what about the use of language in today's society that in times gone by would have 'made the soldiers blush!'

Can we blame one thing alone or are we all just as confused as some of the children mentioned in this chapter? What are the right kinds of advice, education and processes that we need? Don't forget, I am one voice in this, bringing anecdotal evidence here because we haven't got any robust research to provide us with the answers yet.

References

Knibbs, C. (2022). *Children, technology, and healthy development.* Routledge.

Knibbs, C. (forthcoming). *Online harms and cybertrauma: Legal and harmful issues with children and young people.* Routledge.

References

American Psychiatric Association. (2013). *Diagnostic and statistical manual of mental disorders* (5th ed.). APA.

Anti Bullying Alliance. (2022). Cyberbullying definition. https://anti-bullyingalliance. org.uk/.

Atrill-Smith, A., Fullwood, C., Keep, M., & Kuss, D. (2019). *The Oxford handbook of cyberpsychology*. Oxford University Press.

Baddeley, A. (2007). *Working memory thought and action*. Oxford University Press.

Bailenson, J. (2021). Nonverbal overload: A theoretical argument for the causes of Zoom fatigue. *Technology, Mind and Behaviour, 2(1)*, https://doi.org/10.1037/ tmb0000030.

Baker, P., & Norton, L. (2019). *Fat loss forever*. Amazon print on demand.

Ball, M. (2022). *The Metaverse and how it will revolutionise everything*. Liveright Publishing Corporation.

Bandura, A. (1973). *Aggression: A social learning analysis*. Prentice Hall.

Bandura, A., & Walters, R. H. (1977). *Social learning theory* (Vol. 1). Prentice Hall.

Bandura, A., Ross, D., & Ross, S. A. (1961). Transmission of aggression through imitation of aggressive models. *The Journal of Abnormal and Social Psychology, 63(3)*, 575.

Barret, L., Dunbar, R., & Lycett, J. (2002). *Human evolutionary psychology*. Palgrave Macmillan.

Bauman, S. (2011). *Cyberbullying: What counselors need to know*. American Counseling Organization.

Bean, A., Daniel, E., & Hays, S. (2020). *Integrating geek culture into therapeutic practice: The clinician's guide to geek therapy*. Leyline Publishing.

Benton, D., & Young, H. (2016). A meta-analysis of the relationship between brain dopamine receptors and obesity: A matter of changes in behaviour rather than food addiction? *International Journal of Obesity, 40(1)*, S12–S21.

Berne, E. (1964). *Games people play: The psychology of human relationships*. Penguin.

Berne, E. (1970). *Sex in human loving*. Penguin.

Besharat Mann, R., & Blumberg, F. (2022). Adolescents and social media: The effects of frequency of use, self-presentation, social comparison, and self-esteem on possible self-imagery. *Acta Psychologica, 228*, 103629. https://doi.org/10.1016/j. actpsy.2022.103629.

Boffey, P. (1987). *Infants' sense of pain is recognized, finally*. www.nytimes. com/1987/11/24/science/infants-sense-of-pain-is-recognized-finally.html.

Bradshaw, S., & Howard, P. (2019). *The global disinformation order: 2019 Global Inventory of Organised Social Media Manipulation*. Oxford Internet. https://demtech.oii. ox.ac.uk/wp-content/uploads/sites/93/2019/09/CyberTroop-Report19.pdf.

British Board of Film Classification. (2020). *Young people, pornography & age-verification*. Accessed via BBFC directly, Personal Communication: Email, 2020.

Brown, B. (2017). *Braving the wilderness: The quest for true belonging and the courage to stand alone*. Random House.

Burgess, J., & Green, J. (2019). *YouTube* (2nd ed.). Polity Press.

Burrow, A., & Rainone, N. (2017). How many *likes* did I get?: Purpose moderates links between positive social media feedback and self-esteem. *Journal of Experimental Social Psychology, 69*, 232–236.

Buss, D. (2004). *Evolutionary psychology: The new science of the mind* (2nd ed.). Pearson.

Buss, D. (2016). *The evolution of desire: Strategies of human mating*. Basic Books.

Buss, D. (2021). *Bad men: The hidden roots of sexual deception, harassment and assault*. Robinson.

Cantor, J. (2009). *Conquer cyber overload: Get more done, boost your creativity and reduce stress*. Cyberoutlook Press.

Carse, J. (1986). *Finite and Infinite Games. A vision of life as play and possibility*. Free Press.

Carter, S., & Getz, L. (1993). Monogamy and the prairie vole. *Scientific American, 268*, 100–106.

Centre For Disease Control. (2010). *National intimate partner and sexual violence survey*. www.cdc.gov/violenceprevention/pdf/nisvs_report2010-a.pdf.

Children's Commissioner UK. (2022). *The things I wish my parents had known: Young people's advice on talking to your child about online sexual harassment*. www.childrenscommissioner.gov.uk/report/talking-to-your-child-about-online-sexual-harassment-a-guide-for-parents/.

Christiansen, A., DeKloet, A., Ulrich-Lai, Y., & Herman, J. (2011). 'Snacking' causes long-term attenuation of HPA axis stress responses and enhancement of brain FosB/deltaFosB expression in rats. *Physiology & Behavior, 103*, 111–116.

Coleman, J. (2019). *Why won't my teenager talk to me?* (2nd ed.). Routledge.

Coles, M. (2015). *Towards the compassionate school: From golden rule to golden thread*. University College London.

Coles, M., & Gent, B. (Eds.). (2022). *Education for survival: The pedagogy of compassion*. University College London.

Collins Dictionary. 'Muckbang' definition. www.collinsdictionary.com/dictionary/english/mukbang.

Collins Dictionary. Information, misinformation and disinformation. www.collinsdictionary.com/dictionary/english/information.

Collins, M. (n.d.). www.mariecollinsfoundation.org.uk/.

Consilience Project. Technology is not values neutral. https://consilienceproject.org/technology-is-not-values-neutral/.

Cozolino, L. (2006). *The neuroscience of human relationships: Attachment and the developing social brain* (2nd ed.). W.W. Norton.

Crown Prosecution Service. (2017). *Revenge porn: The legal definitions in respect of criminal prosecutions*. www.cps.gov.uk/legal-guidance/revenge-pornography-guidelines-prosecuting-offence-disclosing-private-sexual.

Csikszentmihalyi, M. (1992, 2002). *Flow: The classic work on how to achieve happiness*. Rider.

Csikszentmihalyi, M. (1997). *Creativity: The psychology of discovery and invention*. Harper Perennial.

Culata, R. (2021). *Digital for good: Raising kids to thrive in an online world*. Harvard Business Review Press.

Culloty, E., & Suiter, J. (2021). *Disinformation and manipulation in digital media: Information pathologies.* Routledge.

Davidson, J., & Gottschalk, P. (2011). *Internet child sexual abuse: Current research and policy.* Routledge.

de Becker, G. (1997). *The gift of fear: Survival signals that protect us from violence.* Dell Publishing.

Delahooke, M. (2020). *Beyond behaviours: Using brain science and compassion to understand and solve children's behavioural challenges.* John Murray Learning.

Delahooke, M. (2022). *Brain–body parenting: How to stop managing behavior and start raising joyful, resilient kids.* Harper Wave.

Department for Education. (2018). Working together to safeguard children: a guide to inter-agency working to safeguard and promote the welfare of children. https://assets.publishing.service.gov.uk/government/uploads/system/uploads/attachment_data/file/942454/Working_together_to_safeguard_children_inter_agency_guidance.pdf.

Department for Education. (2021). Harmful online challenges and hoaxes. www.gov.uk/government/publications/harmful-online-challenges-and-online-hoaxes/harmful-online-challenges-and-online-hoaxes.

Dick, P. (1962). *The man in the high castle.* Putnam.

Dick, P. (1968). *Do androids dream of electric sheep?* Doubleday.

Digital, Culture, Media and Sport Committee. (2021). *Second Report of Session 2019–21, Misinformation in the COVID-19 Infodemic (HC 234).* https://committees.parliament.uk/publications/1954/documents/19089/default/.

Dines, G. (2010). *Pornland: How porn has hijacked our sexuality.* Beacon Press.

Donovan, S. (2022). *The strange and curious guide to trauma.* Jessica Kingsley.

Duffy, J. (2019). *Parenting the new teen in the age of anxiety: A complete guide to your child's stressed, depressed, expanded amazing adolescence.* Mango Publishing.

Edwards, D. (2018). *Animal moves: How to move like an animal to get you leaner, fitter, stronger and healthier for life.* Explorer Publishing.

Erikson, E. (1998). *The life cycle completed: The extended version.* W.W. Norton.

Ernst, F. (1971). The OK corral: The grid or get-on-with. *Transactional Analysis Journal, 1(4),* 33–42.

Etchells, P. (2019). *Lost in a good game: Why we play video games and what they can do for us.* Icon Books.

Ey, L., & McInnes, E. (2020). *Harmful sexual behaviour in young children and pre-teens: An education issue.* Routledge Focus.

Eysenk, M., & Keane, M. (2000). *Cognitive Psychology: A Student's Handbook* (4th ed.). Psychology Press.

Feldman, Barratt L., Lewis M., & Haviland-Jones, J. (2016). *The handbook of emotions* (4th ed.). Guilford Press.

Ferrari, P. F., & Coudé, G. (2018). Mirror neurons, embodied emotions, and empathy. In *Neuronal correlates of empathy* (pp. 67–77). Elsevier.

Festinger, L., Riecken, H., & Schacter, S. (2009). *When prophecy fails.* Martino Publishing.

Fetzer, J. (2004). Information, misinformation, and disinformation. *Minds and Machines, 14* (2), 223–229.

Finkelhor, D. (1984). *Child sexual abuse: New theory and research.* Macmillan.

Fonagy, P. (2001). *Attachment theory and psychoanalysis.* Routledge.

Fonagy, P., Gergely, G., Jurist, E., & Target, M. (2004). *Affect regulation, mentalization and the development of the self.* Routledge.

Freud, S. (1955). Beyond the pleasure principle. In *The standard edition of the complete psychological works of Sigmund Freud, Volume XVIII (1920–1922): Beyond the pleasure principle, group psychology and other works* (pp. 1–64). Hogarth.

Gayle, D. (2017). Claims of child-on-child sexual offences soar in England and Wales. *The Guardian*. www.theguardian.com/uk-news/2017/feb/03/claims-child-sexual-offences-soar-england-and-wales-police-barnardos.

Gazzelay, A., & Rosen, L. (2016). *A distracted mind: Ancient brains in a technological world*. MIT Press.

Geher, G., & Kaufman, S. (2013). *Mating intelligence unleashed: The role of the mind in sex, dating and love*. Oxford University Press.

Gerhardt, S. (2014). *Why love matters: How affection shapes a baby's brain*. Routledge.

Gilbert, P. (2010). *The compassionate mind: A new approach to life's challenges* (revised edition). Constable.

Goldacre, B. (2008). *Bad science*. Fourth Estate.

Goldsmith, J., & Wu, T. (2008). *Who controls the internet: Illusions of a borderless world*. Oxford University Press.

Goleman, D. (1995),.*Emotional intelligence*. Bloomsbury.

Goleman, D., & Davidson, R. (2017). *Altered traits: Science reveals how meditation changes your mind, brain and body*. Avery.

Goodyear-Brown, P. (2012). *The handbook of child sexual abuse: Identification, assessment and treatment*. John Wiley & Sons.

Grant, R., & Naylor, D. (1990). *Better than life*. Viking.

Greenberg, D. M., Firestone, P., Bradford, J. M., & Broom, I. (2000). Infantophiles. In L. Schlesinger (Ed.), *Serial offenders: Current thoughts, recent findings* (pp. 229–246). CRC Press.

Greenfield, S. (2014). *Brain change: How digital technologies are leaving their mark on our brains*. Rider.

Gregory, R. (1997). *Eye and brain: The psychology of seeing* (5th ed.). Princeton University Press.

Haidt, J. (2012). *The righteous mind: Why good people are divided by politics and religion*. Penguin.

Hanson, R. (2018). *Resilient: Find your inner strength*. Rider.

Harding, D. (2006). *On having no head: Zen and the rediscovery of the obvious*. Inner Directions Publishing.

Hare, S. (2022). *Technology is not neutral: A short guide to technology ethics*. London Publishing Partnership.

Hargittai, E., & Sandvig, C. (2015). *Digital research confidential: The secrets of studying behaviour online*. MIT Press.

Hay, J. (2015). *Windows to the world*. United Kingdom Association Transactional Analysis Conference, Blackpool.

Haye, S., & Jeffries, S. (2015). Romantic terrorism. In *Romantic terrorism: An auto-ethnography of domestic violence, victimization and survival*. Palgrave Pivot.

Hebb, D. (1966). *The organization of behavior: A neuropsychological theory*. John Wiley & Sons.

Hibberd, G. H. (2022). *The art of cybersecurity: A practical guide to winning the war on cybercrime*. IT Governance Publishing.

Hirrons, P. (2020). Viewers horrified at erect penis onscreen. www.entertainment-daily.co.uk/tv/viewers-horrified-at-unacceptable-channel-4-documentary-that-showed-erect-penises-onscreen/.

Horton, D., & Wohl, R. R. (1956). Mass communication and para-social interaction. *Psychiatry: Journal for the Study of Interpersonal Processes, 19*, 215–229.

Hughes, D. (2011). *Attachment-focused family therapy workbook.* W.W. Norton.

Huxley, A. (1932, printed 1994). *Brave new world.* Vintage.

Information Commissioners Office. (2020). *The children's code of practice.* https://ico.org.uk/about-the-ico/media-centre/news-and-blogs/2020/01/ico-publishes-code-of-practice-to-protect-children-s-privacy-online/.

Internet Watch Foundation. (2018). Once upon a year, annual report. www.iwf.org.uk/media/tthh3woi/once-upon-a-year-iwf-annual-report-2018.pdf.

Jaegle, A., Mehrpour, V., & Rust, N. (2019). Visual novelty, curiosity, and intrinsic reward in machine learning and the brain. *Current opinion in neurobiology, 58*, 167–174.

James, E. (2012). *Fifty shades of grey.* Cornerstone Publishing.

Joyce, H. (2021). *Trans: When ideology meets reality.* Oneworld.

Kahneman, D. (2012). *Thinking fast and slow.* Penguin.

Kain, K., & Terrel, S. (2018). *Nurturing resilience: Helping clients move forward from developmental trauma. An integrative somatic approach.* North Atlantic Books.

Kandel, E., Scwartz, J., Jessel, T., Seigelbaum, S., & Hudspeth, A. (2013). *Principles of neuroscience* (5th ed.). McGraw Hill Medical.

Karpman, S. (1968). Drama triangle script drama analysis. *Transactional Analysis Bulletin, 7(26)*, 39–43.

Kaufman, S. (2020). *Transcend: The new science of self-actualization.* TarcherPerigree.

Kaufman, S., & Gregoire, C. (2016). *Wired to create: Unravelling the mysteries of the creative mind.* TarcherPerigree.

Kaufman, S. B. (2013). *Ungifted: The truth about talent, practice, creativity, and many paths to greatness.* Basic Books.

Kaufman, S. B. (2020). *Transcend: The new science of self-actualization.* Tarcherperigree.

Kaur, P., Dhir, A., Tandon, A., Alzeiby, E., & Abohassan, A. (2021). A systematic literature review on cyberstalking: An analysis of past achievements and future promises. *Technological Forecasting and Social Change, 163.* https://doi.org/ 10.1016/j.techfore.2020.120426.

Kaye, L. (2017). What your emoji says about you. TEDx Vienna. www.ted.com/talks/linda_kaye_what_your_emoji_says_about_you.

Kaye, L. (2022). *Issues and debates in cyberpsychology.* Oxford University Press.

Kerig, P., Ludlow, A., & Wenar, C. (2012). *Developmental psychopathology: From infancy through to adolescence* (6th ed.). McGraw-Hill Education.

Kidd, C., & Hayden, B. (2015). The psychology and neuroscience of curiosity. *Neuron, 88(3)*, 449–460.

Kimmel, S. B., & Mahalik, J. R. (2004). Measuring masculine body ideal distress: Development of a measure. *International Journal of Men's Health, 3*, 1–10.

Kirby, J. (2022). *Choose compassion: Why it matters and how it works.* University of Queensland Press.

Knibbs, C. (2012). Sex, lies and social networking. Workshop for UKCP CYP Conference, London.

Knibbs, C. (2016). *Cybertrauma: The darker side of the internet.* Self-published and available on Amazon kindle and Blurb Books.

Knibbs, C., Goss, S., & Anthony, K. (2017). Counsellors' phenomenological experiences of working with children or young people who have been cyberbullied: Using thematic analysis of semi structured interviews. *International Journal of Technoethics, 8*, 68–86.

Knibbs, C. (2018). *Presenters, media and conferences: Cybertrauma by the experts.* https://childrenandtech.co.uk/2021/05/21/presenters-media-and-conferences-cybertrauma-by-experts-the-shock-factor/.

Knibbs, C. (2019). Fit, fat or frumpy? The effects of social media (writ large). BACP Private Practitioners Conference, 28 September, London BACP.

Knibbs, C. (2019). The human algorithm. https://childrenandtech.co.uk/2021/05/21/the-human-algorithm-that-schools-and-parents-feed-through-fear-concerning-social-media-trends/.

Knibbs, C. (2022). *Children, technology, and healthy development.* Routledge.

Knibbs, C. (forthcoming). *Online harms and cybertrauma: Legal and harmful issues with children and young people.* Routledge.

Kohlberg, L., & Turiel, E. (1971). Moral development and moral education. In: L. Kohlberg (Ed.), *Collected papers on moral development and moral education* (pp. 410–465). Scott, Foresman & Company.

Kotler, S. (2014). *The rise of superman: Decoding the science of ultimate human performance.* Houghton Mifflin Harcourt.

Kowert, R. (2021). Jargon schmargon: Parasocial relationships. Psychgeist channel on YouTube. www.youtube.com/watch?v=Zjl2BFv0Z74.

Kuhn, K. (2022). The constant mirror: Self-view and attitudes to virtual meetings. *Computers n Human Behaviour.* https://doi.org/10.1016/j.chb.2021.107110.

Kurzweil, R. (2005). *The singularity is near: When humans transcend biology.* Viking.

Lamb, S., & Gilbert, J. (2019). *The Cambridge handbook of sexual development: Childhood and adolescence.* Cambridge University Press.

Lanier, J. (2010). *You are not a gadget.* Alfred A. Knopf.

Lanier, J. (2013). *Who owns the future?* Penguin.

Lanier, J. (2017). *Dawn of the new everything. A journey through virtual reality.* Bodley Head.

Lanier, J. (2018). *Ten arguments for deleting your social media accounts right now.* Bodley Head.

Le Doux, J. (2015). *Anxious: The modern mind In the age of anxiety.* Oneworld.

Lembke, A. (2021). *Dopamine nation: Finding balance in the age of indulgence.* Headline.

Levine, P. (2005). *Healing trauma: Restoring the wisdom of your body.* Sounds True.

Levine P. (2008). *Healing trauma: A pioneering program for restoring the wisdom of your body.* Sounds True.

Lieberman, D., & Long, M. (2019). *The molecule of more: How a single chemical in your brain drives, love sex, creativity, and will determine the fate of the human race.* Benbella Books.

Livingstone, M. (2002). *Vision and art: The biology of seeing.* Harry N. Abrahams.

Longo, V. (2018). *The longevity diet" Discover the new science to slow aging fight disease and manage your weight.* Penguin Press.

LSE Consulting. (2021). Rapid evidence assessment on online misinformation and media literacy. www.ofcom.org.uk/__data/assets/pdf_file/0011/220403/rea-online-misinformation.pdf.

Lukianoff, G., & Haidt, J. (2018). *The coddling of the American mind: How good intentions and bad ideas are setting up a generation for failure.* Penguin.

Maslow, A. H. (1943). A theory of human motivation. *Psychological Review, 50*(4), 370–396.

Maslow, A. H. (1962). *Toward a psychology of being.* D. Van Nostrand.

Matos, N., & Winsley, R. J. (2007). The trainability of young athletes and overtraining. *Journal of Sports Science & Medicine, 6*(3), 353.

McGilchrist, I. (2019). *The master and his emissary: The divided brain and the making of the western world*. Yale University Press.

McGilchrist, I. (2021). *The matter with things: Our brains, our delusions and the unmaking of the world*. Perspectiva Press.

Megele, C. (2018). *Safeguarding children and young people online: A guide for practitioners*. Policy Press.

Merleau-Ponty, M. (2002). *Husserl at the limits of phenomenology* (Including texts by Edmund Husserl). North Western University Press.

Merriam-Webster Dictionary. www.merriam-webster.com/dictionary/consent.

Merzencich, M. (2013). *Soft-wired: How the new science of brain plasticity can change your life*. Parnassus Publishing.

Miller, G. (1956). The magical number seven, plus or minus two: Some limits on our capacity for processing information. *Psychological Review, 63*, 81–89.

Moss, M. (2013). *Salt, sugar, fat: How the food giants hooked us*. Random House.

Music, G. (2017). *Nurturing natures: Attachment and children's emotional, sociocultural and brain development* (2nd ed.). Routledge.

Music, G. (2022). *Respark: Igniting hope and joy after trauma and depression*. Mind Nurturing Books.

Nagasoki, E. (2015, revised 2021). *Come as you are: The surprising new science that will transform your sex life*. Scribe.

Naidoo, U. (2020). *This is your brain on food: An indispensable guide to the surprising foods that fights depression, PTSD, anxiety, OCD and more*. Little Brown Spark.

National Centre for Missing and Exploited Children. www.missingkids.org/HOME.

National Society for the Protection of Children. www.nspcc.org.uk/.

Nelson, R., & Kriegsfeld, L. (2023). *An introduction to behavioural endocrinology* (6th ed.). Oxford University Press.

Neufeld, G., & Mate, G. (2019). *Hold onto your kids: Why parents need to matter more than peers*. Vermillion.

New York Times. (2022). A dad took photos of His Naked Toddler for the Doctor. Google Flagged Him as a Criminal. www.nytimes.com/2022/08/21/technology/google-surveillance-toddler-photo.html.

Nielsen Hibbing, A., & Rankin-Erickson, J. (2003). A picture is worth a thousand words: Using visual images to improve comprehension for middle school struggling readers. *The Reading Teacher, 56(8)*, 758–770.

Nissenbaum, H. (2004). Hackers and the contested ontology of cyberspace. *New media & Society, 6(2)*, 195–217.

Ofcom, Life Online Podcast. (2022). The genuine article: Tackling misinformation. www.gov.uk/find-digital-market-research/life-online-podcast-the-genunine-article-tackling-misinformation-ofcom.

Office for National Statistics. (2022). www.ons.gov.uk/peoplepopulationandcommunity/crimeandjustice/datasets/stalkingfindingsfromthecrimesurveyforenglandandwales.

Ogas, O., & Gaddam, S. (2012). *A billion wicked thoughts: What the internet tells us about sexual relationships*. Plume.

Orwell, G. (1949, republished 2008). *1984*. Penguin in association with Martin Secker & Warburg.

Owens, L., Shute, R., & Slee, P. (2000). 'Guess what I just heard!': Indirect aggression among teenage girls in Australia. *Aggressive Behavior: Official Journal of the International Society for Research on Aggression, 26(1)*, 67–83.

Panksepp, J. (2004). *Affective neuroscience: The foundations of human and animal emotions.* Oxford University Press.

Panksepp, J., & Biven, L. (2012). *The archeology of mind: Neuroevolutionary origins of human emotion.* W.W. Norton.

Paulhus, D., & Williams, K. (2002). The dark triad of personality: Narcissism, Machiavellianism, and psychopathy. *Journal of Research in Personality, 36*(6), 556–563.

Pearce, J. (2019). *Child sexual exploitation: Why theory matters.* Policy Press.

Peper, E., & Harvey, R. (2020). *Tech stress: How technology is hijacking our lives, strategies for coping and pragmatic ergonomics.* North Atlantic Press.

Pernecky, T. (2016). *Epistemology and metaphysics for qualitative research.* Sage.

Piaget, J. (1926), cited in Piaget, J. (2002). *The language and thought of the child.* Routledge.

Piaget, J. (1969). *The psychology of the child.* Presse Universitaire de France. Translated to English, Perseus Books.

Pierre, J. (2022). Mistrust and the possibility of civil war. *Psychology Today.* www.psychologytoday.com/us/blog/psych-unseen/202209/mistrust-misinformation-and-the-possibility-civil-war-in-america.

PinkNews. (2018). Literotica: 5 websites to quench your online erotica thirst. www.pinknews.co.uk/2018/09/25/literotica-online-erotica-websites/.

Pinker, S. (2012). *Better angels of our nature: The history of violence and humanity.* Penguin.

Plomin, R. (2018). *Blueprint: How DNA makes us who we are.* MIT Press.

Plomin, R., DeFries, J., & Fulker, D. (1988). *Nature and nurture during infancy and early childhood.* Cambridge University Press.

Porges, S. (2017). *Polyvagal theory in practice.* 2-day seminar. Breath of Life Conference, London.

Porges, S. (2011). *The polyvagal theory: Neurophysiological foundations of emotions, attachment, communication and self-regulation.* W.W. Norton.

Porges, S. (2021). *Polyvagal Safety: Attachment, communication, self-regulation.* W.W. Norton.

Pratchett, T. (2000). *The truth.* (25th Discworld Novel). Doubleday.

Przybylski, A., & Nash, V. (2018). Internet filtering and adolescent exposure to online sexual material. *Original Articles, 21*(7). www.liebertpub.com/doi/pdf/10.1089/cyber.2017.0466

Rettenmund, M. (2012). Playgirl magazine history. www.esquire.com/entertainment/a55592/playgirl-magazine-history/.

Robertson, A. (2021). *Taming gaming: Guide your child to healthy video game habits.* Blackwell.

Roper, C. (2022). *Sex dolls, robots and women hating: The case for resistance.* Spinifex.

Rosen, L. (2012). *iDisorder: Understanding our obsession with technology and overcoming its hold on us.* Palgrave Macmillan.

Rothschild B ((2003) The Body Remembers. Casebook. Unifying methods and models in the treatment of trauma and PTSD. WW Norton and Co. New York

Rudolph, J., Zimmer-Gembeck, M., & Walsh, K. (2022). Recall of sexual abuse prevention education at school and home: Associations with sexual abuse experience, disclosure, protective parenting, and knowledge. *Child Abuse and Neglect, 129.* https://doi.org/10.1016/j.chiabu.2022.105680.

Rushkoff, D. (2019). *Team human.* W.W. Norton.

Science and Media Museum. (2020). A brief history of cinema. www.scienceandmediamuseum.org.uk/objects-and-stories/very-short-history-of-cinema.

Shanahan, C. (2008). *Deep nutrition: Why your genes need traditional food.* Flatiron Books.

Short, E., Guppy, A., Hart, A., Barnes, & J. (2015). The impact of cyberstalking. *Studies in Media and Communication, 3*(2). www.researchgate.net/publication/282201099_The_Impact_of_Cyberstalking.

Siegel, D. (2010). *The mindful therapist: A clinician's guide to mindsight and neural integration.* W.W. Norton.

Siegel, D. (2014). *Brainstorm: The power and purpose of the teenage brain.* Jeremy P. Tarcher.

Siegel, D. (2016). *Mind: A journey to the heart of being human* (Norton Series on Interpersonal Neurobiology). W.W. Norton.

Siegel, D. (1999, 2020). *The developing mind* (3rd ed.). Guilford Press.

South West Grid for Learning. (2015). Revenge porn and non-consensual intimate image abuse. https://swgfl.org.uk/helplines/revenge-porn-helpline/.

Staminov, M., & Gallese, V. (2002). *Mirror neurons and the evolution of brains and language.* John Benjamins Publishing.

Steiner-Adair, C. (2013). *The big disconnect: Protecting childhood and family relationships in the digital age.* Harper Collins.

Steinmetz, K. F. (2015). Becoming a hacker: Demographic characteristics and developmental factors. *Journal of Qualitative Criminal Justice & Criminology, 3*(1), 31–60.

Stephens-Davidowitz, S. (2017). *Everybody lies: What the internet can tell us about who we really are.* Bloomsbury.

Stilman, R. (2022). Attached to technology: Exploring identity and human relating in a virtual and corporeal world. *Transactional Analysis Journal, 52*(2), 93–105.

Strassman, R. (2022). *The psychedelic handbook: A practical guide to Psylocibin, LDS, ketamine, MDMA and DMT/Ayahuasca.* Ulysses Press.

Sugarman, S. (2016). Beyond the pleasure principle: Beyond the pleasure principle. In *What Freud really meant: A chronological reconstruction of his theory of the mind* (pp. 87–104). Cambridge University Press.

Taffel, R. (2020). The myth of micro-aggression. *Contemporary Psychoanalysis, 56*(2–3), 375–393.

Tancer, B. (2009). *Click: What we do online and why it matters.* Harper Collins.

Tester, K. (1994). *Media, culture and morality.* Routledge.

Tester, K. (2001). *Compassion, morality and the media.* Open University Press.

The Education People. (2021). Online safety alerts: Think before you scare. www.theeducationpeople.org/blog/online-safety-alerts-think-before-you-scare/.

The Internet Watch Foundation. (2018). Once upon a year, annual report. www.iwf.org.uk/media/tthh3woi/once-upon-a-year-iwf-annual-report-2018.pdf.

Tovee, M. (2008). *Physiology of vision and the visual system* (2nd ed.). MIT Press.

Turkle, S. (2015). *reclaiming conversation: The power of talk in a digital age.* Penguin.

United Kingdom Parliament. (2022). Online Harms and Disinformation. https://committees.parliament.uk/committee/438/digital-culture-media-and-sport-sub-committee-on-online-harms-and-disinformation/.

United Kingdom Programme of VAWG. (2013–to date). www.gov.uk/government/publications/what-works-in-preventing-violence-against-women-and-girls-review-of-the-evidence-from-the-programme.

United Nations Convention on the Rights of Children. (1989). www.unicef.org/child-rights-convention.

United Nations Convention on the Rights of Children. (1989). Comment 25. www.unicef.org.au/united-nations-convention-on-the-rights-of-the-child.

Van der Kolk, B. (1994). The body keeps the score: Memory and the evolving psychobiology of post-traumatic stress. *Harvard Review of Psychiatry, 1*(5), 253–265.

Vervaeke, J., Mastropietro, C., & Miscevic, F. (2017). *Zombies in western culture: A twenty-first century crisis.* Openbook Publishers.

Vygotsky, L. S. (1967). Play and its role in the mental development of the child. *Soviet Psychology, 5*(3), 6–18.

Wall, H., Kaye, L., & Malone, S. (2016). An exploration of psychological factors on emoticon usage and implications for judgement accuracy. *Computers in Human Behaviour, 62*, 70–78.

Walsh, W. (2012). *Nutrient power: Heal your biochemistry and heal your brain.* Skyhorse Publishing.

Wandell, B. (2011). The neurobiological basis of seeing words. *Annals of the New York Academy of Science, 1224*(1), 63–80.

Wang, H., Tao, X., Huang, S., Wu, L., Tang, H., Song, Y., Zhang, G., & Zhang, Y. (2016). Chronic stress is associated with pain precipitation and elevation in DeltaFosb expression. *Frontiers in Pharmacology, 7*(138). https://doi.org/10.3389/fphar.2016.00138.

Wiener, N. (1954). *The human use of human beings.* De Capo Press.

Wiener, N. (1988). *The human use of human beings: Cybernetics and society.* De Capo Press.

Wheal, J. (2021). *Recapture the rapture: Rethinking god, sex, and death in a world that's lost its mind.* Harper Collins.

Wilber, K. (2000). *Integral psychology: Consciousness, spirit, psychology, therapy.* Shambala.

Williamson, C. (2022) *Modern Wisdom Podcast, #444.* Mary Harrington: Modern society is failing men & women. https://modernwisdom.libsyn.com/episode-444.

Wilson, G. (2014). *Your brain on porn: Internet pornography and the emerging science of addiction.* Commonwealth Publishing.

Wilson, R. A. (1990). *Quantum psychology: How brain software programs you and your world.* Hilarity's Press.

Wilson, E. O. (1975). *Sociobiology: The new synthesis.* Belknapp Press of Harvard University Press.

Winnicott, D. (1971, republished 2005). *Playing and reality.* Routledge Classics. Routledge.

Winsley, R., & Matos, N. (2011). Overtraining and elite young athletes. *The elite young athlete, 56*, 97–105.

Wiseman, R. (2004). *Did you spot the gorilla? How to recognise hidden opportunities.* Penguin.

Women's Aid. (n.d.). Why don't women leave? www.womensaid.org.uk/information-support/what-is-domestic-abuse/women-leave/.

Wu, T. (2010). *The master switch: The rise and fall of information empires.* Alfred A. Knopf.

Wu, T. (2016). *The attention merchants. The epic struggle to get inside our heads.* Atlantic Books.

Yasko, A. (2017). *Nutrigenomics. Your roadmap to health.* Neurological Research Institute.

Yunkaporta, T. (2019). *Sand talk: How indigenous thinking can save the world.* Text Publishing.

Zuboff, S. (2019). *The age of surveillance capitalism: The fight for a new human future at the new frontier of power.* Profile Books.

People, websites and organisations

Aitkin, M. (2015). Cyberpsychologist. www.maryaitkin.com.

British Psychological Society Cyberpsychology Section. www.bps.org.uk/member-networks/cyberpsychology-section.

Centre for Humane Technology. www.humanetech.com/.

Digitaltrends.www.digitaltrends.com/social-media/take-this-lollipop-makes-facebook-stalking-personal-and-horrifying/.

Guardian. www.theguardian.com/uk-news/2022/jun/03/met-police-project-alpha-profiling-children-documents-show.

Pageu, J. https://thesymbolicworld.com/.

Perel, E. www.estherperel.com/.

Rebel Wisdom. https://rebelwisdom.co.uk/.

Samaritans. www.samaritans.org/about-samaritans/media-guidelines/.

Schmachtenberger, D. https://civilizationemerging.com/articles/personal-blog-posts/.

South West Grid for Learning. https://swgfl.org.uk/magazine/digital-ghost-stories/.

The Intellectual Darkweb. www.nytimes.com/2018/05/08/opinion/intellectual-dark-web.html.

Vervaeke, J. (n.d.). http://johnvervaeke.com/.

Vice. www.vice.com/en/article/bvnp8v/met-police-youtube-drill-music-removal.

Vox. www.vox.com/the-big-idea/2018/5/10/17338290/intellectual-dark-web-rogan-peterson-harris-times-weiss.

Video links

American Pie (1999). 3rd base feels like Apple Pie. www.youtube.com/watch?v=Ik1NKkN0ysI.

Gamechangers Movie. (2021). https://gamechangersmovie.com/.

Newhart, B. (2010). *Stop it.* www.youtube.com/watch?v=Ow0lr63y4Mw.

Netflix. (2022). *The most hated man on the internet.* www.netflix.com/gb/title/81387065.

Wiseman video of gorilla. www.youtube.com/watch?v=y6qgoM89ekM.

Newspapers

New York Times. (1987). www.nytimes.com/1987/11/24/science/infants-sense-of-pain-is-recognized-finally.html.

New York Times. (2022). A dad took photos of his naked toddler for the doctor. Google flagged him as a criminal. www.nytimes.com/2022/08/21/technology/google-surveillance-toddler-photo.html.

Resources

Knibbs, C. (2020). Safeguarding children online: A guide for practitioners. https://childrenandtech.co.uk/product/practitioners-guide-to-safeguarding-when-working-online-remotely/.

Knibbs, C. (2023). Tech Talk IT. Cards for onboarding your client: Helpful terminology for practitioners and parents. www.childrenandtech.co.uk.

Knibbs, C. (2023). Talking about adult material to children and young people: Resource cards for professionals. www.childrenandtech.co.uk.

Helplines and Organisations mentioned during the book

www.ceop.police.uk
www.childnet.com
www.gloablkidsonline.net
www.internetmatters.co.uk
https://www.iwf.org.uk
https://www.lgbthealth.org.uk/
https://www.mind.org.uk/
www.nspcc.org.uk
www.parentzone.org.uk
www.safeinternet.org.uk
https://www.samaritans.org/
http://www.stopitnow.org.uk
www.swgfl.org.uk

Services dedicated to the removal of and protection against CSAEM

IWF = The Internet Watch Foundation @ https://www.iwf.org.uk/

INHOPE = The International hotline for removal of CSAM @ https://www.in-hope.org/EN?locale=en

NCMEC= National Centre for Missing and Exploited Children @ https://www.missingkids.org/HOME

ICMEC-= International Centre for missing and exploited children @ https://www.icmec.org/

INTERPOL = International Crime Agency @ https://www.interpol.int/en

WeProtect = Global Alliance for Protection against CSAM @ https://www.weprotect.org/

Index

For Product Safety Concerns and Information please contact our EU
representative GPSR@taylorandfrancis.com
Taylor & Francis Verlag GmbH, Kaufingerstraße 24, 80331 München, Germany